THE PEDIATRICIAN AND THE DEVELOPMENTALLY DELAYED CHILD

THE PEDIATRICIAN AND THE DEVELOPMENTALLY DELAYED CHILD is the second volume in the new **Monographs in Developmental Pediatrics** Series. Other volumes in this series include:

Published:

Primitive Reflex Profile

Proposed:

Early Language Development and the Pediatrician
Reading Retardation: A Clinical Approach to the Evaluation of Dyslexic Children
The Multiply Handicapped Child and the Physician
Early Infantile Autism
The Natural History and Treatment of Epilepsy in the Handicapped
Cerebral Palsy: The Natural History of a Childhood Disability
The Embryology of Behavior
Infant Behavior Scales
Developmental Assessment of the Preschool Child
An Epidemiological Study of Developmental Disabilities

THE PEDIATRICIAN AND THE DEVELOPMENTALLY DELAYED CHILD

A Clinical Textbook on Mental Retardation

Pasquale J. Accardo, M.D.
Assistant Professor of Pediatrics
The Johns Hopkins University
School of Medicine
Developmental Pediatrician
The John F. Kennedy Institute for Handicapped Children
Director, Child Development Clinic
Baltimore City Hospitals

and

Arnold J. Capute, M.D., M.P.H.
Associate Professor of Pediatrics
The Johns Hopkins University
School of Medicine
Deputy Director
The John F. Kennedy Institute for Handicapped Children

University Park Press
Baltimore

UNIVERSITY PARK PRESS
International Publishers in Science, Medicine, and Education
233 East Redwood Street
Baltimore, Maryland 21202

Typeset by American Graphic Arts Corporation
Manufactured in the United States of America by
The Maple Press Company

Library of Congress Cataloging in Publication Data

Accardo, Pasquale J.
The pediatrician and the developmentally delayed child.

(Monographs in developmental pediatrics; 2)
Bibliography: p.
Includes index.
1. Mentally handicapped children. 2. Mental deficiency. 3. Pediatrics. I. Capute, Arnold J., joint author. II. Title. III. Series.
[DNLM: 1. Mental retardation. W1 Mo567LP v. 2/ WS107.3 C255p]

RJ506.M4A23 362.7′8′3 78-11238
ISBN 0-8391-1331-5

Marion Katz

People, even more than things, have to be restored, renewed, revived, reclaimed, and redeemed, and redeemed, and redeemed . . . Never throw out anybody.

Sam Levenson

Contents

Preface ix

History 1

Epidemiology 11

Theory 25

Pathology 43

Biomedical Assessment 57

Developmental Assessment 105

Language Assessment 133

Therapy 153

Parent Counseling 165

Social Policy and Ethical Issues 179

References 187

Index 239

Preface

> Thus they are often obliged to do things which they have imperfectly learned, to say things which they imperfectly understand, and to devote themselves to work for which they are unprepared by long apprenticeship.
>
> de Tocqueville

Medicine in general and the traditional pediatric training program in particular have demonstrated a preponderant interest in the diagnosis and treatment of acute organic illness. Although the importance of developmental and behavioral phenomena to the understanding of the whole patient has always received more than adequate lip service, the tremendous personal and social impact of chronic disease has failed to produce a truly valetudinarian medicine. At the beginning of the Christian era, the Methodist School did make brief inroads against the descendants of Hippocrates, the Dogmatic theorists and the Empirical skeptics. Adopting a peculiar middle position, the Methodists attempted to reform the attitude of physicians toward the treatment of the patient with chronic disease. In the long history of medicine, this movement was an abortive effort with no lasting effects.

Technologic and public health advances have today dramatically reduced the burden of organic childhood disease. Early diagnosis, parent education, more specific therapies, and regionalization of services have all allowed for striking reductions in the mortality and morbidity rates associated with classic pediatric disorders. The concern of society has now begun to focus more on the problems of chronic handicapping conditions, but scientific medicine has remained isolated and aloof from all but a minimal response to this trend.

For this and other reasons, it has become increasingly fashionable to decry the "medical model" in the evaluation and treatment of developmental disabilities. Usually the model that is under attack is a parody of the organ-localization pathology of late nineteenth-century medicine—an arrogant, quantitative mentality. It is unfortunate that traces of this orientation have survived in medical education and practice up to the present time, but it is an egregious error of historical interpretation for patients, physicians, or other professionals to identify this anomalous distortion with medicine proper. Medicine is an art whose proper goal is the use (and, if necessary, abuse) of science to help those suffering from bodily or mental disorders. Its proper study is, in Osler's phrase, the patient who happens to have a disease, and not the disease the patient happens to have. Numbers (such as IQ scores) and organ localization (such as brain cell heterotopia) are not the end, but rather some of the starting points of a comprehensive understanding of the handicapped child. The reduction of a human being to a number or a disease label cannot be justified as a shorthand description in the absence of a working knowledge of the processes of abnormal development.

A clarification of the reference to an "abuse of science" would appear to be in order. Scientific theories frequently fall victim to a vacillating faddishness (witness the history of the corpuscular and wave theories of light, the emotional and organic theories of autism, the genetic and environmental theories of intelligence, etc.); ivory tower researchers demonstrate amazing about-faces in their public pronouncements. As the pendulum swings to and fro, irrefutable (that is, statistically significant, but usually quite refutable) data are mustered to support first one hypothesis and then its antithesis. It is one of the more honorable tasks of humanistic medicine to steer a middle course between such extremes—keeping up to date on the latest clinical and laboratory advances, not subjecting patients to risky or difficult innovations based on tenuous hypotheses, and never being the cause of false hope or false despair.

The present text focuses on the clinical signs and symptoms of developmental delay in young children and attempts to aid the practicing pediatrician in the early diagnosis and habilitation of mental retardation. Serviceable guidelines to the understanding of developmental deviations seem to be a practical goal despite the absence of a unified theory of normal child development. In other words, a completely uniform and generally accepted "developmental physiology" is not a prerequisite to the understanding of developmental pathology. Stress upon early language milestones and such developmental phenomena as dissociation and coupling should make the book of practical value to all professionals working with young children. The concluding chapter analyzes sterilization as a debated issue which may signal clashes between social and ethical goals.

The material presented is part of a core curriculum in Developmental Disabilities in the Department of Pediatrics of The Johns Hopkins University School of Medicine. Medical students, pediatric housestaff, and postdoctoral fellows in Developmental Pediatrics receive formal instruction at their respective levels of training along with intensive experience in the workings of the interdisciplinary team. Interest in historical and ethical issues is a pervasive characteristic of the program.

A necessary part of the education of a pediatrician is a thorough grounding in the roles various nonmedical disciplines play in the diagnosis and treatment of handicapped children. A refusal to enter into meaningful dialogue with such paramedical professionals can only contribute to further handicap the child. The boundaries of traditional medicine need to be considerably extended so that the following fictional (but all too true) account may evolve from the typical to the obsolete:

> I could tell stories. An outsider wouldn't believe the number of conflicting opinions the different doctors gave us and the backbiting judgments they made of each other, but we did. We believed them all, the good and the bad. And disbelieved as well (we had no choice) and had no choice but to search for others, like wandering supplicants.
>
> "It's organic."
>
> "It's functional."
>
> "It's largely organic with functional complications now."
>
> "He is not deaf but may not be able to hear."
>
> "At least he's alive."
>
> "The prognosis is good."
>
> "For what?"
>
> "The prognosis is bad."
>
> "It would not be possible to offer a prognosis at this time."
>
> Not one of them ever had the candor, the courage, the common sense, the character to say:
>
> "Jesus—I really don't know."
>
> It began with:
>
> "You're making too much of it."
>
> And moved to:
>
> "He will never speak."
>
> "He probably will not surpass a mental age of five, if he attains that. His coordination and muscular control will never be good.
>
> It will require tremendous patience."
>
> We hate them all, the ones who were wrong and the ones who were right. After awhile, that made no difference. The cause didn't matter. The prognosis was absolute.[1]

It is too easy a defense against such charges to reply that the experts involved were themselves misdiagnosed and mislabeled.

[1] Reprinted by permission from *Something Happened* by Joseph Heller, 1975, pp. 497–498. Ballantine Books, New York.

The more appropriate response is the establishment of high professional standards. The subspecialty area of developmental pediatrics has the major goal of fostering professional education and interdisciplinary communication in the field of developmental disabilities. It is hoped that the present text, although aimed predominantly at the practicing pediatrician, will fulfill this dual role by clarifying to the nonphysician the contribution that medicine can make to the multidisciplinary team approach to mental retardation.

This work was supported in part by Project 917, Maternal and Child Health Service. Figures and line drawings were prepared under the supervision of Mr. Leon Schlossberg. Instruments were photographed by Mr. William Diehl. The photograph of the young child with Down syndrome on the dedication page is taken from a photographic exhibit of handicapped children entitled "A Different Beauty" by Marion Katz. Zuhair Kareem, Chief of Biomedical Photography at The Johns Hopkins Medical Institutions, prepared all the prints for publication. Barbara Kelner, MLS, hunted up many of the references. The handwritten manuscript was reduced to a legible typescript by Karen A. Torbit. To all those who contributed their support (moral and otherwise) the authors wish to extend their gratitude.

Pasquale J. Accardo
Arnold J. Capute

HISTORY

> You may alter the place to which you are going; but you cannot alter the place from which you have come.
>
> Chesterton

The recognition of childhood as a distinct phase of human development is a recent phenomenon—so recent that its social, legal, and educational implications have yet to be fully worked out. Some historians optimistically view the evolution of childhood as a rational progression toward more humane conditions (Figure 1). But, in the same way that the history of medicine can be said to be the history of humanity itself, the history of mental retardation is but a special aspect of the history of childhood. The major roles of deviant persons (Table 1) which Wolfensberger (1972) used to stereotype past attitudes toward retardation can easily be extended to serve as a descriptive typology of the place children occupy in different cultures. These deviancy roles, whether applied to normal children or to the retarded, evidence relatively little linear progress. Rather, they seem to be cyclic with different roles being dominant at different time periods in the same culture. Thus when the deviant individual was viewed as a social menace during the "genetic scare" (1890–1925), laws for the sterilization and euthanasia of the retarded were passed. More refined genetic theory discredited the pseudoscientific aspects of this movement, but utilitarian social planners are currently attempting to revive the menace role by employing more palatable euphemisms. In a similar vein, Haffter (1968) documents some of the modern survivals of the ancient concept of the "changeling"; attitudes toward children and the retarded seem to be grounded in the more primitive levels of the psyche. The real history of mental retardation would seem to lie in the most recent historical subspeciality—psychohistory, the history of childhood and family life. Attempts to understand the complex evolution of social attitudes toward developmental incompetence should have significant impact on the future of mental retardation.

Ancient and medieval medicine rarely attempted to distinguish between retardation (a permanent, hereditary condition) and lunacy (in which there was some hope of a cure or temporary remission) because there existed no effective therapies for either

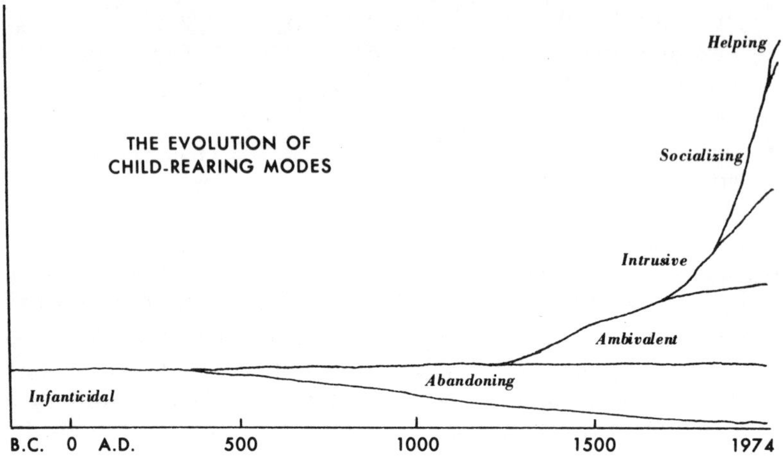

Figure 1. The progressive evolution of parent-child interactional modes. From DeMause (1974) by permission.

condition. However, ancient and medieval law evolved careful distinctions between natural fools (idiots) and lunatics because the disposition of such persons' property by the crown turned on the existence of lucid intervals (Neaman, 1975). Thus in 1534, the jurist Sir Anthony Fitz-Herbert declared:

> And he who shall be said to be a sot [i.e., simpleton] and idiot from his birth, is such a person who cannot account or number twenty pence, nor can tell who was his father or mother, nor how old he is, etc., so as it may appear that he hath no understanding of reason what shall be for his profit nor what for his loss. But if he hath such understanding, that he know and understand his letters, and do read by teaching or information of another man, then it seemeth he is not a sot nor a natural idiot (Doll, 1972, pp. 49–50).

Table 1. Major historic roles of deviant persons

Subhuman Organism
Menace
Unspeakable Object of Dread
Object of Pity
Holy Innocent
Diseased Organism
Object of Ridicule
Eternal Child

It is important to note that the legal focus has until recently been exclusively centered on the protection of property rights with little or no consideration for the person of the mentally handicapped. The literacy criterion in the passage cited above would not have much relevance for the nonpropertied commoner class. Nevertheless, even this early, one can observe a consideration of social and adaptive behaviors in addition to purely cognitive performance. The legal distinction was clear to philosophers such as John Locke (1632–1704), who wrote in his book titled *An Essay Concerning Human Understanding* (1690):

> Herein seems to lie the difference between idiots and madmen, that madmen put wrong ideas together, and so make wrong propositions, but argue and reason right from them, but idiots make very few or no propositions, and reasons scarce at all (1959, Vol. 1, p. 210).

The above examples notwithstanding, throughout most of recorded history disorders of the mind have been confused—St. Dymphna of Gheel (feastday May 15) became the patroness of both the emotionally disturbed and the mentally retarded.

Psychiatry was one of the first of the modern branches of medicine to enter its scientific phase late in the eighteenth century; it recognized the retarded as a distinct type of mental disorder and promptly discarded them as incurable. Within less than a century neurology would establish itself as a specialty and follow psychiatry in abandoning the retarded except for that minority demonstrating interesting neuropathology.

But there was another stream of medical interest that went its way quietly and succeeded in revolutionizing the area of behavioral science. Jean Marc Gaspard Itard (1775–1838) received a grant from the French government to educate Victor, a "wild child" found roaming in the woods of Aveyron. Itard spent 5 years applying a program of graded stimulus discrimination in an attempt to civilize his pupil. This "physiologic method" drew its theoretical inspiration from the erratic speculations of Rousseau's *Emile*, but it was much more firmly grounded in Itard's practical experience with deaf children and his creative responses to his daily interactions with Victor. At the end of the experiment, Itard considered that he had failed; by norm-referenced standards Victor could neither talk nor function independently in society—he was still not normal, still retarded. The French government felt otherwise; compared to his functional level before his sojourn with Itard, Victor had made dramatic progress. The government implicitly used a criterion-referenced standard in honoring the physician's achievement. Dr. Itard went on to become one of the founders of otolaryngology; in his youthful idealism he had fathered special education. One of Itard's physician pupils, Edouard Seguin (1812–1880), further refined the physiologic method, elaborating the sensorimotor drills and exercises and inventing some of the hardware still in use today (Figure 2). After his emigration to the United States in 1848, Seguin became one of the architects of the institutional movement in this country. His classic text on the principles of educating the retarded, *Idiocy and Its Treatment by the Physiological Method* (1866; reprinted in 1971), contains some of the earliest descriptions of Down syndrome and the fetal alcohol syndrome. Maria Montessori (1870–1952) was the first woman to receive a medical degree in Italy. The Montessori method extended the techniques Itard and Seguin had devised for the education of the retarded to the acceleration of the development of the normal child.

In 1877, William Ireland (1832–1909) published *On Idiocy and Imbecility,* the first medical textbook of mental retardation. His classification of idiocy was the first attempt at a comprehensive medical nosology (Table 2). Genetous did not refer to genetics because that branch of science did not yet exist in 1877; rather it was what today would be called idiopathic. It was Ireland's largest category; his observations supported a study of Langdon Down's which described the frequent occurrence of high-arched palate in this group. Absolute microcephaly was an adult head circumference below 17 inches; it was noted to be much more common in males. Ireland recognized that there was no constant relationship between intelligence and head size; he compared the head

Table 2. Classification of idiocy

Genetous
Microcephalic
Eclampsic
Epileptic
Hydrocephalic
Paralytic
Cretinism
Traumatic
Inflammatory
Idiocy by Deprivation

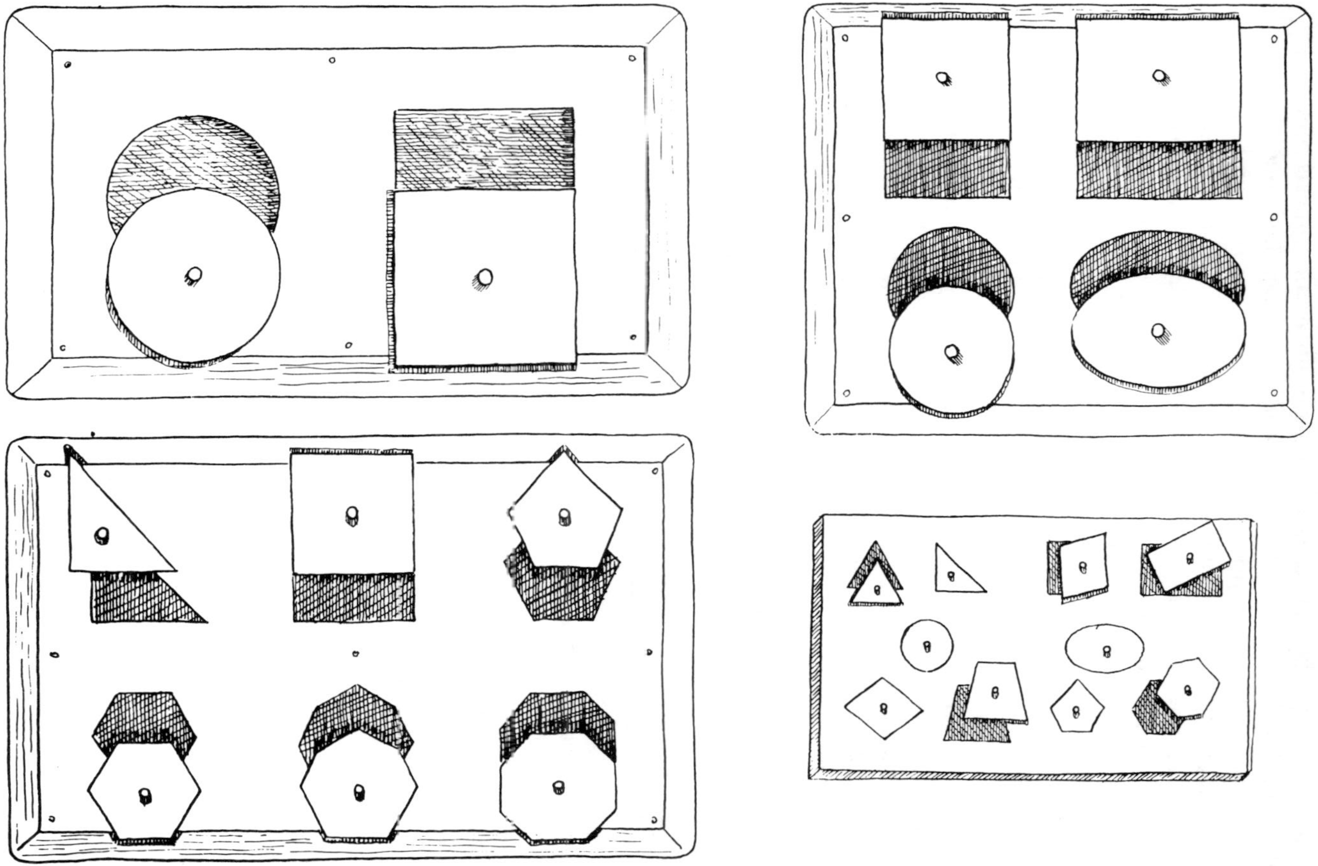

Figure 2. Seguin form boards. Several of the form boards devised by Seguin as educational hardware. From Talbot (1964) by permission.

measurement to the weight of a "nugget of uncertain mineral composition." Both the eclampsic and epileptic types had seizures, but whereas the epileptic had infrequent seizures regularly throughout life, the eclampsic had bursts of life-threatening seizures around the time of teething, after which the convulsive disorder seemed to burn itself out. The descriptive case histories of this latter type suggest infantile spasms. The hydrocephalic (large but light brain) was distinguished from the rarer megancephalic retardate with a large heavy brain. Paralysis referred to the association of various types of cerebral palsy with mental retardation; cretinism is now preventable by the use of thyroid extracts. Traumatic idiocy followed on severe head injury; inflammatory idiocy was post-meningitic or post-encephalitic. Idiocy by deprivation was a unique category of what today would be considered pseudoretardation since the deprivation referred to was the loss of two or more senses, such as hearing and vision. Unfortunately, exceptional "deprived" students such as Helen Keller and Laura Bridgman were presented to the public as examples of the power of the new educational technology to make the retarded normal—if only the right educational key could be discovered to fit the odd-shaped lock of the retardate's brain.

The record of the early training schools was indeed impressive in the large numbers of retardates reintegrated into the community (Seguin, 1971). But the psychologist Alfred Binet (1857–1911) and the physician Theophile Simon (1873–1961) were not to produce the first standardized intelligence test until 1905, and it is conceivable that many of those previously diagnosed retarded were mislabeled. It is an irony that the modern descendents of this early objective test are now under attack for the very same reason that first led to its construction: distrust of teacher bias in identifying cases of mental deficiency (Cronbach, 1970, 1975). Despite its later abuse, the Binet-Simon represented a significant step forward, a liberation from arbitrary and subjective classification. Newer process-oriented evaluation techniques demonstrate functional advances over simpler IQ measurement; their potential for abuse remains to be discovered.

In the early part of the present century, the training schools found themselves left with a self-selected hard core residuum of subtrainables. Their initial optimism gradually clouded over into a pseudoscientific pessimism; they became institutions in the modern sense—permanent residential facilities for the custodial care of the severely impaired. Studies by Goddard and Dugdale suggested that mental retardation was either an autosomal dominant or recessive trait. Thus, if all the retardates in one generation were prevented from reproducing, the disorder would be significantly decreased in the next generation and virtually eradicated within several generations. A eugenics movement led to the passage of sterilization laws in the United States and euthanasia laws in Germany (Binding and Hoche, 1975).

Sigmund Freud stressed the theoretical importance of early childhood and the necessity for a careful developmental history. Twentieth-century medicine has continued to pursue the elaboration of biochemical and genetic etiologies for mental retardation. Although its successes have been on an unprecedented scale, correlation of the discovered abnormalities to behavioral observations have been sadly lacking.

A pediatrician, Arnold Gesell (1888–1961), was the first to document the development of infants and young children. His meticulous observations have served as the basis for all succeeding infant tests and are still a useful reservoir of clinical information for the practicing pediatrician. The importance of the developmental pediatrician, the new specialist envisioned by Gesell, was slow in finding acceptance. The major obstacle to the training of such personnel was solved in the late 1960s by the establishment of University Affiliated Facilities (UAF), with their triple goal of training, service, and research in the area of developmental disabilities. Government support of such interdisciplinary centers mirrors the more general phenomenon of increasing social awareness of the plight of the handicapped; normalization, deinstitutionalization, and education for all (PL 94-142) similarly reflect a heightened public conscience.

Long-range predictions as to the future of mental retardation are at the least unscientific. In historical retrospect, the extremes of optimism and pessimism on the part of our predecessors seem to have been unwarranted. They are still unwarranted today.

BIBLIOGRAPHIC NOTE

Garrison's (1923) history of pediatrics remains eminently readable; part two of Despert's (1970) book on emotional disorders reviews past attitudes toward children. Jackson (1970) and

DeMause (1974) provide brief overviews of the history of childhood; Aries (1962) is still the classic introduction to the field. Chase (1977) provides a scholarly review of the nature-nurture controversy and its social implications.

Itard's (1962) classic reports are still an excellent introduction to special education; Lane's (1977) reinterpretation of the tale of the wild boy of Aveyron gives the modern reader the advantage of copious extracts from other contemporary documents. Malson's (1972) review of feral children is interesting if somewhat marred by an obtrusive Marxism. The original texts by Seguin (1971) and Ireland (1877) make fascinating reading today. Kanner's (1964) historical outline possesses an excellent bibliography, and a fine collection of American documents on mental retardation has recently been published (Rosen, Clark, and Kivitz, 1976).

EPIDEMIOLOGY

A name can be given to anything that can be understood.

Aquinas

Before the late nineteenth century, children were classified as being retarded by an unusual physiognomy (facial appearance) and other peculiar morphologic features. With the development of intelligence tests in the early part of the twentieth century there evolved the concept of a fixed IQ for each person. Today it is recognized that there is no one IQ for any person; rather, intelligence is composed of a number of different cognitive and perceptual skills which can be measured by formal psychologic tests. Although the IQ has declined as the sole criterion for defining mental retardation, intelligence tests still serve the purpose for which they were originally designed—prediction of school performance.

The American Association on Mental Deficiency (AAMD) currently defines mental retardation as "significantly subaverage general intellectual functioning existing concurrently with deficits in adaptive behavior, and manifested during the developmental period" (Grossman, 1973).

"Significantly subaverage general intellectual functioning" refers to an intelligence quotient that is below 70 and represents 2 or more standard deviations (1 standard deviation = 15 points on the Wechsler scales; see Figure 3) below the mean (usually 100). During the early years of life, infant development tests focus on sensorimotor skills. The most commonly used scales include the Gesell (Revised Yale Developmental Schedules; 4 weeks to 5 years), the Bayley Scales of Infant Development (Bayley, 1969; 2 months to 30 months) and the Cattell (Cattell, 1940; 2 months to 30 months); from 22 months upward the Cattell duplicates items from the Stanford-Binet. In preschool and school age children, the Stanford-Binet Intelligence Scale (2 years to adult), the Wechsler Preschool and Primary Scale of Intelligence (WPPSI; 4 years to 6½ years), and the Wechsler Intelligence Scale for Children (WISC; 5 years to 16 years) are used to measure levels of mental functioning. The WISC is reported with full-scale verbal and performance IQ scores; these represent summations of a dozen subscores (Table 3). The learning deficit in the retarded refers to

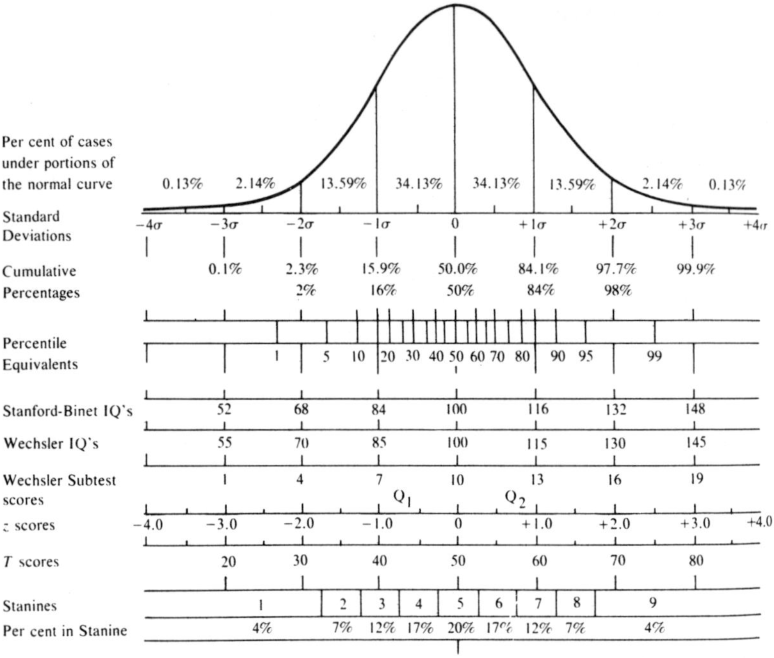

Figure 3. Relationship of normal curve to various types of standard scores. From Sattler (1974) by permission.

an overall depression of cognitive skills (i.e., low full-scale IQ) whereas "learning disability" occurs in children with normal global intelligence (full-scale IQ) but with accompanying perceptual-cognitive deficits (usually reflected in verbal IQ-performance, IQ discrepancies, and subscore scatter) and school underachievement. Many retarded children do not have homogeneous test scores, but rather demonstrate a significant variability

Table 3. Wechsler Intelligence Scale for Children subscores

Verbal	Performance
General information	Picture completion
General comprehension	Picture arrangement
Arithmetic	Block design
Similarities	Object assembly
Vocabulary	Coding
Digit span	Mazes

in the different skills tested: high splinter skills may lead to unrealistic expectations (and pressures) for the child; low subscores in key areas may give the impression that the child is more retarded than is the case. A significant scatter of abilities can make accurate long-term prediction difficult. One hopes that a child with discrepant abilities will ultimately function at the level of his highest abilities, but his poorer skills often severely limit the use of his higher ones. It is still a debated issue in special education whether to teach to a child's strengths or weaknesses; whichever option is chosen, the teacher needs to be aware of the entire pattern. Thus, there is no one IQ score for every child, but rather a careful functional description of each child's strengths and weaknesses as evaluated by a tester experienced in working with children. Such a functional evaluation is useful to the educator in designing an appropriate curriculum. IQ scores and subscores can only remain useful if it is remembered that they are shorthand for a comprehensive assessment process that attempts a synthesis of many other nonmeasured variables that contribute to the whole child.

The second part of the definition, "existing concurrently with deficits in adaptive behavior," implies that the individual lacks the personal independence and social responsibility expected for his age and cultural group. For the most part, clinicians do not employ social quotients in the classification of mental retardation (Adams, 1973). Social competence is strongly correlated with intelligence (Johnson, 1970; MacAndrew and Edgerton, 1964), and good measures of adaptive behavior, as independent from cognitive behavior, seem to be lacking. The Vineland Social Maturity Scale yields social quotients consistently 10 to 20 points higher than simultaneously administered intelligence quotients (Erickson, Johnson, and Campbell, 1970); the Alpern-Boll Developmental Profile (Alpern and Boll, 1972) includes a measure of social behavior but is not well standardized. Although such instruments need further refinement, it remains doubtful whether adaptive behavior can progress much in advance of the child's mental age.

The final part of the definition, "during the developmental period," recognizes the upper developmental age limit as 18 years. Thus, someone who after 18 years of age suffers a serious cerebral insult leading to severe cognitive and adpative impairment would be considered brain damaged, but not mentally retarded. There is an unspoken assumption that, despite similarly impaired levels of functioning, the person whose pathologic lesion occurs during the developmental period will be qualitatively different from one whose insult occurs after maturity.

Thus, for an individual to be considered mentally retarded, he must satisfy all three criteria: 1) an IQ score at least 2 standard deviations below the mean, 2) manifested before 18 years of age, and 3) accompanied by impairments in adaptive behavior.

The overall prevalence of mental retardation is 3%; with a population of 200 million there are approximately 6 million retardates. But this global statistic conceals a skewed distribution: the majority of the mentally retarded are only mildly involved, with very few retardates occupying the more severe end of the spectrum. For every 1000 persons, a 3% prevalence of mental retardation predicts 30 retarded individuals. The distribution of these 30, however, is skewed toward the normal: 26 are mildly retarded, three are moderately retarded, and only one is profoundly retarded (Figure 4). The more severely retarded have a

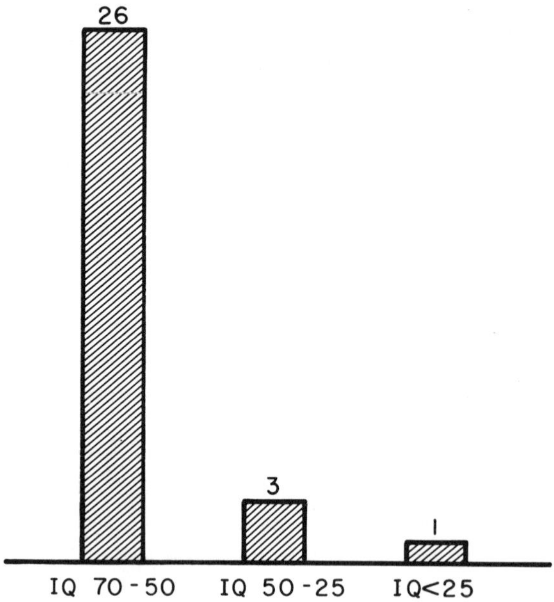

Figure 4. Relative distribution of mental retardation. For every 1000 population, a 3% prevalence of mental retardation predicts 30 retardates; their distribution is skewed toward normal.

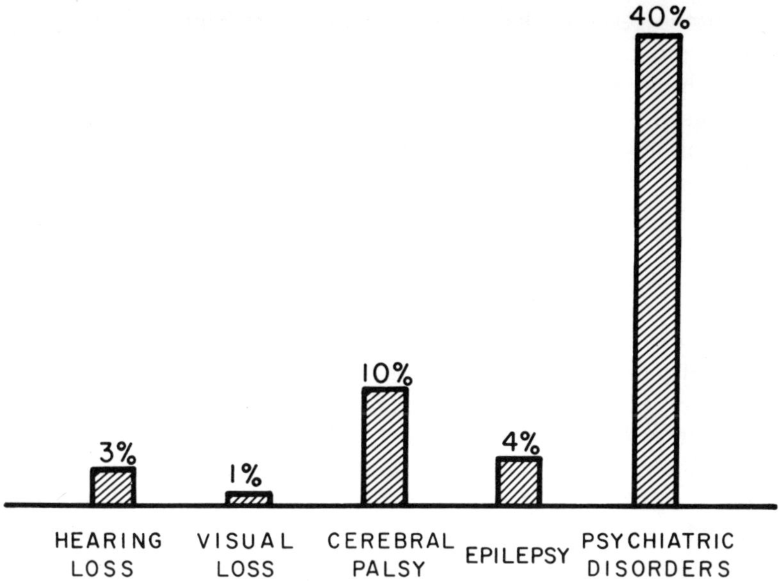

Figure 5. Prevalence of various associated handicaps in the retarded population. Data pooled from Conley (1973).

higher prevalence of associated handicaps and therefore a higher mortality. Conley (1973) estimates the relative mortality for those with an IQ below 25 to be three times that of the general population, and for those with an IQ between 25 and 50, twice that of the general population. Because of this increased mortality there is a decrease in the prevalence of severe mental retardation with increasing age. Similarly, many mildly retarded persons are not identified until close to school age and therefore the prevalence of mild mental retardation may show an increase with age (Tarjan et al., 1973).

To be retarded is to be at significant risk for other disabilities. Of all developmentally disabled children, approximately one-third have one handicap, another third have two handicaps, and the remaining third have three or more handicaps. Thus approximately two-thirds of handicapped children have more than one handicap. The more severe the retardation, the greater the probability of an associated disability. Pooling data from various population studies, one can arrive at an approximate prevalence for different disabilities in the retarded (Figure 5); for example,

3% of the retarded have a significant hearing loss. If one starts from epidemiologic studies of the other disabilities, one can approximate the prevalence of mental retardation associated with each disability (Figure 6); for example, 15% of the deaf population are mentally retarded. Such pooled figures may mask significant variations within fairly mixed samples. Thus the prevalence of mental retardation is much lower than 50% in the hemiplegic cerebral palsied population, but much higher (approximating 100%) in those patients with the rigid variety of cerebral palsy. Specific etiologies may vary the rate within a single type of cerebral palsy: several decades ago the majority of patients with choreoathetoid cerebral palsy had their brain lesion localized to the basal ganglia (secondary to neonatal hyperbilirubinemia) and therefore demonstrated an almost pure motor disability with little cognitive impairment. Now that phototherapy and exchange transfusion have virtually eradicated the more damaging levels of newborn jaundice, most choreoathetoid cerebral palsied patients are survivors of extreme neonatal asphyxia; this anoxic insult produces a

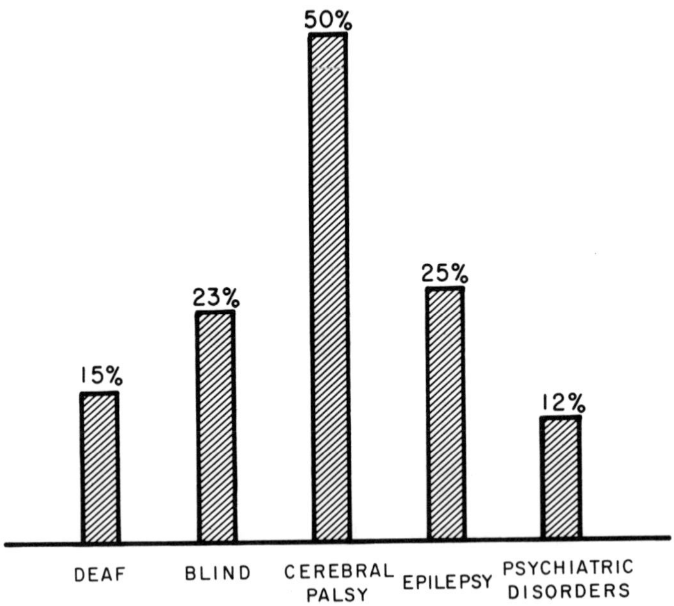

Figure 6. Prevalence of mental retardation associated with other handicapping conditions. Data pooled from Conley (1973).

diffuse type of brain damage that is associated with a high incidence of severe mental retardation.

The grades of mental retardation are defined by the number of standard deviations from the mean. Almost all current intelligence tests are based on the refined statistical concept of a standard deviation for each age level tested; that is, each child is compared with his own age group. Nevertheless, for the pediatrician the older developmental quotient (developmental quotient = mental age/chronologic age × 100; DQ = MA/CA × 100) can serve as a rule of thumb adequate to most clinical situations. Although there is some degree of variability of the IQ over time, the most striking characteristic of retardate IQs is their stability. Many dramatic variations in IQ scores can be attributed to improperly performed tests or to the use of tests with different measurement biases. For example, young infants with Down syndrome normally have a strong imitative tendency; this makes them appear very sociable for their age and increases their IQ on infant sensorimotor tests. However, when they get older and are tested on an instrument such as the Stanford-Binet, with its strong language bias, their IQ seems to plateau and then decline.

The IQ ranges for the different levels of retardation are presented in Table 4 and Figure 7. More recently educators are moving away from the negative implication of the term "subtrainable" and are adopting the psychologic classifications of severe and profound (e.g., SPH/SPR, severe and profoundly handicapped/severe and profoundly retarded). There are many regional variations in usage that each practitioner will need to familiarize himself with. The last column is presented only for antiquarian interest. Although some scientific papers in the last two decades still use such terms, they are highly imprecise

Table 4. Levels of retardation

IQ range	Educational terminology	Psychologic terminology	Archaic terminology
84–70	Slow learner	Borderline	Feebleminded
69–55	Educable	Mild	Moron
54–40	Trainable	Moderate	Imbecile
39–25 <25	Subtrainable	Severe Profound	Idiot

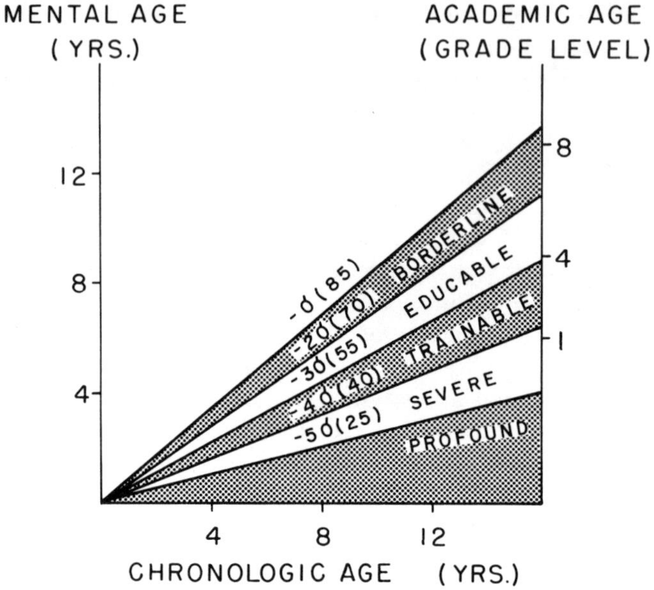

Figure 7. Academic achievement for different levels of retardation. The left ordinate gives the mental age (MA), the abscissa the chronologic age (CA), and the right ordinate the academic age (AA) or grade level for the different degrees of mental retardation. "Rule of five": AA = MA − 5 for all populations. (AA = CA − 5 for the normal population where MA = CA). From Capute and Accardo (1967a) by permission.

(they antedate the development of formal psychometrics) and derogatory.

The educable (or mild) mentally retarded (EMR) comprise that group of persons with IQs between 2 and 3 standard deviations below the mean (69–55). The prototype for the EMR group is the psychosocially or culturally deprived individual. With an ultimate academic achievement level equivalent to a fourth to sixth grade education, the goal for the EMR is social and economic independence. These children develop at a rate between one-half and three-quarters of normal; they are not usually identified until kindergarten or the first grade, when confronted with academics or given IQ tests. Because they 1) are not considered retarded before school, 2) disappear into the normal population at maturity, and 3) demonstrate reasonable social adaptability outside of school, they are often considered "six-hour retarded children."

The special educator plays a prominent role in the formative years of the EMR, preparing the child with the important academic and behavioral skills requisite for job training. Later vocational training readies him for a suitable occupation. Successful integration into society depends on the appropriateness of the educational curriculum. Although segregation from normal peers is undesirable, the optimal degree of mainstreaming needs to be individualized for each child. A very useful rule of thumb for the pediatric consultant is the child's attitude toward school; boredom from too much busy work and frustration from being over-challenged both quickly produce negativism toward going to school. It would be very unusual to find that a child happy and positive about attending school was inappropriately placed.

One may use the "rule of five" to estimate the ultimate level of academic achievement: subtract 5 from the mental age (MA) at maturity (16 years) to obtain the academic age (AA) or grade level (Dunn, 1963). The majority of educables will become functionally literate (i.e., reading comprehension at fourth grade level or above); they will be able to read want ads, fill out applications, and travel to and from work. Approximately 80% of EMR marry (usually spouses with higher IQs) and have normal children (Charles, 1957).

When jobs are plentiful, the rate of employment for the EMR is fairly high. However, when there is a business recession, the incidence of unemployment increases (Dunn, 1963). Four-fifths of the mildly retarded are employed in semiskilled, unskilled, and domestic occupations; men are readily employed as laborers, whereas women follow domestic pursuits. Up to one-fifth of EMRs may work at skilled occupations (Johnson, 1968). In its revised classification system the American Association on Mental Deficiency (AAMD) deleted the borderline category (IQ range 84–70); however, in an increasingly technological society, the learning disabled, borderline, and mildly retarded are experiencing growing difficulties in blending into the normal population.

One of the most difficult problems facing the clinician is the professional family with a borderline to mildly retarded child; such a child is relatively more retarded compared to parental expectations than a similar child from a lower class family. The behavior problems generated by viewing the child's problem as one of motivation may well prevent him from achieving his full potential; skillful parent counseling is a prerequisite to habilitation.

The trainable (or mildly) mentally retarded (TMR) comprise that group of persons with IQs between 3 and 4 standard deviations below the mean (54–40). The TMR develops at a rate between one-third and one-half of normal, reaching a mental age of 4 to 8 years by maturity; he remains functionally illiterate although he can be taught survival words (e.g., traffic signs and signals, safety warnings, lavatory labels). The ability of the TMR to acquire early academic skills sometimes fosters the illusion that with enough time and work the trainable child can achieve literacy. What is forgotten is that in both normal and retarded persons there is a plateauing of cognitive structures at about age 16; this places a significant limitation on the retardate's ability to "catch up" (Figure 8). It is tragic to encounter adult TMRs who have spent their entire academic careers working on literacy to the exclusion of needed self-help, vocational, and social skills.

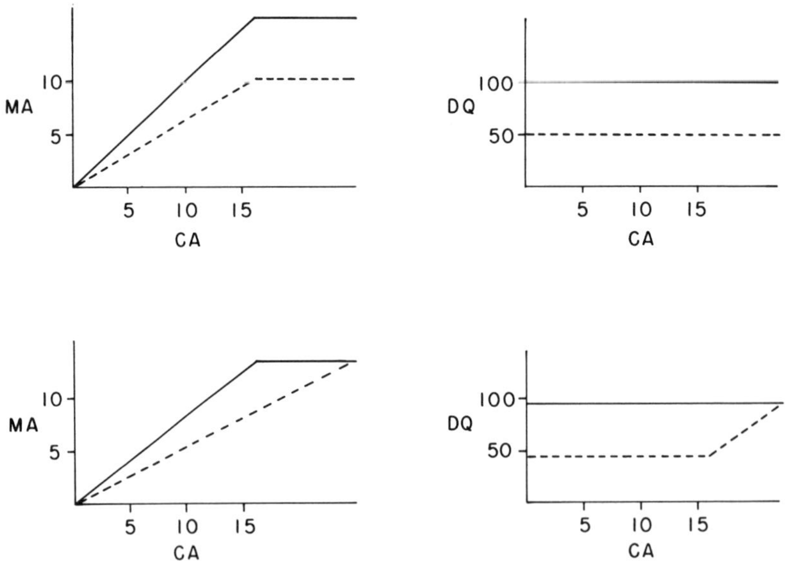

Figure 8. Development in the moderately retarded. The upper two graphs compare the development of a normal (solid line) to a moderately retarded (dashed line) subject. The lower two graphs depict what would happen if the evolution of cognitive structures did not plateau at maturity (approximately 16 years) for the retarded.

The severe (SMR) and profound (PMR) mentally retarded comprise that group of persons whose IQs are more than 4 standard deviations below the mean. These children do not fit into the usual special education curricula; they need help in feeding, dressing, and toileting as well as language and motor stimulation. Under the impetus of PL 94-142, Education for All Handicapped Children Act, educators are working with physical and occupational therapists, behavioral psychologists, and speech therapists to design responsive and innovative programs. In the not too distant past children with this degree of retardation had only one option as adults—institutionalization. In the past decade movements toward normalization and deinstitutionalization have both broadened and humanized the alternatives for integration into the community. The range of choices available is continually expanding (Wehbring and Ogren, 1976; Wolfensberger, 1973), and it is very difficult for the practitioner dealing with a young retarded child to conceive the possible life-styles that may be available in the next several decades. Even retardation complicated by significant physical disability may not necessitate custodial care.

There is much controversy surrounding the issue of labeling retarded children. According to the "Rosenthal effect" (Rosenthal and Jacobson, 1968) a diagnostic label may become a self-fulfilling prophecy to the detriment of the child. However, research with retarded children reveals little evidence for such a bias among psychologists (Dangel, 1972), teachers (Soule, 1972), or peers (Gottlieb, 1974). Babad (1977) found that the expectations of special education teachers were too complex for such a simplistic formula, and MacMillan et al. (1974) concluded that detrimental effects of labeling have not been documented. Although mislabeling is a genuine danger that one must always guard against, labeling itself often assumes the role of a pseudo-issue. The ultimate concern is appropriate educational programming for the individual and society. Labels should ideally contribute toward that planning as a shorthand; their potential misuse should not be used to mask more fundamental inadequacies in the educational service system.

BIBLIOGRAPHIC NOTE

The AAMD Manual on Terminology and Classification (Grossman, 1973) is essential reading. Conley (1973) and Fotheringham and Morrison (1976) review a wealth of epidemiologic data; Lemkau and Imre (1969) and Tarjan et al. (1973) are interesting individual studies. The apparent decline of IQ in Down syndrome is discussed by Koch et al. (1963) and Cornwell and Birch (1969).

THEORY

> Don't let us forget that the causes of human actions are usually immeasurably more complex and varied than our subsequent explanations of them.
>
> Dostoyevsky, *The Idiot*

The same facts can have very different interpretations given different theoretical assumptions. This provides something of a challenge to the clinician working with handicapped children because there is no one generally accepted theoretical perspective for either normal or abnormal development. One is forced to be eclectic, to pick and choose the more pragmatic, the more heuristic, the more intelligible, the more available.

The medical model is frequently identified with a disease-oriented approach. Its goal would then be the diagnosis of the sick versus the well, the identification of the abnormal versus the normal. If available, a treatment would be applied and a prognosis given. In the area of mental retardation, the medical model views retardation along a spectrum of other chronic neurologic handicaps. One way of depicting this complex brain damage matrix is illustrated in Figure 9; this diagram has the peculiar characteristic of completely reversing the usual psychometric bias in which the normal occupy a wide range and the retarded are represented by a point at one extreme.

If instead of the theoretical distribution of IQ scores as given in Figure 3 one looks at the actual distribution (Figure 10), the basis for the "two-group" theory of retardation can be observed. Five-sixths of the retarded population are only mildly involved; most of these are located on the tail end of the predicted normal distribution. Only one-sixth of the retarded have IQs below 55 and they may be viewed as occupying their own distribution curve. The latter group has a much higher prevalence of organic findings whereas the former is composed mostly of sociocultural or familial retardates.

The "two-group" model of mental retardation receives further support from studies of relatives of the retarded. The severely retarded tend to have families with IQs forming a normal distribution. These patients are like unexpected mutations within the pedigree; the etiology of their retardation is more likely to be accidental and unique. The mildly retarded, on the other hand, have

DEVELOPMENTAL DISABILITIES MATRIX

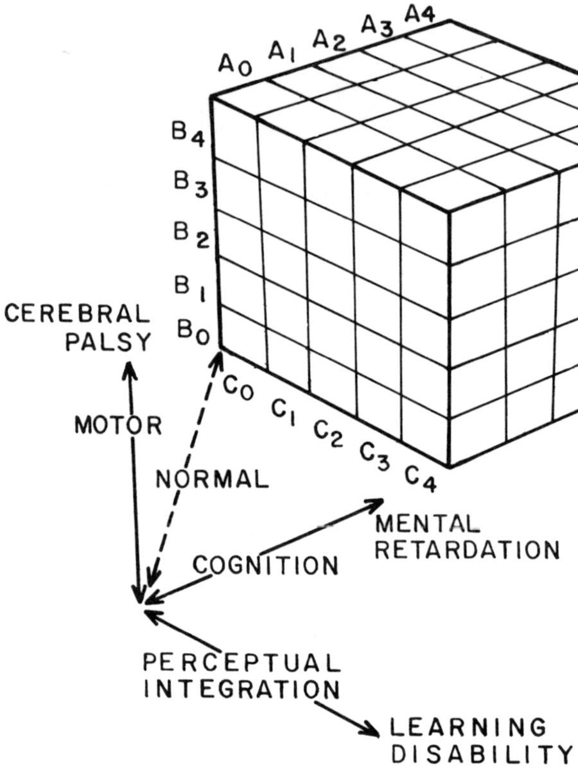

Figure 9. Developmental disabilities matrix. Although the number of variables could easily be multiplied to produce an *n*-dimensional figure, this cubic matrix allows one to approximate the interrelationships among the various developmental disabilities. A fourth dimension (time) is obligatory: the matrix should be visualized as a plastic structure that demonstrates slight distortions in shape as it moves to the right. The location of various chronic neurologic conditions on the matrix may be illustrated by the following examples: $A_0B_0C_0$ = normal child; $A_4B_4C_4$ = severely retarded, severely motor impaired child with significant perceptual dysfunction; $A_3B_0C_0$ = moderate global retardation with no motor disability or perceptual dysfunction; $A_0B_2C_1$ = mild cerebral palsy with normal intelligence and minimal perceptual dysfunction; $A_0B_0C_4$ = severe dyslexic with normal intelligence and no soft neurologic signs; $A_0B_1C_3$ = MBD child with normal intelligence, "clumsy child" syndrome, and moderate perceptual dysfunction; $A_3B_0C_4$ = moderate retardation with severe central communication disorder ("autistic" child).

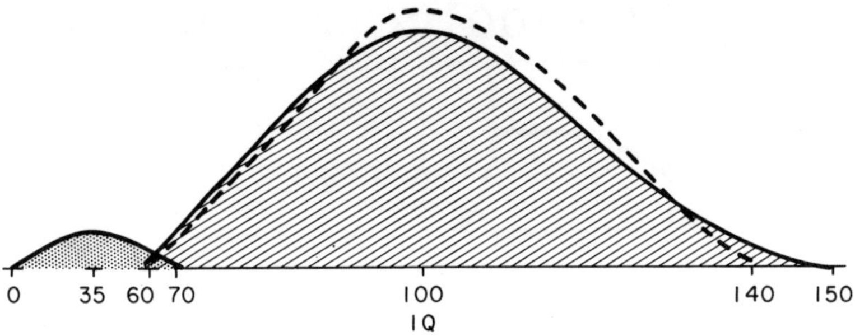

Figure 10. Two-group theory of mental retardation. The theoretical distribution of intelligence (predicted on the basis of a normal distribution) is shown by the broken line; the two solid curves present the actual distribution. The hatched curve (an almost normal distribution) emphasizes that there are more subjects at both extremes than predicted; the smaller (but still exaggerated) shaded curve represents that group of persons whose retardation has an organic basis.

families with IQs forming a distribution shifted toward the retarded range (Figure 11). These patients are likely to have siblings and parents with a similar degree of retardation; whether this is on a polygenetic basis (poor gene pool) or represents part of a vicious cycle of sociocultural deprivation is difficult to say.

The Lewin-Kounin model (Figure 12) posits that the mentally retarded are inherently more rigid in their thought processes (Kounin, 1941 a,b, 1948). Thus, a 10-year-old retardate with a mental age of 5 years will pass the same items on an IQ test as a

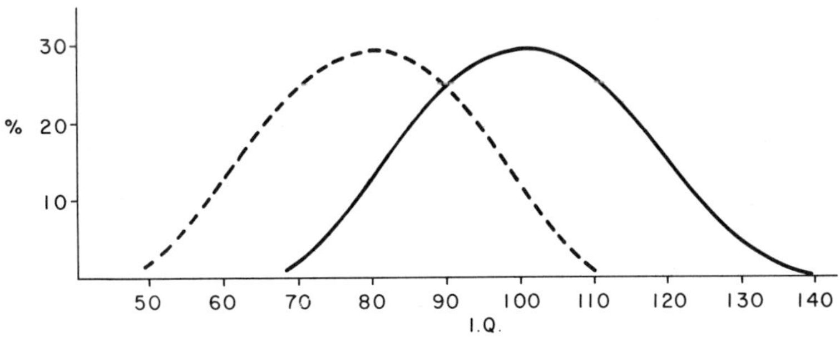

Figure 11. Distribution of IQ scores in families with a retarded member. In accordance with the "two-group theory" of mental retardation, the IQ scores of parents and siblings of the more severely retarded will tend to have a normal distribution (solid line), whereas the IQ distribution of parents and siblings of the mildly retarded will tend to have a mean in the borderline range (broken line). Redrawn from Roberts (1952) by permission.

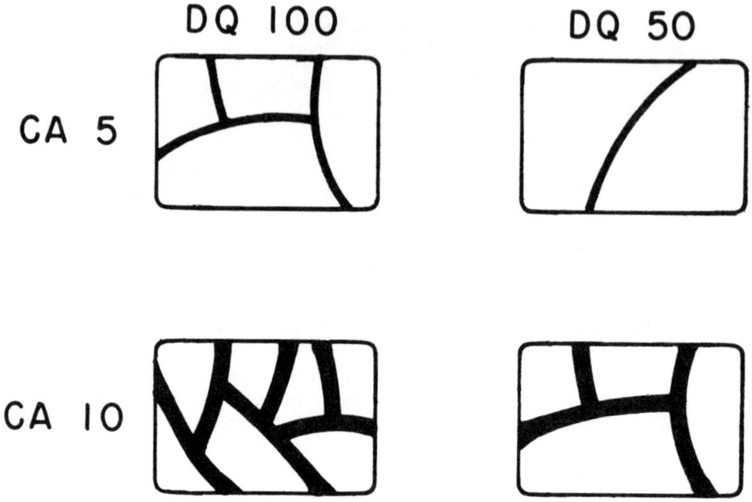

Figure 12. The Lewin-Kounin model. With increasing age, the structure and function of the mind increase in complexity but at the price of a decrease in adaptability or flexibility. Thus, a child with an IQ of 50 at 10 years of age passes almost the same test items as a normal 5-year-old but the quality of his performance is distinct from that of the normal 5-year-old and his potential for further development is much more limited. Redrawn from Zigler (1969) by permission.

normal 5-year-old, but the quality of his behavior will be deviant: his performance will be slower, less verbal, and more concrete. This defect or difference approach is certainly applicable to the small number of organically brain damaged retardates. However, the larger number of mild sociocultural retardates may be more open to a developmental approach in which the above qualitative differences are secondary to noncognitive factors such as motivation, past experience, and personality (Milgram, 1969; Shepps and Zigler, 1962; Weisz, 1976; Zigler, 1967, 1969; Zigler and Butterfield, 1966). Although the effect of such experiences as institutionalization is fairly complex (Birch and Belmont, 1961), it certainly involves lowered expectations and performance (Lyle, 1959). Both difference/defect and development hypotheses are probably true, but relate predominantly to different (although sometimes overlapping) populations.

The genetic contribution to intelligence is unfortunately either overplayed or ignored. With exceptions (the rare genius or retardate), children given an "average expectable environment" tend to take after their parents and demonstrate a generally predictable course of development. With extreme swings in the quality of the environment it should be possible to alter the tempo of developmental progress. Indeed it is one of the hallmarks of the normal child that he will respond to such variations. Thus a child with a genetic potential in the normal range (say, between curves C and D in Figure 13) can with environmental enrichment do better than predicted on a purely genetic basis; the ceiling for this effect is not known. On the other hand, a severely deprivational environment may depress a child's performance; but, in the absence of serious head trauma and malnutrition during the period of brain growth, such deprivation cannot depress the child into the retarded range. For example, language in childhood seems to be relatively resistant to a wide range of variables before demonstrating significant delay: "unless a child is literally raised in a closet he will make use of the language stimuli surrounding him, however impoverished these might be" (Lenneberg, 1964). A child with a chromosomal aberration or severe brain malformation

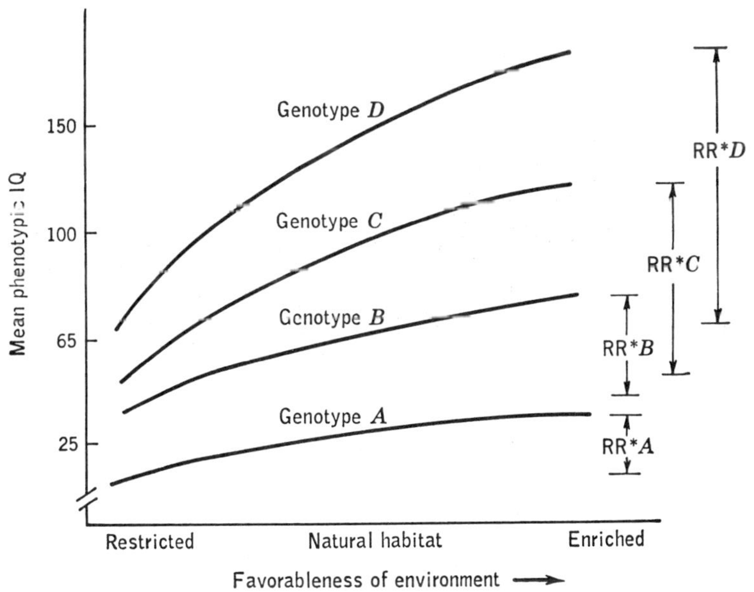

Figure 13. Reaction range. Given a genetic potential in the normal range, the effect of environment on the phenotype can be considerable. However, with a genetic potential increasingly within the retarded range, environmental effects become minimized. From Gottesman (1963) by permission.

may have a low genetic potential (say, curve A in Figure 13); environmental stimulation/deprivation will certainly affect behavior but overall cognitive/adaptive functioning will be little influenced. A striking characteristic of retardate development is its degree of stability (and predictability) as compared to normals. As an alternative to Figure 13, the enhancing and limiting effects of environmental quality over time may be depicted by Figure 14.

The psychometric model assumes that developmental variables are linear and continuous and that milestones are statistically additive. Such a theory is incrementalist and in reality nondevelopmental. The practical substrate for a medical approach to development is neural maturation. A maturational explanation for developmental phenomena requires certain structural changes in the developing central nervous system; similarly, brain damage from any cause will influence the behavioral expression of developmental phenomena. Many theories have attempted a comprehensive association between behavior and the structural levels of the brain (Figure 15). The most clinically useful observa-

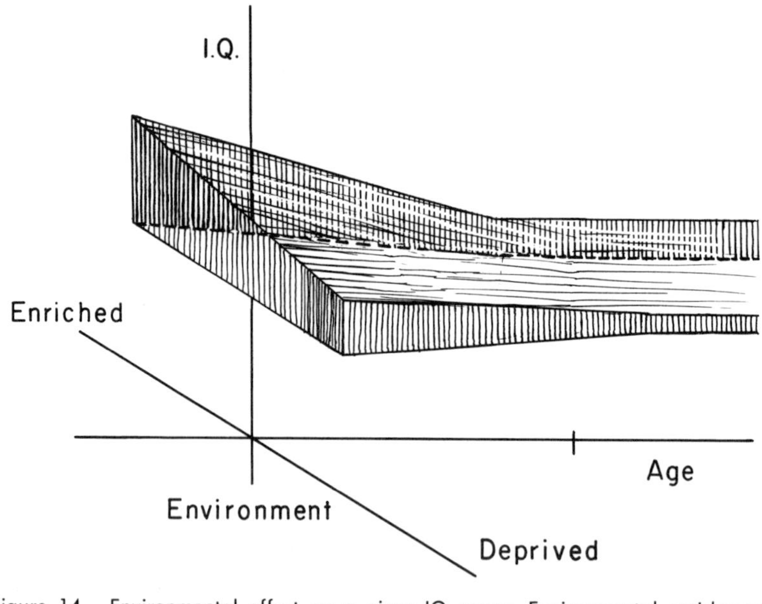

Figure 14. Environmental effect on a given IQ range. Environmental enrichment tends to increase the observed variability; environmental deprivation decreases mean performance and narrows the variability bandwidth. Similarly, time's arrow narrows the range of options except to the very brightest.

ENGLISH NEUROLOGY Hughlings Jackson	RUSSIAN NEUROPHYSIOLOGY Ivan P. Pavlov	COMPARATIVE NEUROANATOMY Edinger, Kappers, Herrick	PSYCHOANALYTIC PSYCHIATRY Sigmund Freud	SYNTHESIS
HIGHEST LEVEL	SECOND SIGNAL SYSTEM		SUPER EGO	ABSTRACTION DISCRIMINATION SYMBOLIZATION COMMUNICATION
MIDDLE LEVEL	CONDITIONED REFLEX	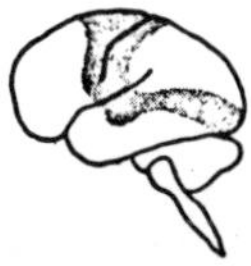	EGO	ACQUIRED ADAPTIVE BEHAVIOR
LOWEST LEVEL	UNCONDITIONED REFLEXES		ID	INNATE STEREOTYPED PERFORMANCE

Figure 15. Evolutionary concepts of brain function. Structural analogies among different theories of brain organization and function. From Magoun (1960) by permission.

tions are derived from data on the timetable for myelination: pediatricians involved in the assessment of infants recognize that visual orienting skills develop before auditory orienting skills (see Figure 16).

Brain damage models and the neuropsychology that depends on them are limited by the fact that the localization of a defect is not the same as the localization of a function (Zangwill, 1963). There is still some truth to Lashley's (1963) concept of mass action, in which more complex behaviors are a function of the whole cortex. Thus, a lesion to the motor strip will cause localized paralysis, but the voluntary production of complex motor patterns cannot be said to originate at any one place in the brain. Luria's (1973) neuropsychology illustrates this problem of localization by presenting "centers" that are actually scattered throughout the different areas of the brain and more or less loosely associated by multiple resonating pathways. The most fundamental weakness of modern neuropsychology is its lack of a firm developmental data

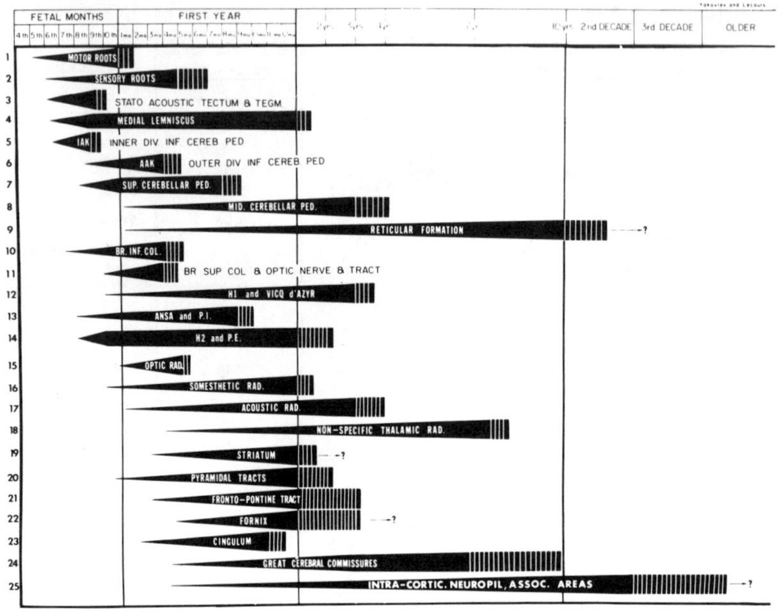

Figure 16. Cycles of myelination. Vertical stripes indicate the approximate age ranges for termination of myelination. Note that the visual pathways (11, 15) are myelinated before the auditory ones (17). From Yakovlev and Lecours (1967) by permission.

base. This is much more difficult than establishing psychometric norms because research is lending increasing support to the idea that identical lesions need not have the same effect on different patients; the multiple sources of individual variability have yet to be elucidated.

Sameroff (1975) reviewed many retrospective and prospective studies purporting to demonstrate correlations between perinatal insults and later developmental outcome. The documentation for this presumed association was found to be poor and the correlation with early environment was noted to be much more significant. To replace the older "continuum of reproductive casualty," Sameroff proposed a "continuum of caretaking casualty." But the classic neuromaturational perspective never did exclude environmental factors. Gesell (1940) had stressed the interaction between the organism and its environment—cultural milieu, siblings, parents, nutrition, illness, trauma, education—and had suggested that the distinction between the two should never be drawn too sharply.

Knobloch and Pasamanick (1959; Pasamanick and Knobloch, 1966) recognized the vicious cycle that readily occurs when infants with neurologic damage increase tension in their mothers and thus facilitate their own development of behavior problems. Such irritable babies may provoke their parents to child abuse or neglect, which is then misinterpreted as a primary cause of developmental delay (Sandgrund, Gaines, and Green, 1974). Postnatal exposure to toxins such as lead may reflect a similar circular association: prolonged mouthing behavior in retarded children increases the liklihood of their ingesting paint chips.

Prechtl, who has noted consistent associations between newborn evaluations and certain neurobehavioral syndromes in late childhood (1965), concluded that neurologically impaired babies do not make adequate partners in the infant-maternal interaction. He noted that the mothers of babies with gross brain damage (obviously abnormal) often adjusted better than the mothers of babies with only minimal damage when problems would frequently be blamed on the mother's handling of the child (Prechtl, 1963).

The New York Longitudinal Study demonstrated striking consistency of temperament from infancy to maturity (Thomas and Chess, 1977). Starting with nine different behavioral categories, Thomas and Chess were able to classify the majority (65%) of subjects into one of three temperament constellations: the Easy Child (40%), the Difficult Child (10%), and the Slow to Warm Up Child (15%). The Difficult Child with his slow adaptation to change, his intense (and frequently negative) mood expressions, and his irregular sleeping/feeding schedules, was especially vulnerable to the development of behavioral disorders. This Difficult Child temperament was found to be much more common in the retarded population, and when associated with another handicap further increased the child's vulnerability. These conclusions are further supported by the Kauai Study (Werner, Bierman, and French, 1971; Werner and Smith, 1977), which demonstrated that perinatally stressed infants were biologically more vulnerable to further environmental stresses; i.e., there was a cumulative interaction between perinatal stress and the quality of the caregiving environment (cf. Holden and Willerman, 1972).

The above studies by Prechtl, Thomas and Chess, Werner, Bierman, and French, and Werner and Smith all suggest that early anticipatory guidance of parents of brain damaged infants may alleviate if not prevent the later development of behavior disorders. However, higher scores on the Difficult Child temperament in retarded children imply both a greater degree of brain damage and a lesser response to environmental manipulation. Strauss and Lehtinen (1947), working with a population of retarded and cerebral palsied children, described the behavioral constellation of the "brain damage syndrome": distractibility, perseveration, conceptual rigidity, emotional lability, and difficulties with figure-ground perception. Later, when some children were found to exhibit this behavioral syndrome without cerebral palsy or mental retardation, they were assumed to have "minimal" brain damage. Finally, when neuropathology could demonstrate no structural lesions, they were reclassified as minimal brain "dysfunction"; i.e., they acted *as if* they had minimal brain damage even if they did not. Again, this behavioral constellation, known as the Strauss syndrome, becomes more common as one progresses toward the more severe levels of retardation. It describes essentially the same phenomena as the Difficult Child temperament.

Psychoanalytic theory, with its emphasis on the affective and irrational, has little to contribute to an understanding of mental retardation (Table 5). That profoundly retarded children will persist in mouthing objects (oral stage) or are not yet toilet trained (anal stage) are factual observations not functionally enhanced by attempting to fit them into an analytic framework. One of the fundamental truths of psychiatry does not seem to hold with regard to most behavior problems in the retarded: symptoms do not have to be traced back to and resolved at the infantile level of their origin. Rather, they may be extinguished immediately with little risk of alternative symptom formation. Erikson's (1963) rephrasing of basic psychoanalytic concepts within a perspective of cultural relativism has made them somewhat more palatable but of no greater relevance to a theory of retardation. The idea that some kind of emotional block can produce global developmental delay is deservedly waning. Although young children can certainly demonstrate specific emotional problems, the earlier that general retardation manifests itself, the less likely that it is secondary to emotional causes (Figure 17). Family discord can just as easily be the *result* of having a retarded child. Finally, whenever an emotional etiology is considered for any pediatric diagnosis, one must heed Apley and MacKeith's (1968) dictum that such an etiology

Table 5. Theories of development

Age (years)	Sexual (Freud)	Social (Erikson)	Cognitive (Piaget)	Moral (Kohlberg)
0–1	Oral—sensory	Basic trust/mistrust	Sensorimotor primary circular reaction 1–4.5 secondary circular reaction 4.5–9 coordination of secondary schemata 9–12	
1–2	Anal—muscular		tertiary circular reaction 12–18 invention of new means 18–24	
2–3		Autonomy/shame, doubt	Preoperational preconceptual 2–4	
3–4	Genital—locomotor	Initiative/guilt		
4–7			intuitive 4–7	Preconventional punishment reward
7–12	Latency	Industry/inferiority	Concrete operations 7–11	Conventional social approaval respect for authority ("law and order")
Adolescence	Puberty	Identity/role confusion	Formal operations	Autonomous social contract personal ethics

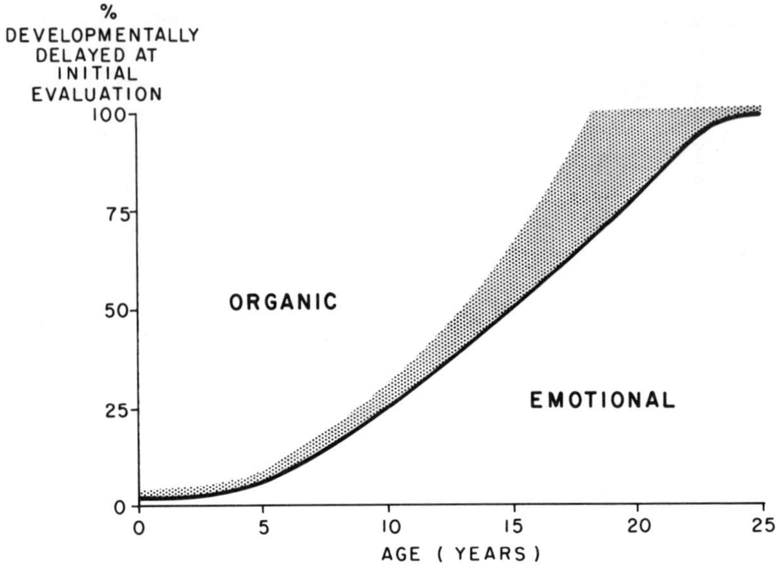

Figure 17. Organic versus emotional etiologies at different ages. The older school age child who has previously experienced academic success and who then begins to fail is much more likely to be suffering from a primary emotional disorder (Rutter, 1974). (Degenerative diseases are uncommon at all ages.) The younger child with global developmental delay is more commonly mentally retarded; the degree of psychopathology necessary to produce generalized delay is rarely seen in clinical practice. Secondary emotional problems complicating a primary neurologic deficit such as mental retardation tend to increase with age (shaded area).

cannot be established by exclusion but needs positive supporting data.

Cognitive theorists place much less stress on motivation; given the structure of the human mind and minimal environmental input, they posit an intrinsic drive to learn. Piaget has provided the model pattern (see Table 5) for the evolution of qualitatively different cognitive structures in childhood. The two basic adaptive processes of assimilation (by which experience or reality is modified to fit into existing cognitive schemas or structures) and accommodation (by which existing schemas are modified to incorporate discrepant experiences) contribute toward a fluctuating equilibrium. This cognitive homeostasis progresses through an invariant sequence of developmental stages, each of which is characterized by its own particular set of logical rules. Despite theoretical differences in construction, Piagetian scales correlate highly with formal intelligence tests (Dudek et al., 1969), and Piagetian stages effectively describe the adult functional levels for the different degrees of retardation. Thus the profoundly retarded ultimately function at the sensorimotor stage, the moderately to severely retarded at the preoperational level, and the mildly retarded at the level of concrete operations; to achieve the stage of formal operations (the use of induction and deduction) is to not be retarded. Because Piagetian theory recognizes perception and sensorimotor activity as stages in cognition, it has stimulated the proliferation of more refined infant tests. When older profoundly retarded children are found to be "off the scale," "untestable," or demonstrating no progress or even a declining IQ with formal psychometric instruments, Piagetian scales can often demonstrate developmental advances.

Although many American interpreters see Piaget as supporting a strongly environmentalist position (e.g., Hunt, 1961), his structuralism is much closer to Gesell's maturational perspective than to Skinner's behaviorism. Cognitive structures are essentially self-generating given minimal environmental input, and massive general types of experience are probably much more significant than specific teaching (Kohlberg, 1968). Nowhere is the limiting influence of genetic and organic factors more clearly seen than in Piagetian research on mental retardation; Inhelder (1966, 1968) refers to premature fixation or blocking at different stages. Although the assumptions of Piagetian theory are at the opposite extreme of those of learning theory (with its extreme form being incrementalist and nondevelopmental; thus, no developmental stages can be given for it in Table 5), it not infrequently supplies behavioral psychology with the cognitive prerequisites for achieving target behaviors. Thus until a child reaches sensorimotor Stage 6 (i.e., demonstrates delayed imitation and symbolic play), language training may program a mechanical increase in vocabulary but will fail to generalize (Kahn, 1975).

Kohlberg has applied Piagetian stage theory to the evolution of moral judgment (Table 5); cognitive structures are seen as necessary but not sufficient conditions for different levels of moral reasoning (Kahn, 1976). Although social experience is an additional requirement, more years of such experience (reflected in the chronologic age of older retardates) does not advance moral judgment beyond the limitation imposed by mental age (Taylor and Achenbach, 1975). The Temple Longitudinal Study demonstrated interrelationships between reasoning and moral conduct in retardates and between reasoning and moral judgment in normals. Although moral conduct improved with increases in mental age and chronologic age, the correlation between moral judgment and moral conduct in normals was surprisingly weak; in other words, normals were much more readily able to dissociate what they knew they ought to do from what they actually did (McLaughlin and Stephens, 1974; Mahaney and Stephens, 1974; Moore and Stephens, 1974). Whereas the mild, sociocultural retardate will violate the law approximately twice as often as the nonretardate, those with IQs below 50 make an insignificant contribution to the crime rate (Conley, 1973).

Theories help generate research questions and can place disparate clinical observations within a larger unifying perspective. But theories should never be used to restrict programs or other options available to handicapped children. Only hard data can bear the weight of that responsibility.

BIBLIOGRAPHIC NOTE

Theories of child development are reviewed in Langer (1969), Mussen (1970), and Rhodes and Tracy (1972). Theories of mental retardation are summarized in Ellis (1963). A neuromaturational perspective is presented by Gesell (1945); an interactional viewpoint is described in Sameroff (1975) and Thomas and Chess (1977). Piagetian theory is outlined in Gruber and Voneche (1977), and a behavioral psychology approach is argued in Skinner (1953) and Watson (1962). Luria (1961) refines the verbal mediation hypothesis. Moral development is outlined in Hoffman (1970).

The relationships between Piagetian theory and mental retardation are analyzed in Klein and Safford (1977), Reiss (1967), Wolinsky (1962), and Woodward (1959). Magary et al. (1977) and the preceding volumes in that series present some practical applications of Piagetian theory. Uzgiris and Hunt (1975) have standardized a Piagetian instrument for qualitative infant assessment. Correlations between achievement tests and Piagetian tests are reviewed in DeVries (1974). Wolff's (1960) attempt to assimilate Freud to Piaget has not generated any significant research

For those interested in assessing infant temperament in a pediatric setting, the Carey (1973) questionnaire is easy to use and correlates highly with the structured interview of the New York Longitudinal Study. Considering the overriding importance some theorists place on environment, the lack of objective measuring instruments in this area is striking. A useful exception is the Home Observation for the Measurement of the Environment (HOME) (Caldwell, Heider, and Kaplan). Baldwin and Baldwin (1973) found it difficult to support a language deprivation hypothesis in a naturalistic setting. Rutter (1972) offers a recent review of some of the complexities of "maternal deprivation" and concludes that the term should be retired. Lorenz (1967, Chapter 7) warns that severe deprivation experiments may have as little relationship to reality as laboratory-induced localized brain lesions. Infant stimulation is critically reviewed by Caldwell, Heider, and Elardo (1975) and Marquis (1976).

One would like to conclude this bibliographic note with a reasonable, balanced reference on the nature-nurture controversy. The absence of such a work is not to be deplored, indeed it is quite expected of such a political issue. For mental retardation, the nature-nurture polemic is something of a straw or pseudo-issue; since it does not admit a solution, it is best avoided in favor of more pragmatic concerns.

PATHOLOGY

Every generation of physicians has overestimated the progress made by medicine in its own time.

Snapper

Although mental retardation is a symptom and not a disease, medical diagnoses still have important etiologic and prognostic significance for retardation. The pathologic lesions associated with retardation may occur before, during, or after birth; the precipitating factors include trauma, asphyxia, malnutrition, toxins, infections, and metabolic and genetic processes. Timing as well as severity of the insult help determine the resulting degree of mental impairment.

The human brain is most vulnerable to injury during its period of maximal growth. Between the second trimester of pregnancy and the second year of age there is a spurt of dendritic arborization and synaptic connections. Approximately five-sixths of this brain growth spurt occurs postnatally. The cerebellar component is relatively later and more rapid and, therefore, most vulnerable to insult (Dobbing and Sands, 1973). Towbin (1971) emphasized mechanical injury at birth as relatively unimportant compared to hypoxia; asphyxia produces venous infarctions which tend to be periventricular in the premature infant and cortical in the term neonate. Towbin concluded that birth is "the most endangering experience to which most individuals are ever exposed."

Brain injury per se is not a unique determinant of behavior. Windle (1968) studied the results of severe hypoxia in newborn monkeys and found that although the structural brain lesions deteriorated over time, there was nevertheless considerable improvememt in the neurologic and behavioral characteristics. This lessening significance of acute insults over time was independent of any therapy and probably reflects the plasticity of the developing brain. This adaptive capacity to utilize alternate pathways is most evident clinically in the dramatic recovery seen in traumatic aphasia of early childhood with its accompanying shift of language dominance from the left to the right cerebral hemisphere. That Gottfried (1973) found poor correlations between perinatal asphyxia and the incidence of subsequent mental retardation is not inconsistent with an "all or none effect" at the more hypoxic end of the spectrum (Thomson, Searle, and Russell, 1977). It remains that anoxia increases the probability of mental retardation, but not all anoxia causes retardation (cf. Marriage and Davies, 1977, and Smith, Reynolds, and Taghizadeh, 1974).

The capacity of the organism to adapt to brain injury makes the neurologic examination of the newborn infant (and the child under 2 years of age) a poor predictor of developmental outcome; the fact that moderate to severe brain damage does contribute significantly to the incidence of retardation allows for the positive correlations found between newborn evaluations and later outcome (Mednick, 1977; Prechtl, 1965). Large-scale studies tend to dilute the effect of severe biologic insults because high variability is the most striking characteristic of the (larger) normal group. Such surveys conclude that low intelligence is better predicted by the level of maternal education, socioeconomic status (SES), and prenatal care than by biomedical and neurologic variables (Broman, Nichols, and Kennedy, 1975).

Gross structural malformations of the brain are associated with the more severe degrees of retardation. Heterotopia of brain cell types is found in certain genetic syndromes and intracranial calcification occurs with intrauterine infections. But most retardation is of unspecified etiology and the neuropathology is freqently nonspecific. Purpura (1974) has demonstrated changes in the dendritic cytoarchitecture in cases of severe mental retardation with nonspecific etiology (Figure 18); he found a decrease in the number of mushroom and stubby spines accompanied by a lengthening of the thin spines. Interestingly, similar structural changes (along with alterations in other biochemical parameters) have been noted in severly deprived rats. In these environmentally deprived animals the cortex weighed less, the RNA/DNA ratio was increased (because of decreased DNA), and there were greater activity levels for acetylcholinesterase and cholinesterase and a decrease in dendritic spines (Rosenzweig, 1976; Rosenzweig, Bennett, and Diamond, 1972). The reverse findings were noted in environmentally stimulated rats (although the magnitude of the change was more striking when compared to rats raised in a more naturalistic setting). Analogies from the rodent to the human cortex are tenuous; however, the lesson to be gleaned is simply that microstructural brain lesions may not be primary.

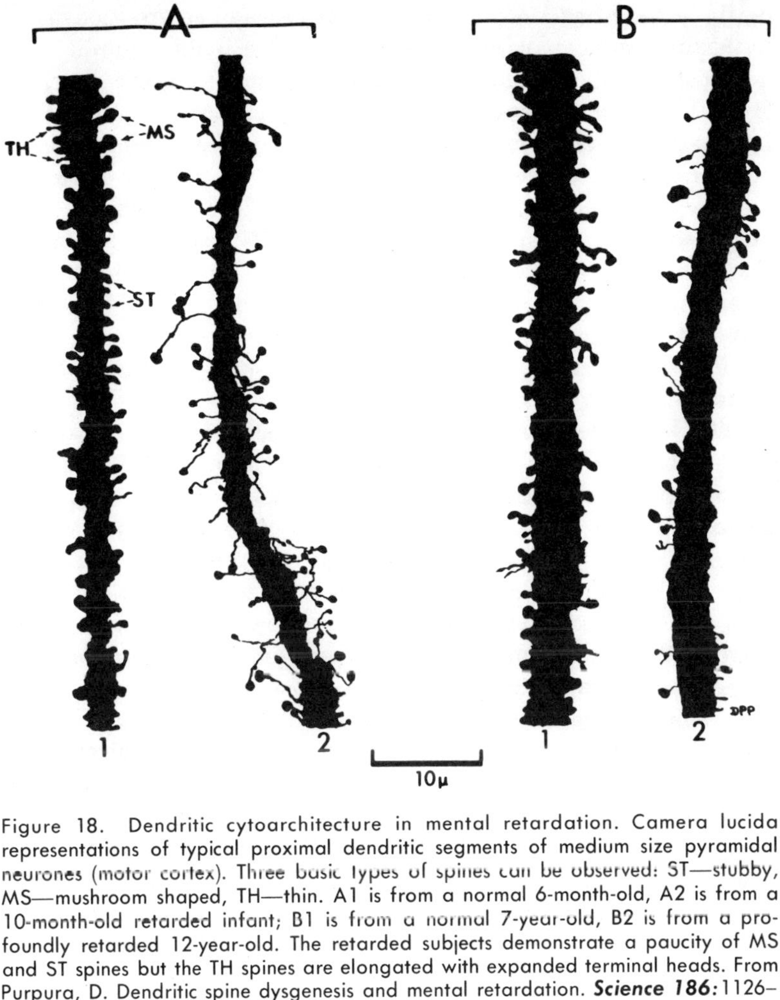

Figure 18. Dendritic cytoarchitecture in mental retardation. Camera lucida representations of typical proximal dendritic segments of medium size pyramidal neurones (motor cortex). Three basic types of spines can be observed: ST—stubby, MS—mushroom shaped, TH—thin. A1 is from a normal 6-month-old, A2 is from a 10-month-old retarded infant; B1 is from a normal 7-year-old, B2 is from a profoundly retarded 12-year-old. The retarded subjects demonstrate a paucity of MS and ST spines but the TH spines are elongated with expanded terminal heads. From Purpura, D. Dendritic spine dysgenesis and mental retardation. ***Science* 186:**1126–1128. Copyright © 1974 by the American Association for the Advancement of Science.

The incidence of identifiable (although nonspecific) neuropathology in the institutionalized (and therefore more severely) retarded approaches 90%. Freytag and Lindenberg (1967) found morphologic disorders in 83% of the brains of 359 autopsied retardates. In 50% of the cases the damage was present before birth, in 16% it was related to the birth process, and in 24% it occurred postnatally. (In 10% of the cases a time of onset could not be established.) Almost half of the cases of retardation which by history would have been attributed to perinatal complications demonstrate brain lesions at autopsy incompatible with such an etiology; the insult must have occurred earlier in utero (Palo, Lydecken, and Kivalo, 1966). Iivanainen (1974), using cerebral angiography and pneumoencephalography as part of a routine diagnostic evaluation for the severely retarded, was able to show neuroradiologic abnormalities in 90% of 334 cases. He too noted that many patients with a history of birth injury actually had cerebral structural defects more compatible with a prenatal etiology. He hypothesized that such infants would be more vulnerable to perinatal stress and more likely to demonstrate symptoms in the newborn period.

This situation makes the task of evaluating the significance of perinatal factors fairly complicated. Hobel et al. (1973) weighted various prenatal, intrapartum, and neonatal factors (Table 6). There was no significant increase in neonatal mortality or perinatal morbidity in those with high risk prenatal scores (total score $\geq$ 10) accompanied by low intrapartum scores. However, high risk intrapartum scores with high or low perinatal scores were correlated with high neonatal scores and high perinatal mortality. In general, intrapartum scores were most predictive of neonatal risk. When trying to associate problems at delivery with long-term outcomes such as mental retardation, the neuropathologic data cited above must not be forgotten; many of the babies who have a difficult delivery had abnormal brains to begin with. Braun, Jones, and Smith (1975) documented that breech delivery per se could be considered an indicator of fetal abnormality; the breech incidence of major malformations was three times that in babies with a normal presentation. Abnormal tone was postulated as limiting the fetus' ability to assume the vertex position.

Low birth weight seems to have a particularly high correlation with retardation: a birth weight under 2500 grams has an incidence of 7% in the general population, but of 25% in the retarded. A birth weight under 1588 grams occurs in 1% of deliveries but in 6% of the retarded population (Katz and Taylor, 1967). Whether appropriate for gestational age (AGA), premature, or weight-matched small for gestational age (SGA) infants have a worse prognosis is undetermined (Davies and Davis, 1970; Fitzhardinge and Steven, 1972; Neligan et al., 1976). To attempt to decide the issue on currently available data may not be very relevant since follow-up studies take a number of years to complete and intensive care nursery techniques are rapidly improving our ability to successfully manage problems of oxygenation and nutrition in these very small babies.

Certain infections in utero affect multiple organ systems, including the developing central nervous system. Because their clinical pictures can be very similar, serologic studies are necessary to distinguish the entities comprising the TORCH complex: toxoplasmosis, rubella, cytomegalovirus, herpes, and others. The impact of congenital cytomegalovirus is particularly intriguing because of the high percentage of unaffected carriers and the existence of "silent" infections which may correlate with mental retardation (Hanshaw et al., 1976; Sinha, Kaveggia, and Gordon, 1972). Other viruses previously thought benign may contribute to neurodevelopmental morbidity. Sells, Carpenter, and Ray (1975) documented that recovery from enteroviral meningoencephalitis in the first year of life was not as complete as supposed; 16% demonstrated definite and 26% possible signs of neurologic impairment such as small head circumference or low IQ scores.

Many gross structural malformations of the brain may have as their primary etiology a nonspecific viral infection during early cerebral morphogenesis (Johnson, 1972). Susceptibility to such infections may be enhanced by the immature immunologic system of the fetus (Sells and Bennett, 1977) or by a specific impairment in cell-mediated immunity in the mother (Rola-Pleszeznski et al., 1975). In the postnatal period children with primary immunodeficiency can develop encephalitis (Bugiani, Toso, and Gatti, 1975); patients with defined mental retardation syndromes do have associated impairments of the B system as in ataxia telangiectasia (Rosenthal, Markowitz, and Medenis, 1965) or of the T system as in Down syndrome (Levin, Nir, and Mogilner, 1975). The interrelationships between immune status and potential insults to the developing brain remain to be elucidated. Models for slow, inapparent, and recurrent viruses (Holland, 1974) suggest that current knowledge may be just the tip of an iceberg. Recurrent infections are a common phenomenon in the severely retarded. They have frequently been attributed to neurologic problems with the swallowing mechanism or to prolonged inactivity; detailed large-scale immunologic surveys are lacking.

The incidence of major nonbanded chromosomal abnormalities in the general population is approximately 1 in 200

Table 6. Prenatal, intrapartum, and neonatal factors

A. Prenatal factors

I. Cardiovascular and renal	
1. Moderate to severe toxemia	10
2. Chronic hypertension	10
3. Moderate to severe renal disease	10
4. Severe heart disease, Class II-IV	10
5. History of eclampsia	5
6. History of pyelitis	5
7. Class I heart diease	5
8. Mild toxemia	5
9. Acute pyelonephritis	5
10. History of cystitis	1
11. Acute cystitis	1
12. History of toxemia	1
II. Metabolic	
1. Diabetes > Class A-II	10
2. Previous endocrine ablation	10
3. Thyroid disease	5
4. Prediabetes (A-I)	5
5. Family history of diabetes	1
III. Previous histories	
1. Previous fetal exchange transfusion for Rh	10
2. Previous stillbirth	10
3. Post-term > 42 weeks	10
4. Previous premature infant	10
5. Previous neonatal death	10
6. Previous cesarean section	5

B. Intrapartum factors

I. Maternal factors	
1. Moderate-severe toxemia	10
2. Hydramnios or oligohydramnios	10
3. Amnionitis	10
4. Uterine rupture	10
5. Mild toxemia	5
6. Premature rupture of membrane > 12 hr.	5
7. Primary dysfunctional labor	5
8. Secondary arrest of dilation	5
9. Demerol > 300 mg.	5
10. $MgSO_4$ > 25 Gm.	5
11. Labor > 20 hours	5
12. Second stage > $2\frac{1}{2}$ hours	5
13. Clinical small pelvis	5
14. Medical induction	5
15. Precipitous labor < 3 hours	5
16. Primary cesarean section	5
17. Repeat cesarean section	5
18. Elective induction	1
19. Prolonged latent phase	1
20. Uterine tetancy	1
21. Pitocin augmentation	1
II. Placental factors	
1. Placenta previa	10
2. Abruptio placentae	10
3. Post-term > 42 weeks	10
4. Meconium stained amniotic fluid	10

C. Neonatal factors

I. General	
1. Prematurity < 2,000 grams	10
2. Apgar at 5 minutes < 5	10
3. Resuscitation at birth	10
4. Fetal anomalies	10
5. Dysmaturity	5
6. Prematurity 2,000–2,500 grams	5
7. Apgar at 1 minute < 5	5
8. Feeding problem	1
9. Multiple birth	1
II. Respiratory	
1. RDS	10
2. Meconium aspiration syndrome	10
3. Congenital pneumonia	10
4. Anomalies of respiratory system	10
5. Apnea	10
6. Other respiratory distress	10
7. Transient tachypnea	5
III. Metabolic disorders	
1. Hypoglycemia	10
2. Hypocalcemia	10
3. Hypomagnesemia or hypermagnesemia	5
4. Hypoparathyroidism	5
5. Failure to gain weight	1
6. Jitteriness or hyperactivity with specific causes	1

Factor	Score
7. Habitual abortion	5
8. Infant $>$ 10 pounds	5
9. Multiparity $>$ 5	5
10. Epilepsy	5
11. Fetal anomalies	1
IV. Anatomic abnormalities	
1. Uterine malformation	10
2. Incompetent cervix	10
3. Abnormal fetal position	10
4. Polyhydramnios	10
5. Small pelvis	5
V. Miscellaneous	
1. Abnormal cervical cytology	10
2. Multiple pregnancy	10
3. Sickle cell disease	10
4. Age $\geq$ 35 or $\leq$ 15	5
5. Viral disease	5
6. Rh sensitization only	5
7. Positive serology	5
8. Severe anemia ($<$9 Gm. Hgb)	5
9. Excessive use of drugs	5
10. History of TB or PPD $\geq$ 10 mm.	5
11. Weight $<$ 100 or $>$ 200 pounds	5
12. Pulmonary disease	5
13. Flu syndrome (severe)	5
14. Vaginal spotting	5
15. Mild anemia (9–10.9 Gm. Hgb)	1
16. Smoking $\geq$ 1 pack per day	1
17. Alcohol (moderate)	1
18. Emotional problem	1
(dark)	
5. Meconium stained amniotic fluid (light)	5
6. Marginal separation	1
II. Fetal factors	
1. Abnormal presentation	10
2. Multiple pregnancy	10
3. Fetal bradycardia $>$ 30 minutes	10
4. Breech delivery total extraction	10
5. Prolapsed cord	10
6. Fetal weight $<$ 2,500 grams	10
7. Fetal acidosis pH $\leq$ 7.25 (Stage I)	10
8. Fetal tachycardia $>$ 30 minutes	10
9. Operative forceps or vacuum extraction	5
10. Breech delivery spontaneous or assisted	5
11. General anesthesia	5
12. Outlet forceps	1
13. Shoulder dystocia	1
IV. Cardiac	
1. Major cardiac anomalies which require immediate catheterization	10
2. CHF	10
3. Persistent cyanosis	5
4. Cardiac anomalies not requiring	5
immediate catheterization	5
5. Murmur	5
V. Hematologic problems	
1. Hyperbilirubinemia	10
2. Hemorrhagic diathesis	10
3. Chromosomal anomalies	10
4. Sepsis	10
5. Anemia	5
VI. CNS	
1. CNS depression $>$ 24 hours	10
2. Seizures	10
3. CNS depression $<$ 24 hours	5

From Hobel et al. (1973). Prenatal and intrapartum high-risk screening. Am. J. Obstet. Gynecol. 117:1–9.

(0.5%). Almost 40% of these are sex chromosome disorders which, although they demonstrate phenotypic changes, are rarely associated with mental retardation (Jacobs, Melville, and Ratcliffe, 1974). This incidence varies strikingly with length of gestation since more than 90% of major chromosomal abnormalities are lost before birth (Hamerton et al., 1975). In very early spontaneous abortions the incidence of chromosomal abnormalities approaches 50%; in term stillbirths it drops to 5% (Hook and Porter, 1977; cf. Carr, 1965). Kim et al. (1975) found that approximately 10% of couples with a history of fetal wastage demonstrated cytogenetic abnormalities; the largest portion of these were balanced reciprocal translocations. Such rearrangements of genetic material (see Figure 19) were previously thought to be harmless. However, Jacobs (1974) hypothesized that euploid rearrangements could represent mutations at the breakage point. Funderburk, Spence, and Sparkes (1977) documented an increase in non-Robertsonian translocations in the severely retarded with normal karyotypes; when this incidence was correlated with parental banding patterns, most of the rearrangements were found to be de novo rather than familial. This would be consistent both with the earlier interpretation of (familial) translocations as usually benign as well as with Jacobs's theory that they may function as mutations. However, banding per se has added relatively little to the identification of genetic disorders in the retarded: severe retardates with normal karyotypes have a 0.6% incidence of banding abnormalities (Funderburk, Spence, and Sparkes, 1977). In contrast, abnormal autosomal karyotypes are found in 9.4% of institutionalized retardates; almost 90% of these are in Down syndrome patients (Newton et al., 1972b). Thus, out of 1000 severely retarded patients with multiple malformations and normal chromosomes, only six would be identified as having an abnormality on banding, and the significance of these findings would remain moot.

When karyotype and banding are normal and specific genetic syndromes are not identified, there remains a significant hereditary contribution to mental deficiency. This is especially important to consider when counseling parents as to recurrence risks for mental retardation. Turner, Collins, and Turner (1971) found a general recurrence rate on the order of 5%; Bundy and Carter (1974) estimated a 2.7% risk for the same type of retardation and added to this a 2.5% random risk to obtain a 5.2% overall

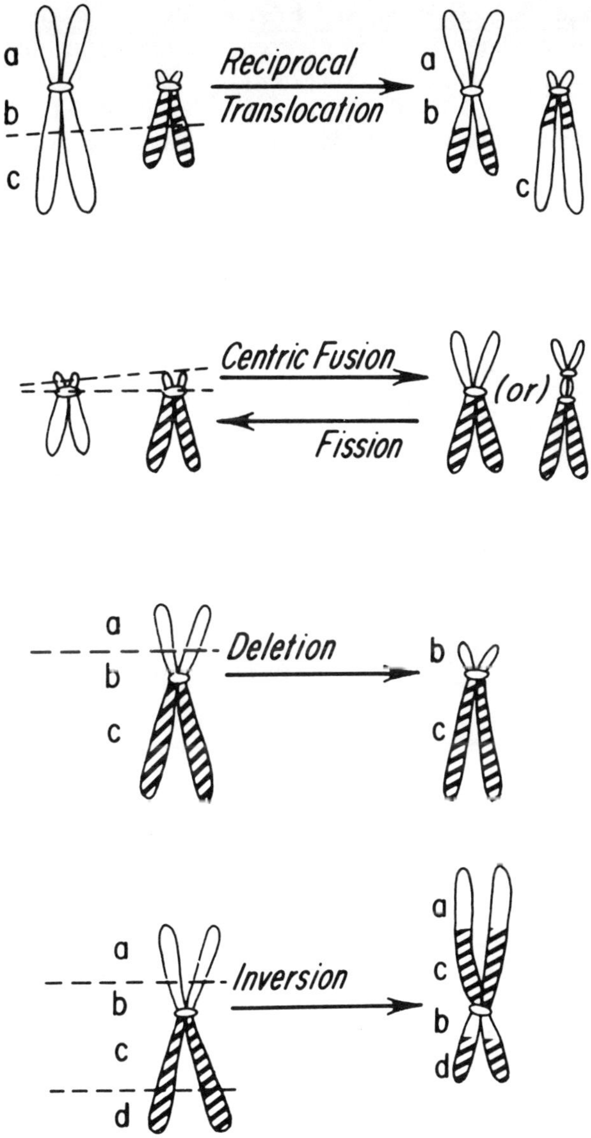

Figure 19. Major structural changes in chromosomes. Balanced structural rearrangements such as translocations and inversions have until recently been considered harmless. Non-Robertsonian translocations (top figure) have now been found to be increased in severe mental retardation. From Miller and Breg (1976) by permission of the ***New England Journal of Medicine 294:596–598.***

recurrence risk (cf. Angeli and Kirman, 1975). Certain categories of children, however, represented higher risks: moderately retarded males with no other specific findings (e.g., seizures, microcephaly, abnormal physiognomy) and patients with symmetrical spasticity not secondary to birth asphyxia had recurrence rates of over 10%. (A familial pattern of severe retardation in males may represent the Martin-Bell (1943) syndrome.) As more currently unrecognized sex-linked and autosomal recessive entities are identified, the recurrence risk for the same type of unspecified retardation should drop to 2% (Bundy and Carter, 1974).

It must be remembered, however, that whatever the numerical risk factor given to the parents, they will be more influenced by their perception of the sense of burden associated with the involved child (Leonard, Chase, and Childs, 1972). For example, if a family with a severely retarded, multiply handicapped, frequently hospitalized child is quoted a recurrence rate of less than 5% they will be less likely to risk another child than a family with a mildly handicapped child and a 25% recurrence rate. The perceived burden far outweighs the quantitative risk.

Identifiable and preventible genetic and metabolic disorders represent a restricted proportion of the total retardation problem. Despite advances such as amniocentesis (Milunsky, 1975, 1976), a marked reduction in the incidence of mental retardation within the next several generations is highly unlikely to result from medical technology alone (cf. Clarke and Clarke, 1977).

BIBLIOGRAPHIC NOTE

The lesions produced by hypoglycemia are analogous to those produced by hypoxia (Anderson, Milner, and Stritch, 1966); abnormal cerebral hemodynamics are fairly common in the more severely retarded (Doust and Podnieks, 1973). Naylor and Warburton (1974) investigated the genetics of obstetric variables and found a large hereditability component for the duration of labor stages. Aladjem, Perrin, and Fanaroff (1972) devised a score for the microscopic pathology of the placenta and correlated this with neonatal outcome. Fujikura and Klionsky (1975) studied the significance of meconium staining. Chik et al. (1977) used intrapartum fetal electroencephalograms and heart rates to predict neurologic status at 1 year of age. Postmaturity as well as prematurity increase the risk of cognitive impairment (Field et al., 1977). An animal model for immune prophylaxis against slow CNS viruses was demonstrated by Doyle and Holland (1973). Despite the possible contribution of slow viruses to mental retardation, the recommended schedule of immunizations is to be followed with retarded children (Report of the Committee on Infectious Diseases, 1974).

Modern genetics is reviewed by Erbe (1976a,b), Gerald (1976), and Miller and Breg (1976). Principles of genetic counseling are outlined in Nitowsky and Legum (1974) and Wilson (1975); recurrence risks are calculated by applications of Bayes' Theorem (Nicholls and Stark, 1971). A classic example of misinterpretation of genetic data was provided recently by the XYY debacle (Witkin et al., 1976); the pathway from chromosomes to human behavior is neither simple or direct. That in the late twentieth century extra genetic material could be associated with "criminal tendencies" will supply the subject for interesting psychoanalytic speculation in the next millenium.

BIOMEDICAL ASSESSMENT

Watson:	For example, how did you deduce that this man was intellectual?
Holmes:	It is a question of cubic capacity; a man with so large a brain must have something in it.

The Adventure of the Blue Carbuncle

There is no routine work-up for all retarded children; Smith and Simons (1975) have rightly criticized the nonrational use of diagnostic tests in the evaluation of mental retardation. The usual inpatient admission battery of CBC, urinalysis, electrolytes, serum chemistries, and chest x-ray is predictably unrewarding. Experienced clinical judgment is necessary to determine the extent of the biomedical evaluation, whether to pursue chromosome studies, measure hormone levels, order tolerance tests, gauge immunologic competence, or perform neuroradiologic procedures. Perhaps the primary emphasis should be placed on referral to a pediatric specialist (i.e., developmentalist) with special competence in the field of retardation rather than on a shotgun approach to diagnosis. Weakly positive or inconclusive laboratory results (usually not indicated in the first place) have the habit of increasing exponentially and thereby escalating hospital costs, multiplying parental anxieties, and contributing to iatrogenic anemia in the child, all without aiding in establishing a diagnosis.

The clinician must remember that the IQ of 55 is a significant demarcation point: five-sixths of the retarded population are above this point, only one-sixth fall below it. But those patients with an IQ greater than 55 are unlikely to yield an identifiable organic etiology, whereas with an IQ below 55 a chromosomal, genetic, metabolic, or encephalopathic etiology is much more probable (Table 7). Although this IQ cutoff can be used as a rough rule of thumb in selecting patients for more exhaustive testing, every case needs to be individualized. Nonbiologic factors will play a role: parents place a high priority on a comprehensive investigation for etiology and a definitive estimate of recurrence risks. Also, if infant stimulation programs are successful, the number of sociocultural retardates should decrease and the proportion of mildly retarded subjects with an organic etiology should increase.

Table 7. Pathology increases as IQ decreases

Increasing pathology 0 ←	IQ 50 to 54	Decreasing pathology → 70
Severe residuals of CNS disease during prenatal, natal, or postnatal periods		Polygenic variability
or		or
Cytogenetic anomalies		Experiential-socioenvironmental
or		or
Major gene effects		Mild residuals of CNS disease
Syndrome frequency: occasional		Syndrome frequency: rare (mild variants: cytogenetic and major gene)

From Garrard (1968) by permission.

Recognizing that there can be no cookbook or flow sheet approach to differential diagnosis in mental retardation, some tentative guidelines may nevertheless be suggested (Table 8). Generally, if genetic studies are positive less than 10% of the time, they are probably being overused and the selection criteria should be tightened; if they are positive in more than 25% of cases, the criteria need to be liberalized because some positives are probably being missed. Regardless of percentage yields, children with IQs below 50 and without a documented severe central nervous system insult should all have an amino acid chromatogram and a metabolic screening survey (cf. Scott and Thomas, 1973; Thomas and Scott, 1973); retarded children with three or more congenital malformations should be considered candidates for chromosomal studies (Daly, 1970; Summitt, 1969).

The medical evaluation of the child with mental retardation is composed of a detailed history (including a genetic pedigree), a physical examination focusing on dysmorphology and syndrome identification, a neurodevelopmental assessment, and indicated laboratory tests and other special procedures.

Whenever possible, the history should be supported by existing medical reports and other behavioral records. This is especially true of the birth history; two-thirds of parents who had been informed of the probability of severe brain damage in the newborn period (documented by detailed counseling notes) later recalled

Table 8. Indications for genetic diagnostic studies in mental retardation

	Banded chromosome analysis	Lysosomal enzyme assays	Amino acid testing	Organic acid testing
Strong indication	Clinical features of specific chromosome disorder Multiple minor or major malformations	Specific clinical evidence such as degenerative course, organomegaly, macrocephaly, macular degeneration, corneal clouding, coarse facies, or other	Clinical findings suggestive of specific amino acid disorder	Normal newborn who becomes acutely ill with metabolic acidosis or neurologic complications Episodic acidosis or neurologic symptoms
Moderate indication	? X-linked mental retardation		Normal at birth with microcephaly or seizures later Consanguinity or affected siblings	
Slight indication	Small for gestational age or microcephalic at birth	Normal at birth with neurologic abnormalities or seizures later	Isolated mental retardation	Normal at birth with microcephaly or seizures later Consanguinity or affected siblings
Insufficient indication	Isolated mental retardation ? Isolated neural tube defect or defect in brain morphogenesis	Isolated mental retardation Multiple malformations	Evidence of prenatal onset Multiple malformations	Isolated mental retardation Evidence of prenatal onset Multiple malformations

From Beaudet, A. L. Genetic diagnostic studies for mental retardation. In L. Gluck et al. (eds.), ***Current Problems in Pediatrics.***

nothing (Drake and Ober, 1963). Although parents will usually know the birth weight, they rarely note the Apgar score, and both of these data are independently significant (Drage et al., 1966). After the stilbestrol time bomb (Herbst et al., 1975) obstetricians have become sensitized to the risks of maternal medication for the fetus during pregnancy; recently Smith (1977) warned of the teratogenic effects of anticonvulsants. The category of substances dangerous to the fetus is enlarging rapidly and, given a retarded child, warrants careful investigation.

Baby books and family photographs can help to structure the developmental history. Historical items that are unlikely to be found in any existing records but that are of diagnostic importance focus on fetal behavior. Research on the quantitative assessment of fetal movement is verifying the older clinical impression of its importance (Dubowitz, 1977; Timor-Tritsch et al., 1976). Even without the use of ultrasound or pressure transducers, Pearson and Weaver (1976) were able to correlate a daily fetal movement count (DFMC) with fetal asphyxia. They let the mothers decide what constituted a "movement" and had them count the number occurring over 12 hours; a DFMC of 10 was low normal (2.5th percentile) between 32 and 40 gestational weeks. With a retarded child who demonstrates poor suck and excessive irritability alternating with extreme quietness in early infancy, a history of hypoactivity in the fetus may be obtained even from a relatively inexperienced mother (primigravida). Approaching term, fetuses may have episodes of hiccups, but hiccups after the seventh month of gestation are highly suspect as intrauterine convulsions.

The most important question one can ask parents is exactly when they began to worry that their child was not normal. The earlier this suspicion starts in the first year of life, the more retarded the child probably is. Experienced mothers will sometimes suspect something is wrong as early as the third trimester, but they usually succeed in suppressing this concern, and it may not surface again unless directly questioned. Establishing a prenatal onset can affect the direction and extent of the diagnostic work-up, and the repressed suspicion, now brought to light as an astute observation, might otherwise have festered as a source of guilt—you couldn't have known that early that the baby was abnormal unless you wanted it so.

Prematurity and its complications contribute not only to the incidence of mental retardation but also to the difficulty of diagnosing developmental delay early. After 1 to 2 years of age, taking account of 1 to 2 months of prematurity in the denominator of the developmental quotient (DQ) has little effect. But estimating DQs in the first year of life for children with different degrees of prematurity still presents the pediatrician with some unresolved difficulties. Should one make full allowance for the infant's biologic immaturity and correct for the short length of gestation in the denominator? Or does the baby's prolonged extrauterine experience (compared to matched chronologic age infants) accelerate neurologic maturation (Figure 20)? The clinical observation that a premature infant, when he reaches his expected date of delivery, appears developmentally more advanced than a full-term newborn suggests that experience does play a role in stimulating certain areas of development such as visual attentiveness. Other milestones such as the social smile (appearing at 46 post-conceptual weeks) follow a stricter biologic timetable (Bower, 1974). Thus although full correction for the degree of prematurity is warranted after 6 months of age, it can lead to overestimation of the rate of development in the first half-year of life (Hunt and Rhodes, 1977).

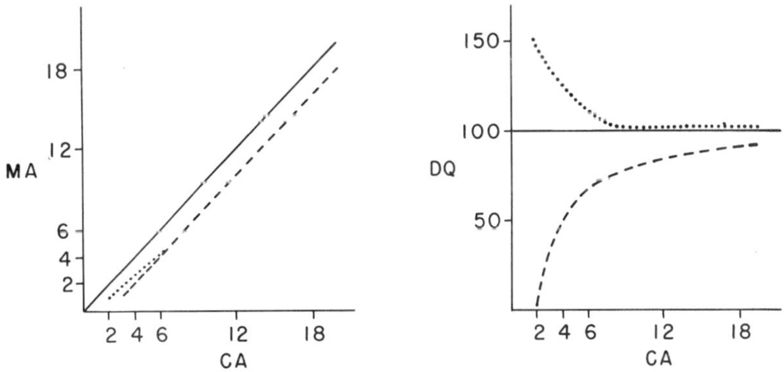

Figure 20. The developmental quotient in premature infants. If development were purely maturational, a baby 2 months premature (left, broken line) would progress with a mental age (MA) consistently 2 months slower than a term infant (left, solid line). If one calculated the developmental quotient (DQ) for this premature using an uncorrected chronologic age (CA), a curve approaching normal (DQ = 100) from below would result (right, broken line). In actual fact, the added experience of being extrauterine longer than a term baby matched for gestational age does accelerate some developmental milestones in the first half-year of life (left, dotted line); if one corrects these items for the full degree of prematurity, normal may be approached from the higher end of the DQ scale (right, dotted line).

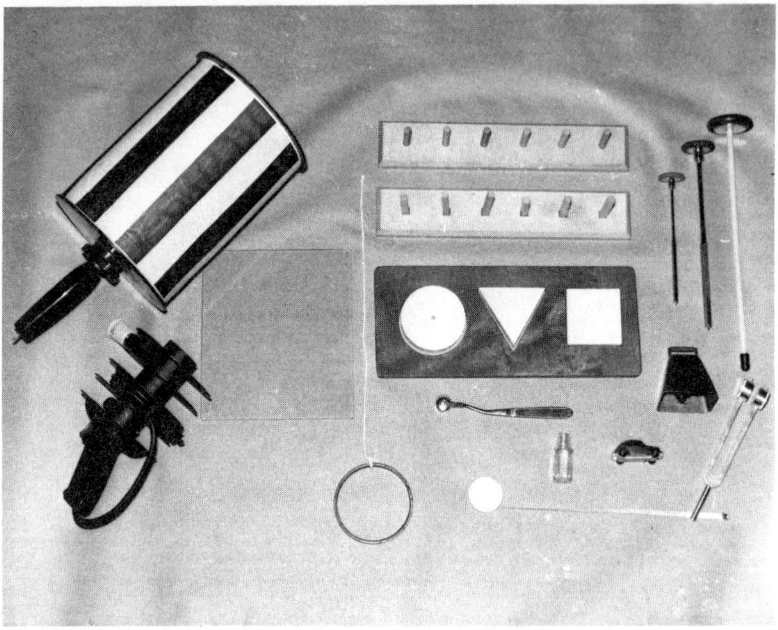

Figure 21. Neurodevelopmental kit. Skull transillumination with an instrument such as the Chun gun should be routine in the newborn evaluation and in the assessment of retarded children. The OKN (optokinetic nystagmus) drum can be used to document the basic integrity of the retinal-occipital pathway. The Queen Square type of reflex hammer is much more sensitive than the commonly used triangular shaped ones. The cow bell is particularly effective in breaking through the habituation seen in retardates. The pegboards, round (Wallin A) and square (Wallin B), are used to assess both problem-solving skills and fine motor coordination.

The neurodevelopmental assessment (Figure 21) includes both a pediatric neurologic examination and a comprehensive developmental evaluation. The classic neurologic examination contributes relatively little to the assessment of mental retardation. The prognostic values for mental retardation of a neurologic evaluation in the newborn period (Donovan, Coues, and Paine, 1962) and in the first year of life (Yang, Ting, and Kennedy, 1968) is very low. Only when more attention is paid to the behavioral component of infant behavior is predictability improved (DeSouza and Milner, 1974; Prechtl, 1965). Hypotonia is commonly associated with mental retardation in infancy; it is frequently referred to as "benign cerebral hypotonia"—the "benign" signifying the absence of cerebral palsy (many motor-impaired infants pass through a transient phase of hypotonia in the first year) and degenerative central nervous system disease. From a cognitive viewpoint it is not nearly so benign. Severe hypotonia may also be observed in late infancy in blind children when their visual impairment has remained unsuspected (Jan et al., 1975); it resolves with appropriate sensorimotor stimulation. Although primitive reflexes persist longer in children with cerebral palsy, their temporal evolution in severe mental retardation without a motor component is unknown (Capute et al., 1978).

In the older retarded child the presence of "soft signs," the involuntary spread (sometimes contralateral) of complex voluntary movement patterns, reflects the mental age: of two children with the same chronologic age, the one with the lower mental age will demonstrate more overflow. This covariation is independent of other evidence for neuromotor impairment (Cohen et al., 1967). These neurologic signs, each with its own developmental age, are certainly not diagnostic of retardation. They would seem to occupy a position similar to the Simian crease in Down syndrome: they are more common in retarded than in normals, but even a low incidence in normals leaves so many of the latter with positive signs that they are useless for screening purposes. As with the Simian crease, finding the sign does not establish the diagnosis, but given the diagnosis it is somewhat silly not to look for the associated signs. Subscore scatter on IQ tests is a cognitive soft sign that suffers from similar limitations (Kaufman, 1976). Studies of laterality (hand, foot, and eye preferences) suggest a higher incidence of sinistrality and crossed laterality in both retarded and learning-disabled children. However, the relationship of these phenomena to cerebral dominance and cortical development is still very confused and will have to await more accurate clinical research (cf. Touwen, 1972).

Degenerative disorders are traditionally divided into those involving predominantly gray matter versus those affecting white matter. The gray matter or neuronal storage group damages higher cortical functions with visual impairment and seizures early on; only late in the course of the disease do motor signs appear. Some of these children may first be referred for evaluation of a cognitive deficit. In the white matter disorders motor signs are among the first to appear with spasticity, Babinski dorsiflexion, hyperreflexia, and ataxia; intellectual deterioration occurs late in the course. These disorders have an almost universally hopeless prognosis ending after a variable time period in death; effective therapy exists only for a handful, such as Wilson's hepatolenticular degeneration, Hartnup's disease, and some hyperammonemia syndromes. Despite the complex biochemical deficiencies that are being unraveled, progress in the understanding of these rare diseases will not decrease the incidence of mental retardation; they affect developmental progress only slightly more directly than other severe organic disorders with a progressively fatal course. Oddly enough, the initial and single most important step in diagnosing these purely neurologic diseases is not, properly speaking, neurologic at all but developmental. When the pediatrician is presented with a case of delay, he needs to carefully assess the child's past rate of development (Figure 22). Until a loss of milestones is documented, vigorous pursuit of a diagnosis of degenerative disease is difficult to justify. Yet it is urgent to reach such a diagnosis as soon as possible because of the strong heredit-ability component in these disorders. As with mental retardation in early infancy, a diagnosis is approached by successive approximations, by increasing suspicion (Ingram, 1969) confirmed by serial examinations.

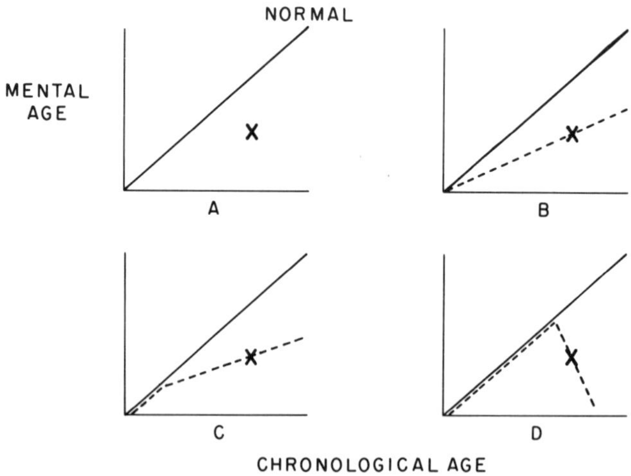

Figure 22. Patternologic diagnosis. When the pediatrician is presented with a child whose development is delayed (A), it may be a case of retardation from birth (B), from postnatal insult (C), or secondary to a degenerative disorder (D). The pattern of development assumes a much greater importance than the simple fact of delay.

Although multiple malformations (major or minor) support a prenatal etiology, similar phenotypes may result from either genetic or intrauterine environmental factors. The concept that even minor physical anomalies are markers for basic neurologic integrity has yielded positive correlations between such malformations and both hyperactivity (Waldrop and Halverson, 1971) and problem-solving behavior (Halverson and Victor, 1976) in normal children. Patterns of malformations are usefully subsumed under different syndrome categories when a common etiology or prognosis can be assigned. But facility in syndrome identification requires more than a simple accretion of isolated malformations; clinical experience allows the pediatrician with a high index of suspicion to develop a gestalt perspective that cannot be learned from books. A coloboma of the eye in a newborn may lead one to check for anal atresia (cat-eye syndrome), but the synophrys (bushy eyebrows that cross the midline) of the Cornelia de Lange syndrome may not be present at birth. In the Williams syndrome by the time the elfin facies develops and the supravalvular aortic stenosis is diagnosed the infantile hypercalcemia has resolved; the cat cry in the cri-du-chat (5p−) syndrome disappears by 1 year of age. The hallmark of Menkes syndrome must wait upon the child's growing some hair; the hypospadias that is one of the distinguishing characteristics of the Smith-Lemli-Opitz syndrome does not aid diagnosis in a female. Two of the most common causes of retardation, Down syndrome (Figure 23) and hypothyroidism (cretinism), do not frequently adhere to the textbook descriptions when involved infants are admitted to the newborn nursery. Although specific diagnosis may sometimes be made on clinical grounds alone, the pediatrician's certainty that something is wrong with this baby often far outweighs his satisfaction with a particular diagnosis in the absence of confirmatory laboratory tests. (Universal thyroid screening is becoming more widespread.) The remainder of this chapter discusses selected clues in the medical evaluation of the retarded child; more comprehensive references are found in the bibliographic note.

General growth failure is a common feature of many kinds of retardation. Kügel and Mohr (1963) and Mosier, Grossman, and Dingman (1965) found a positive correlation between mental and physical (including sexual) development. The more severe the retardation, the greater the growth deficiency; when the growth deficiency was of prenatal onset, it remained relatively more

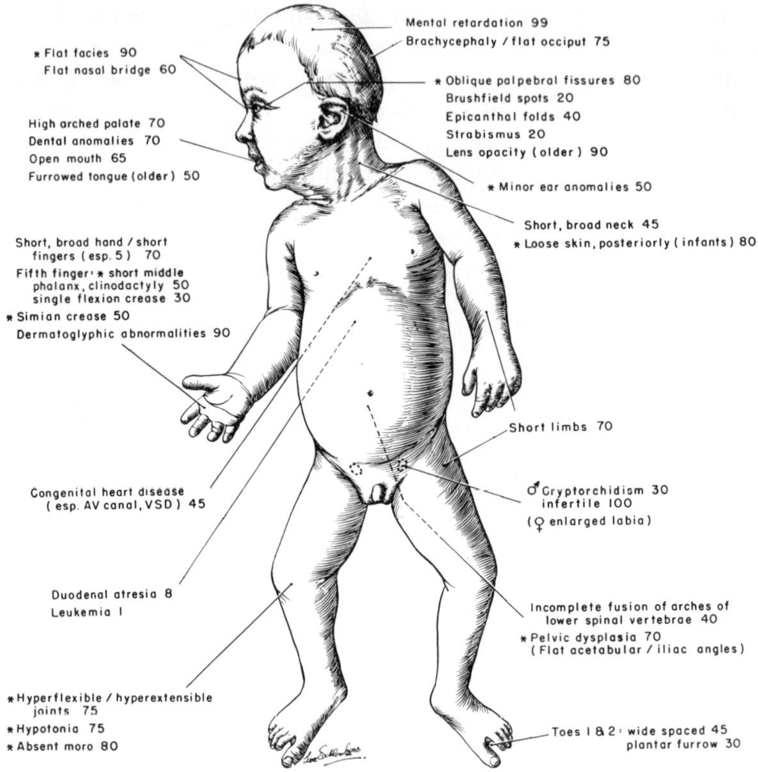

Figure 23. Down syndrome. Percentages for the different components of the syndrome are given above; the asterisked items are Hall's (1966) 10 cardinal signs of Down syndrome in the newborn period: if six or more are present the diagnosis is clinically confirmed; less than six warrants chromosomal studies. Down syndrome accounted for one-quarter to one-half of the population in many older institutions; it accounts for almost 90% of the identifiable chromosomal abnormalities in mental retardation.

marked. Pilot studies (e.g., Lowrey et al., 1968) attempting to identify endocrine abnormalities in the retarded have been negative or inconclusive; the numbers have been small and the populations studied too heterogeneous. (It should be remembered that most dwarf syndromes are associated with normal intelligence.) As endocrinology evolves toward neuroendocrinology, a specific lesion in the hypothalamic-pituitary axis need not be postulated; nonspecific brain damage sufficiently diffuse to cause severe mental retardation can easily alter a delicate neuroendocrine homeostasis.

Genetic retardation syndromes are frequently associated with short stature; Chen et al. (1970) showed that, with other criteria for chromosome studies being constant, a low birth weight multiplied the number of abnormal karyotypes uncovered by a factor of 3 to 4. The association with growth holds if one starts from the other end: a common diagnosis in the wastebasket category "failure to thrive" is mental retardation (Glaser et al., 1968; Riley et al., 1968). Growth deficiency with retardation may also result from combined toxic and nutritional effects of maternal alcohol ingestion. The fetal alcohol syndrome (Jones and Smith, 1973, 1975; Jones et al., 1974) demonstrates a prenatal growth deficiency, developmental delay, small palpebral fissures, and multiple other anomalies; the severity of the manifestations appear dose related. Asymmetrical growth is a prerequisite of the Russell-Silver syndrome with low birth weight, short stature, triangular facies (pseudohydrocephalus), café au lait spots, elevated urinary gonadotropins, and urinary tract abnormalities. Low birth weight should also raise one's index of suspicion for the TORCH complex of intrauterine infections.

Large birth weight is observed in patients with Wiedemann-Beckwith syndrome and Sotos syndrome (cerebral gigantism); the association with a degree of retardation in these cases is mild. Children with normal birth weights who later gain weight rapidly may have the Prader-Willi syndrome (H_3O, hypotonia-hypomentia-hypogonadism-obesity) or the Laurence-Moon-Bardet-Biedl (LMBB) syndrome; the retardation in these syndromes is moderate. It is important to identify the LMBB syndrome early because it is an autosomal recessive. Even if the obese retardate does not have polydactyly or a positive family history, a careful ophthalmologic examination should be made for the earliest signs of the retinal degeneration diagnostic of LMBB.

Among abnormalities of the shape and size of the head, microcephaly has usually been awarded the greatest prominence. Avery, Meneses, and Lodge (1972) and Pryor and Thelander (1968) found that extreme microcephaly correlated with severe retardation. Thus a head circumference between 2 and 3 standard deviations below the mean for age would be compatible with normal but not with superior intelligence; most of the children with OFCs (occipito-frontal circumferences, maximal measurement) in this range would be retarded. As the head circumference measurement drops below 3 standard deviations, the probability and degree of retardation increases (Martin, 1970; O'Connell, Feldt, and Stickler, 1965). MacFarlane et al. (1975) suggested that correlation with intelligence could be improved by taking the head circumference percentile for the child's height age rather than for his chronologic age. That the correlation with IQ must always remain approximate is readily concluded from the fact that large heads rarely signify genius; indeed, the commonest cause of megalocephaly (large head) is hydrocephalus, which can itself lead to retardation. Even true megaloencephaly (large brain) is a familial (autosomal dominant) trait frequently associated with dull normal to mildly retarded intelligence (DeMyer, 1972). Finally, even with a very small head, the brain substance may be smaller still (Figure 24).

Qazi and Reed (1973, 1975) have hypothesized that an autosomal recessive gene for microcephaly may account for 10% of all mental retardation. Heterozygotes for that gene may demonstrate phenotypically only retardation, but an epidemiologic study of this population reveals an increased incidence of consanguinity and mental retardation in first degree relatives, microcephaly at birth (50%), and decreased rates of birth, perinatal complications, and neurologic abnormalities. Smith and Gong (1974) noted that primary microcephaly is frequently (83%) associated with aberrant trichoglyphics: the abnormal hair pattern in microcephaly is an absent or poorly developed parietal whorl (present in 95% of normals, with 80% being clockwise).

The head circumference should be plotted on standardized growth charts (Figure 25) and reported in unit measures (cm), percentile for age, and (when less than the third percentile for age) as that age for which it is fiftieth percentile. One can also attempt to estimate the number of standard deviations below the mean for age a given measure is. Thus, a 5-month-old male with a head circumference of 38 cm is well below the third percentile for age, approximately 4 standard deviations below the mean for age, and at the fiftieth percentile for 1-month-olds. Especially in the first 2 years of life, serial measurements are much more instructive than single ones.

Infants with hydranencephaly can behave much like normal newborns (Halsey, Allen, and Chamberlin, 1968); as a rough first approximation Peiper's (1963) concept of the newborn infant as a subcortical organism thus receives some support. While more refined techniques of observation continue to uncover complex

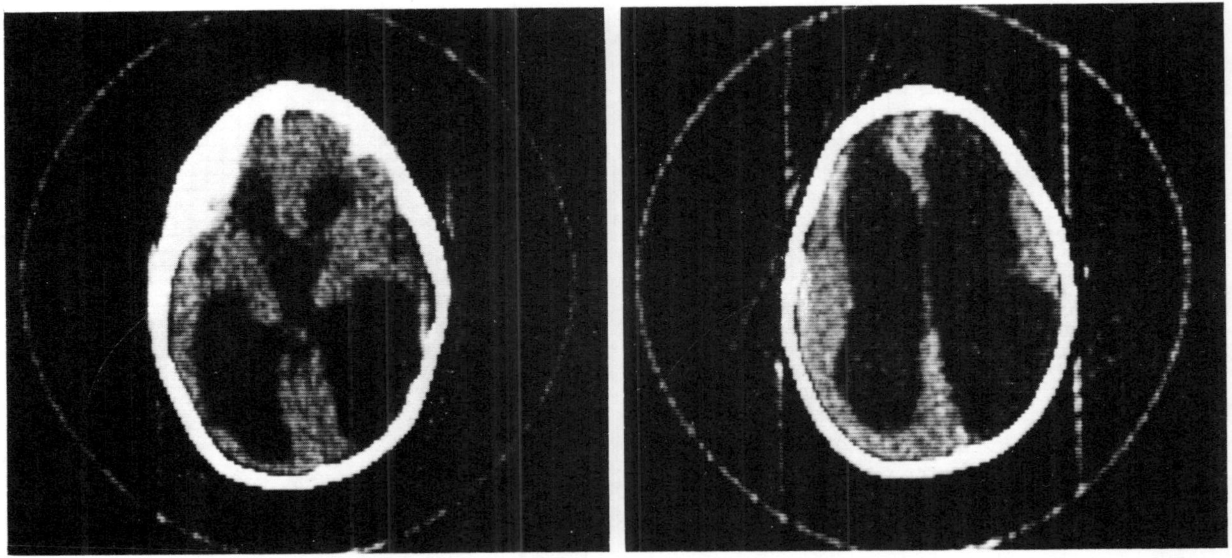

Figure 24. This 4-year-old profoundly retarded child had severe microcephaly with a head circumference 3 standard deviations below the mean for his age. Nevertheless, computerized tomography demonstrated a degree of hydrocephalus ex vacuo such that the actual volume of brain tissue is less than would have been predicted from external skull measurements. Courtesy of Fred J. Hodges, III.

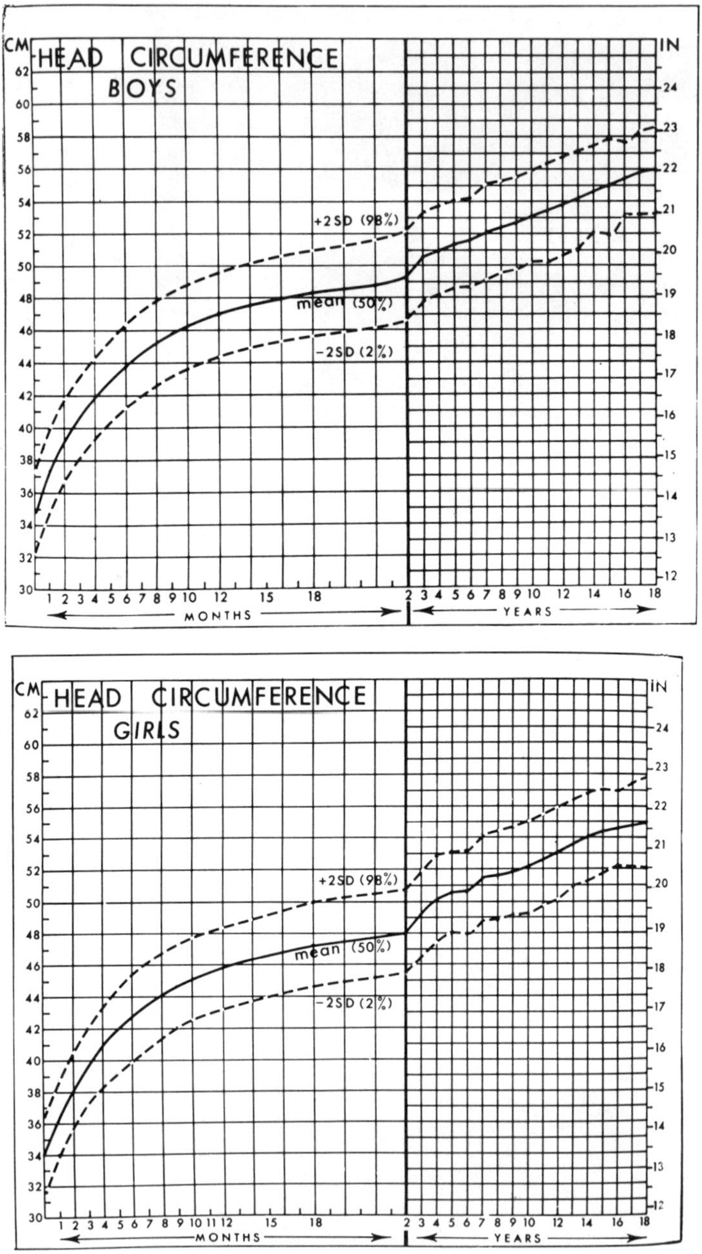

Figure 25. Head circumference in boys and girls. From Nellhaus (1968). ***Pediatrics* 41**:106–114. Copyright © 1968 American Academy of Pediatrics.

learning abilities in the normal neonate (Brazelton, Parker, and Zuckerman, 1976; Robinson, 1966), for the pediatrician, routine transillumination with an instrument such as the Chun gun (standards in Cheldelin, Davis, and Grant, 1975) should be carried out in the first month of life. Fontanel size (standards in Popich and Smith, 1972) can also be followed in the first 2 years of life. Large fontanels may accompany hypothyroidism, Down syndrome, and cleidocranial dysostosis, among others; small fontanels may suggest premature closure of cranial sutures. When only one of the sutures fuses prematurely, the problem is mostly cosmetic; when they all fuse early, surgery may be attempted to relieve pressure on a growing brain and thus prevent retardation. However, the long-term results of such surgery for craniosynostosis (or craniostenosis) are fairly disappointing; in most cases the sutures fuse prematurely secondary to a primary arrest of brain growth (cf. Freeman and Borkowf, 1962; Hemple et al., 1961).

Like hypertelorism, microcephaly is a clinical rather than a radiologic diagnosis. Plain films may show only an altered cranio-facial ratio (Figure 26), or they may reveal distinctive patterns of intracranial calcification (Figure 27; cf. Babbitt et al., 1969; Caffey, 1972). More elaborate neuroradiologic procedures such as cerebral angiography or pneumoencephalography (PEG) may be considered in selected cases, but recent refinements in the technology of computerized tomography (CT) have made available a noninvasive, low risk scan of relatively high resolution (Figure 28; cf. Gomez and Reese, 1976; Harwood-Nash and Breckbill, 1976).

Measurements of the interpupillary distance to determine hypertelorism or hypotelorism may need to be supplemented by inner and outer canthal distances (Feingold and Bossert, 1974). The eye should be carefully examined both externally (Figures 29, 30) and fundoscopically (Figure 31). The retina is the only part of the brain directly accessible to examination without any invasive procedures. Unfortunately, the majority of diagnostically specific patterns belong to the spectrum of degenerative disorders; the most common finding in nonspecific mental retardation is an exaggerated granular quality to the macula. In addition to associations with retardation and various syndromes (Figure 30), abnormalities of the pinna frequently accompany structural anomalies of the middle ear; many of these are surgically correctable with improvement of hearing (Jaffe, 1976).

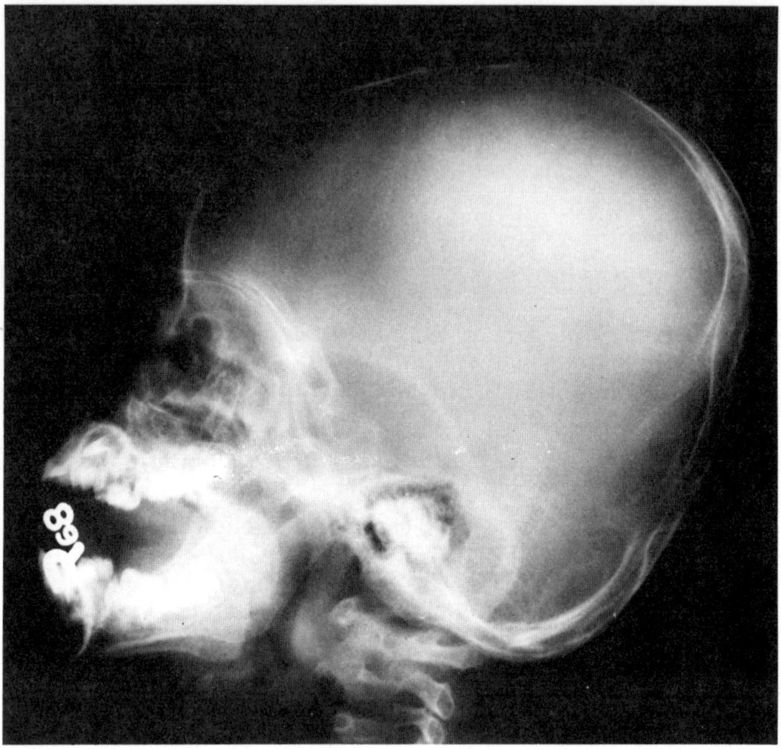

Figure 26. Microcephaly is best diagnosed on physical examination by head circumference measurement. However, x-rays will demonstrate an altered proportion between the facial bones and the contents of the cranial vault. This particular case also shows marked postural flattening of the occiput, a not uncommon finding in the severely to profoundly retarded. Courtesy of John Dorst, M.D.

In the evaluation of the eye and the ear not only must structural defects be ruled out but an attempt should be made to assess intactness of function. The pediatrician must be very careful to identify significant visual or auditory impairments; these may cause a syndrome of pseudoretardation or complicate an existing handicap of retardation. Adequate testing of sensory modalities in the retarded presents multiple difficulties. Nystagmus in response to the OKN drum can be observed in most newborns (Brazelton, Parker, and Zuckerman, 1976) and all older infants, but this phenomenon says nothing with regard to visual acuity. In addition to routine consultation with an ophthalmologist and an audiologist, the pediatrician should familiarize himself

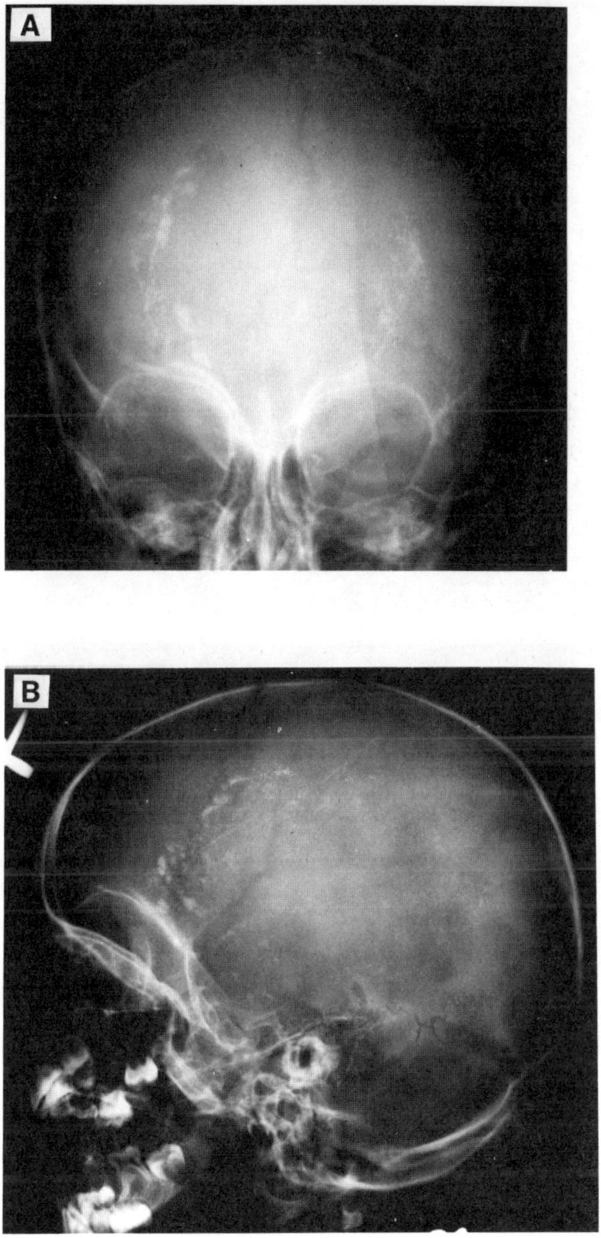

Figure 27. The plain skull radiographs (A, B) demonstrate the sheet-like pattern of intracranial calcification seen in cytomegalic inclusion disease.

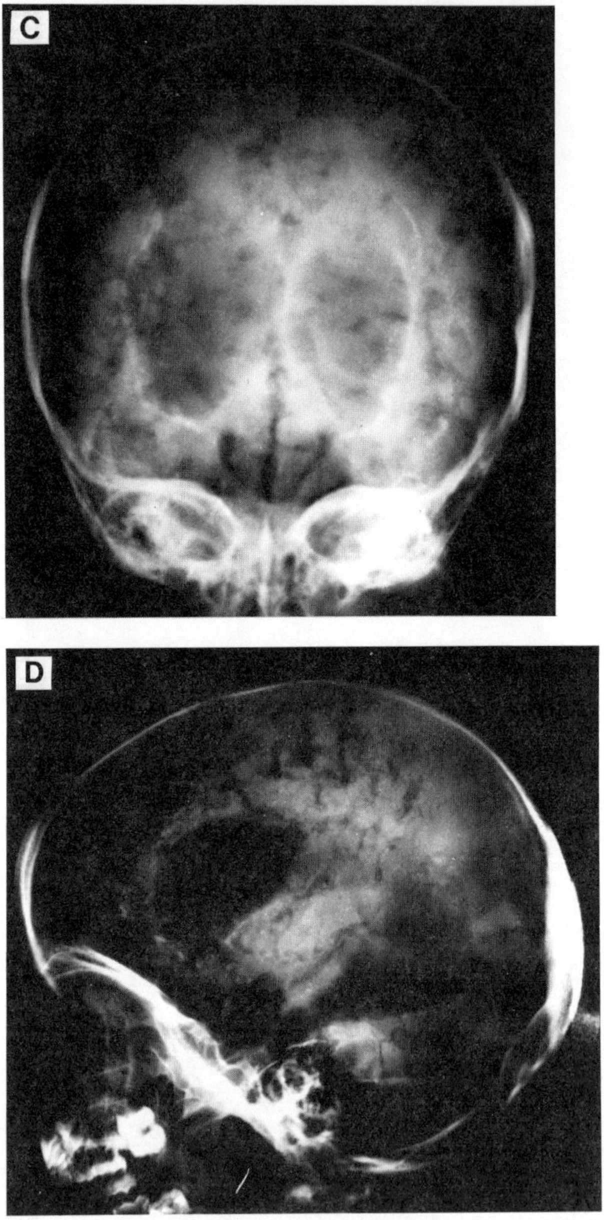

Figure 27. Ventriculography (C, D) confirms the periventricular localization of these calcifications. Courtesy of John Dorst, M.D.

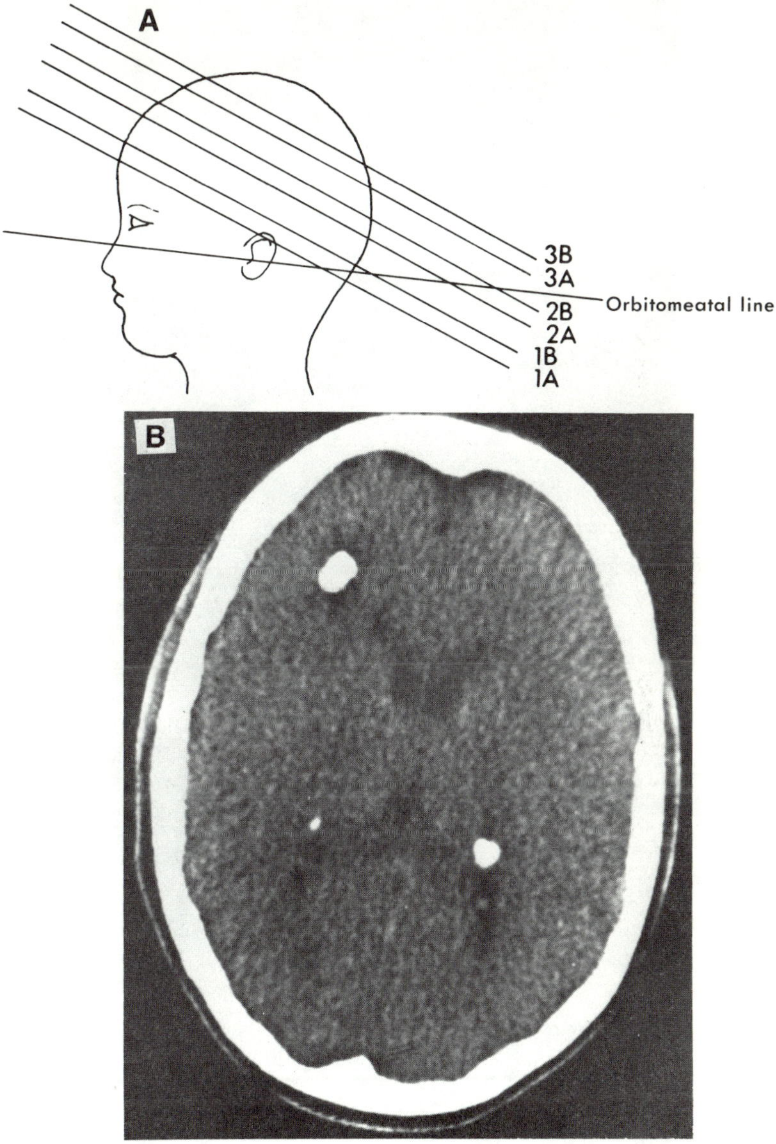

Figure 28. Computerized tomography takes slices through the brain (A) and may demonstrate intracranial calcification earlier than plain films as in this case of tuberous sclerosis (B).

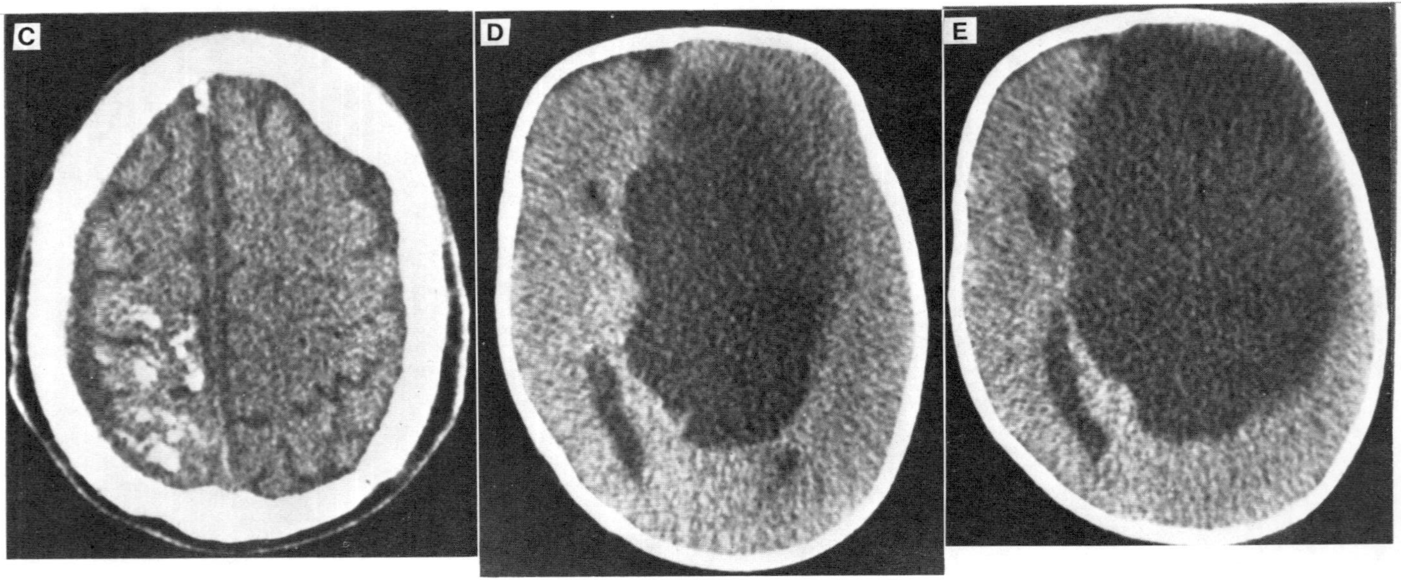

Figure 28. The calcification of Sturge-Weber syndrome is striking even on CT scan (C). Porencephaly (D and E) and other structural malformations can be clearly delineated by this method. (All films are without dye injection.) A, from Gomez and Reese (1976) by permission. B, C, D, E, courtesy of Fred J. Hodges, III.

with Sheridan's Tests for Young Children and Retardates (STYCAR) for both vision and hearing. Sheridan (1958, 1960, 1973a,b) devised a series of ingenious practical tools for the clinical screening of vision and hearing in children (of mental ages) from 6 months to 7 years; these standardized qualitative assessments take into account the child's developmental maturity and the response variability appropriate to these different levels (Figures 32, 33, 34). The test manuals provide a rich source for behavioral observations of the developing child. Impedance audiometry (Henderson, 1975) is becoming almost routine in the evaluation of difficult-to-test children, and a last resort may be made to the use of evoked potentials (Picton and Hink, 1974; Figure 35). The clinical interpretation of evoked visual and auditory potentials on electroencephalography is not always straightforward; if in a controlled setting the child cannot be trained to betray some visual or auditory response, it is doubtful that documenting the presence of evoked potentials will make the child more functional. Parents frequently raise the question of deafness with severely retarded children—"He acts as if he doesn't hear." If the evoked potentials prove that the child does indeed "hear," it

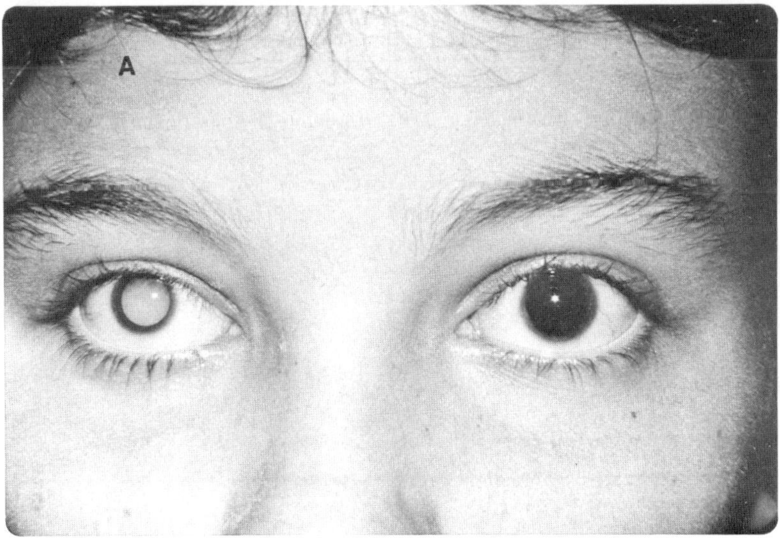

Figure 29. Eye findings. A—The right eye in this rubella patient is microphthalmic with a dense cataract. The differential diagnosis of cataract is reviewed by Kohn (1976).

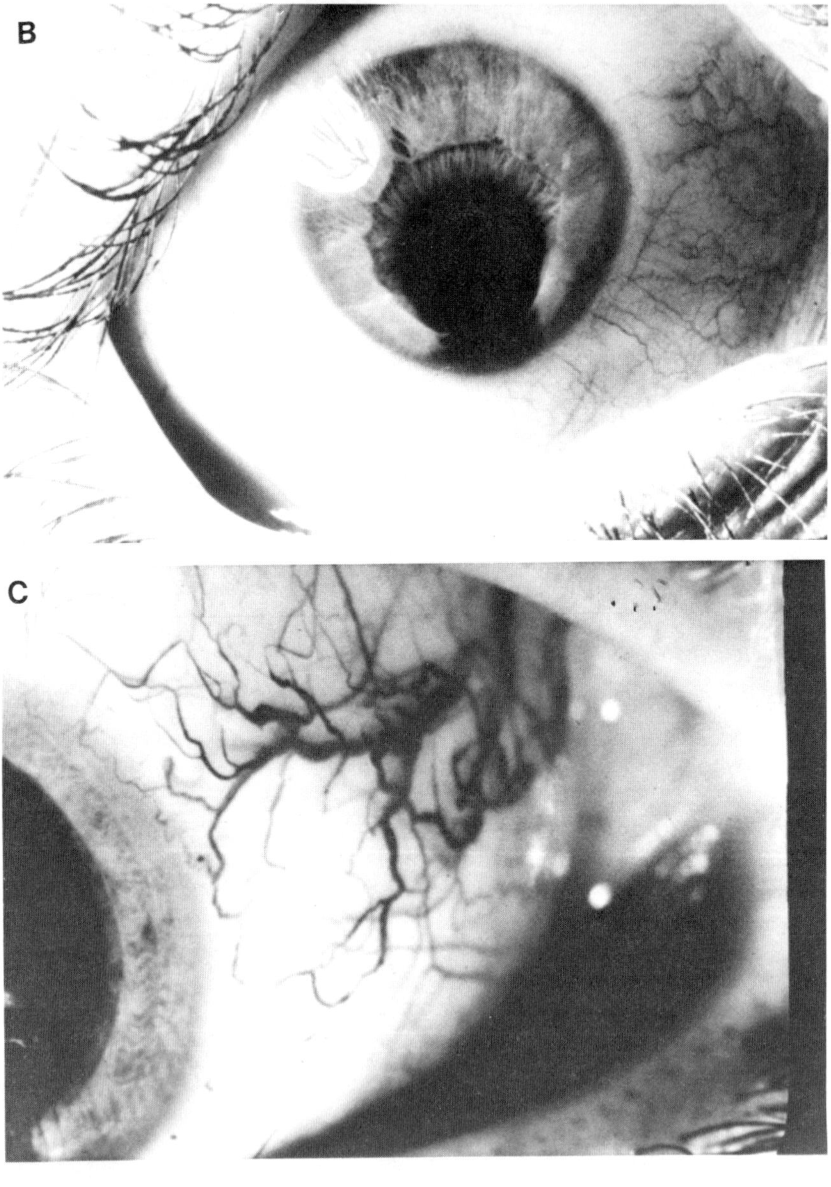

Figure 29. B—Coloboma of iris. C—Conjunctival telangiectasia in ataxia telangiectasia; in this disorder the telangiectasia may first appear on the ear. A, courtesy of Neil R. Miller, M.D; B and C, courtesy of the Wilmer Ophthalmological Institute.

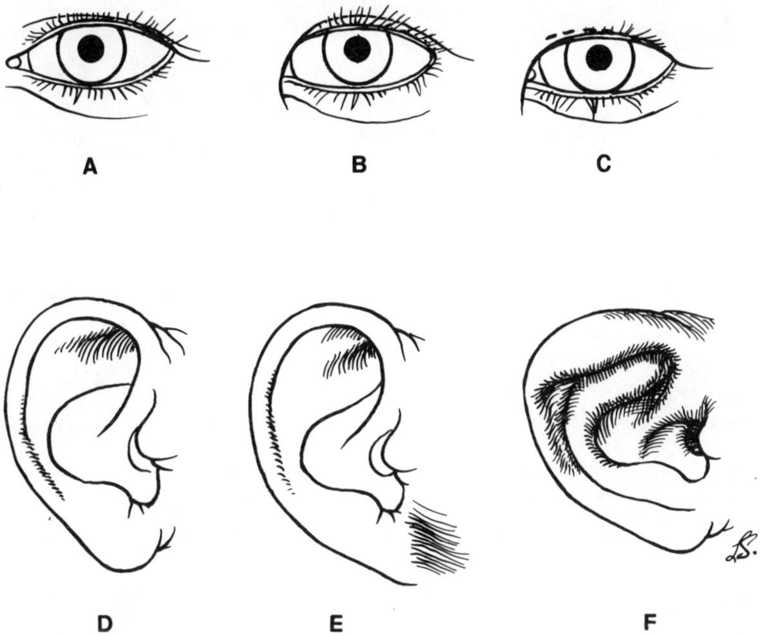

Figure 30. The eye of the child with Down syndrome (B) differs from that of a normal child (A) by the presence of an epicanthal fold. This, in turn, differs from that of a normal Asian (C) by a double fold. The absence of an ear lobule (E) is a minor variant compared to a normal external ear (D); an angular overlapping helix is a common finding in Down syndrome.

must be made clear to the parents that the child's tuning them out is not willful (i.e., malicious) behavior or emotional disturbance but rather behavior reflective of a global cognitive deficit.

Enamel dysplasia has been demonstrated in the primary or decidous teeth of children with cerebral palsy; the hypoplasia correlates both with the time of the insult during gestation and with the severity of the disease (Gordon and Rosenstein, 1965; Watson, Massler, and Perlstein, 1964). Cohen and Diner (1970) documented a spectrum of problems with amelogenesis that paralleled the entire spectrum of developmental disorders. Dysmorphology of the secondary or permanent teeth whose odontogenesis begins in the second trimester is common in mental retardation (approximately 50% of the cases) and in a milder degree is found in children with learning disabilities (Goodwin and Erickson, 1973; Kraus et al., 1967). Unfortunately this kind of odon-

A

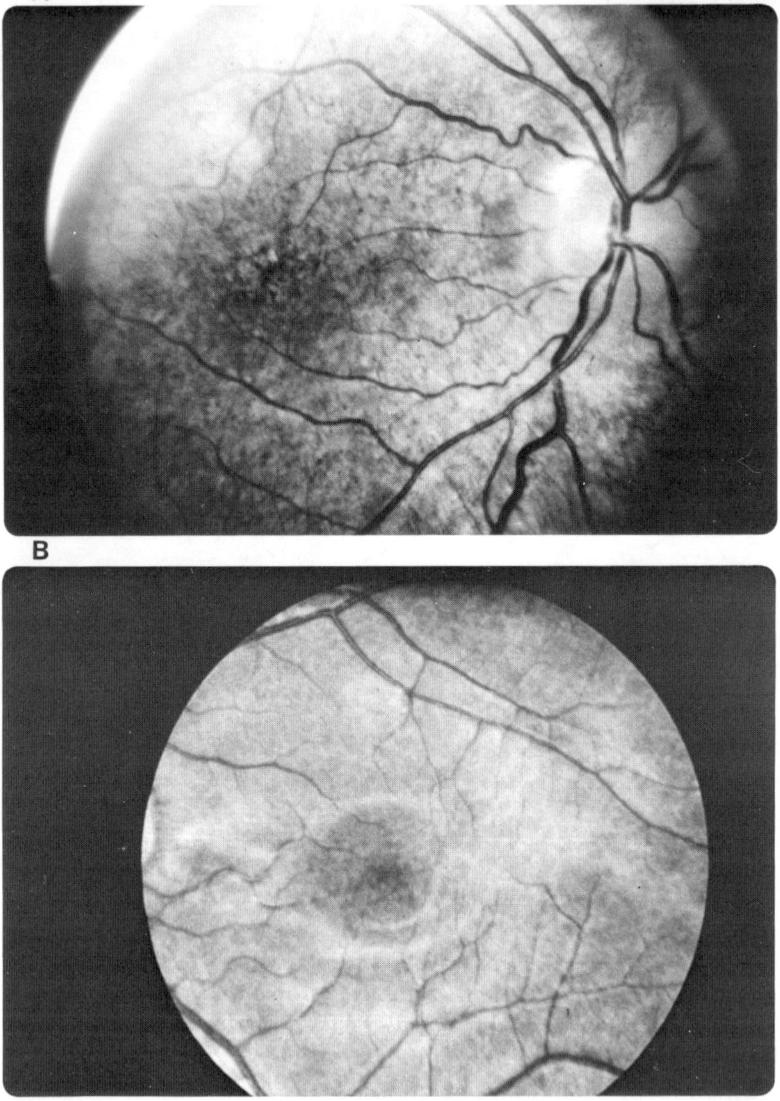

Figure 31. Retinal findings. A—Extensive pigmentary retinopathy in a child with congenital rubella. B—Extensive pigmentary abnormality in the macula. C—Cherry red spot in a patient with Tay-Sachs disease. This abnormality is caused by an accumulation of material in the ganglion cell layer of the retina producing a thickened, whitish retina, except in the fovea where there are no ganglion cells. D—Optic nerve coloboma with extensive pigmentary abnormality in the macula. A, B, C, D, courtesy of Neil R. Miller, M.D.

C

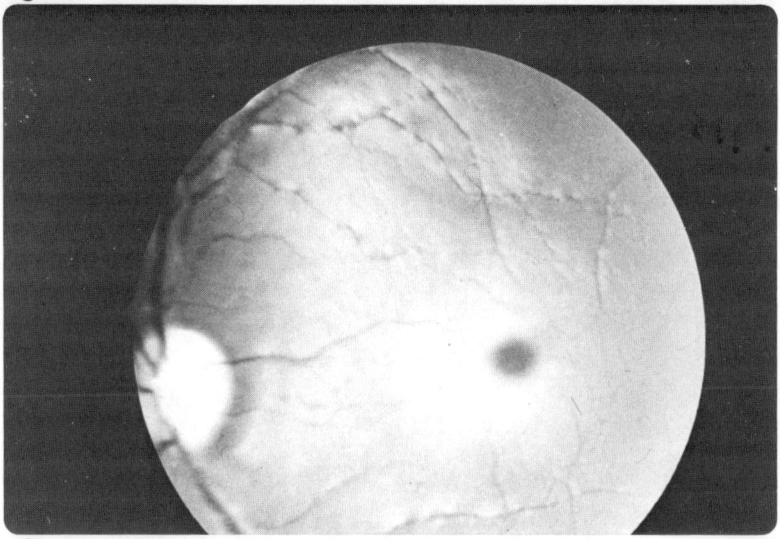

D

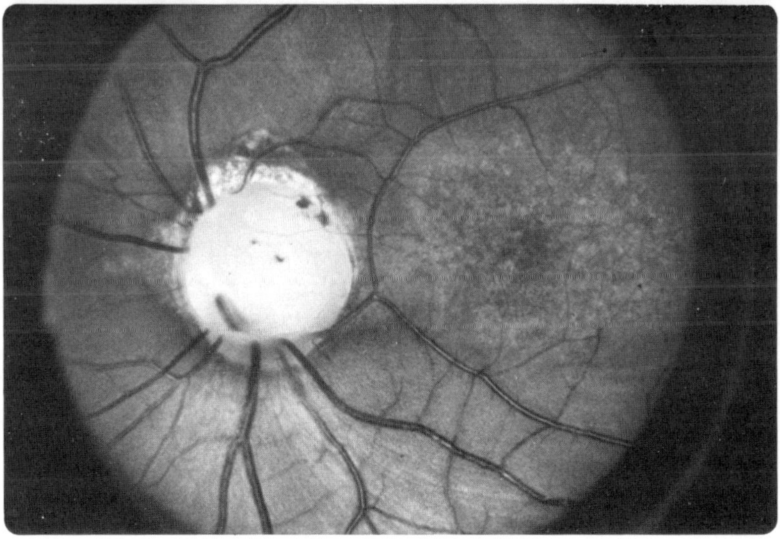

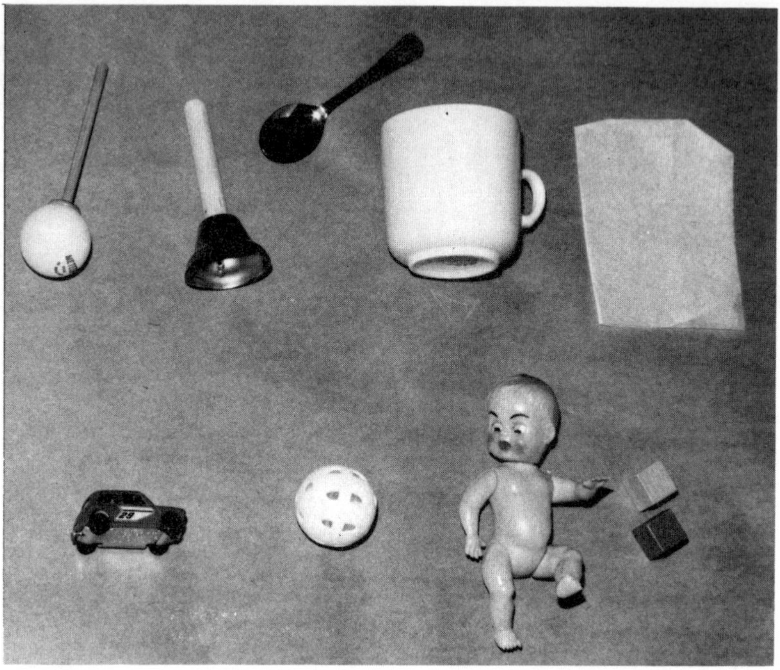

Figure 32. STYCAR hearing tests (selections). The Nuffield rattle imitates delicate high frequency speech sounds. Orienting to voice, rattle, spoon against cup, tissue paper, and handbell is sought. The toys are used for one-step commands voiced at standardized distances.

toglyphic patterning is beyond the expertise of most physicians and dentists except in the case of gross malformations (Figure 36). A high palatal arch (as distinct from torus palatinus, a normal variant) is not well defined but nevertheless does seem to be more frequent in cases of mental retardation. There are no good explanations for the origin of this anomaly, but perhaps the decreased pressure transmitted by an abnormally slow rate of brain growth contributes to this phenomenon. (If this is the case, the finding should be more common with microcephaly.) The complex genetics of cleft lip/cleft palate (Gorlin, Pindborg, and Cohen, 1976) crosses over into that of many other syndromes associated with mental retardation; the child with a cleft palate deserves close developmental follow-up.

Retardation is not infrequent in the presence of gross limb malformations; the association is stronger when the upper extremities are preferentially involved and there is accompanying congenital heart disease (Smith et al., 1970). Hypoplasia of the distal phalanges and nails is a striking finding in the fetal hydantoin syndrome; with older children, the newborn examination will have to be reviewed since the hypoplasia tends to correct over time. Minor abnormalities of the palmar creases and the digits (Figure 37) occur in normals but have a higher incidence in mental retardation. Dermatoglyphics, the study of dermal ridge patterns, is concerned with ectodermal markings (on the terminal pads of the fingers and toes) formed before the sixteenth gestational week. When karyotyping was not as readily available as it is today, dermatoglyphics represented skin dysmorphology and was used as one of the prerequisites for justifying chromosomal studies. Dermatoglyphic analysis is a tedious process that yields path-

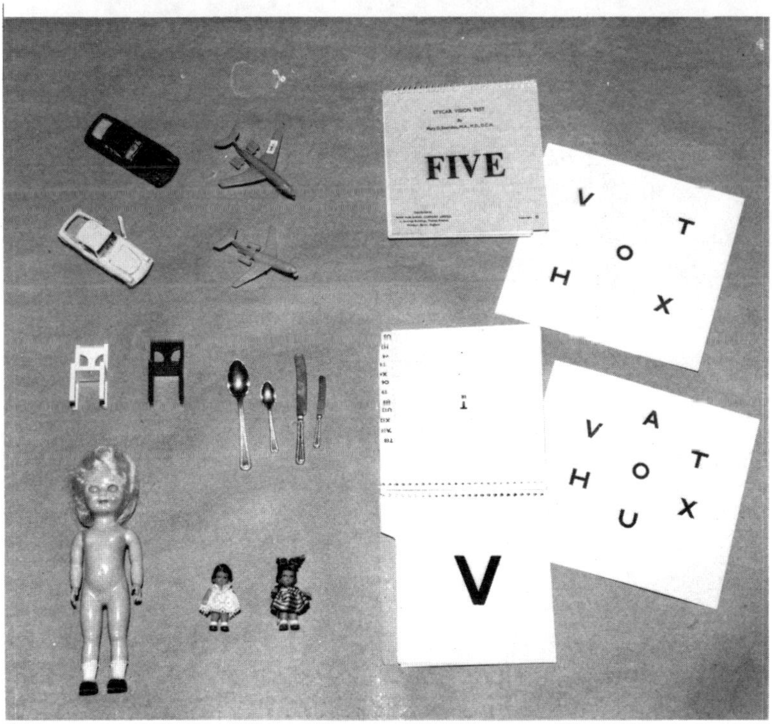

Figure 33. STYCAR vision tests (selections). Paired miniature toys are matched from standardized distances. With children over 3 years of age, the single letters are presented at fixed distances and matched to the appropriate key card by the child. Verbal responses are not necessary.

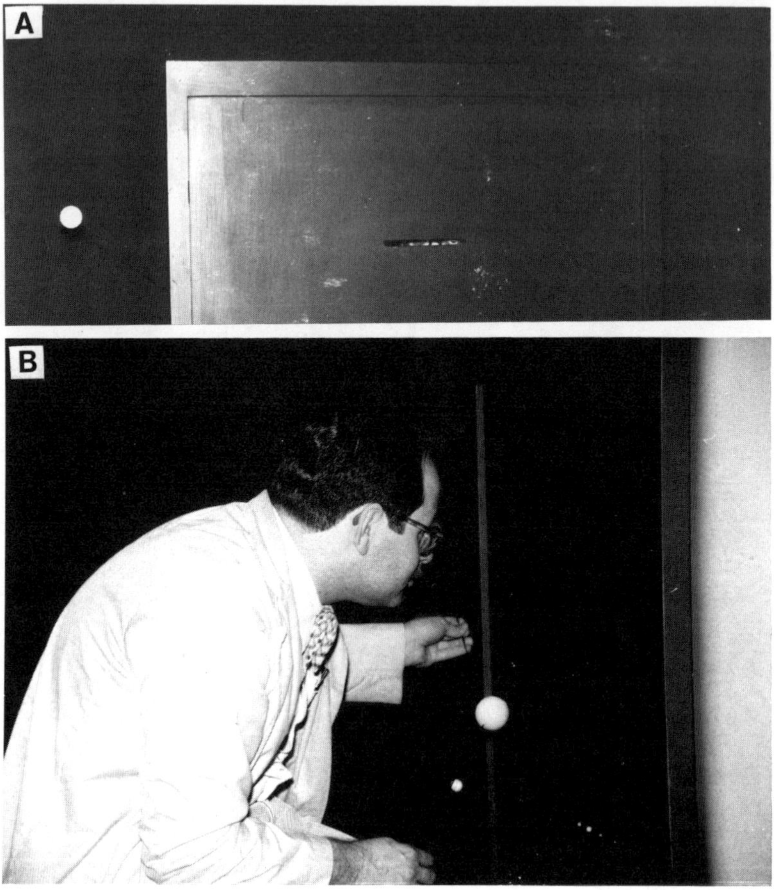

Figure 34. STYCAR graded balls test. White balls mounted on black rods are moved against a black background from behind a black screen; a visual following response is observed.

ognomonic findings in only two disorders, Down syndrome (trisomy 21) and Edwards syndrome (trisomy 18). In most cases, ridge patterns are impressively quantitative, diagnostically suggestive, and clinically superfluous. Abnormal dermatoglyphics in a retarded child supports a causative factor operative before the second trimester.

The skin, an ectodermal derivative like the brain, frequently provides a clue to diagnosis. In multiple neurofibromatosis (von Recklinghausen's disease), long before the pathognomonic fibromata appear, the patient may demonstrate café au lait spots and axillary freckling (Figure 38A and B). This is an autosomal dominant condition with variable expressivity; the more severe end of the spectrum includes mental retardation and a complex seizure disorder. Any child with retardation and seizures should be carefully reexamined for café au lait spots because these tend to increase with age, and the presence of six or more lesions greater than 1.5 cm in diameter is considered highly suggestive of the diagnosis (Crowe's rule; Crowe, Schull, and Neel, 1956). Whitehouse (1966) found that less than 1% of children under 5 years of age had more than two spots larger than 0.5 cm. Tuberous sclerosis (Bourneville's disease, epiloia) is another autosomal dominant phacomatosis associated with mental retardation and a severe seizure disorder. The diagnostic adenoma sebaceum (Figure

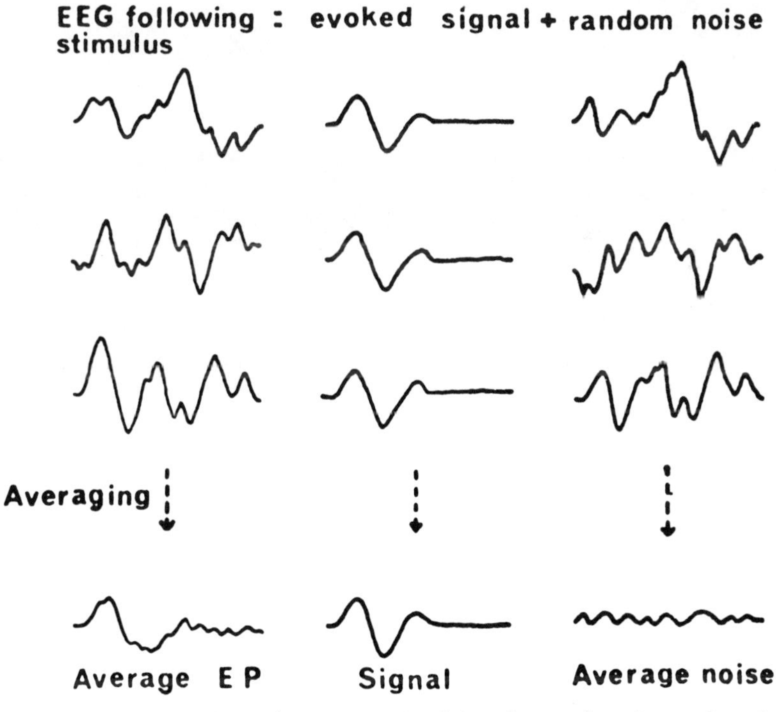

Figure 35. Theory of signal averaging. Random noise can be subtracted out by computer techniques (the average random noise is 0) to reveal the otherwise hidden evoked visual or auditory response on the electroencephalogram. From Picton and Hink (1974) by permission.

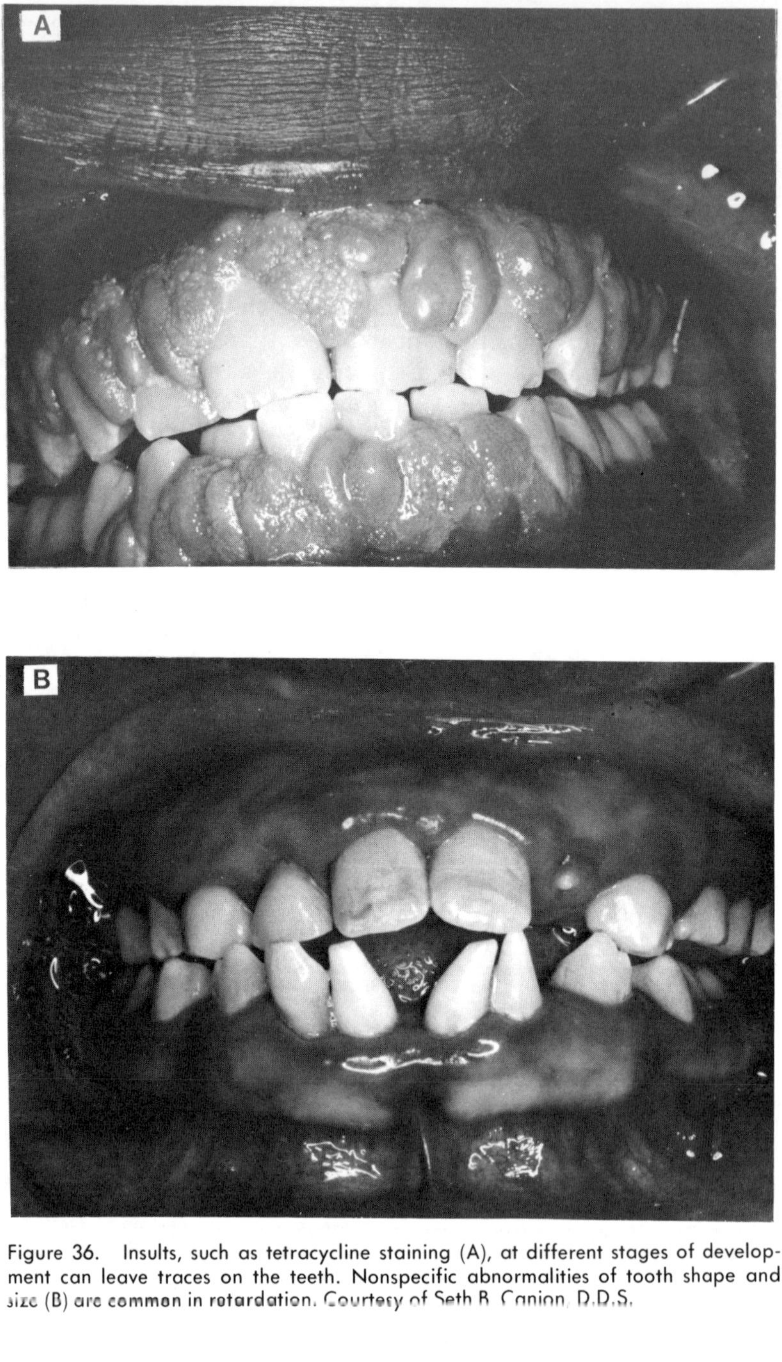

Figure 36. Insults, such as tetracycline staining (A), at different stages of development can leave traces on the teeth. Nonspecific abnormalities of tooth shape and size (B) are common in retardation. Courtesy of Seth B. Canion, D.D.S.

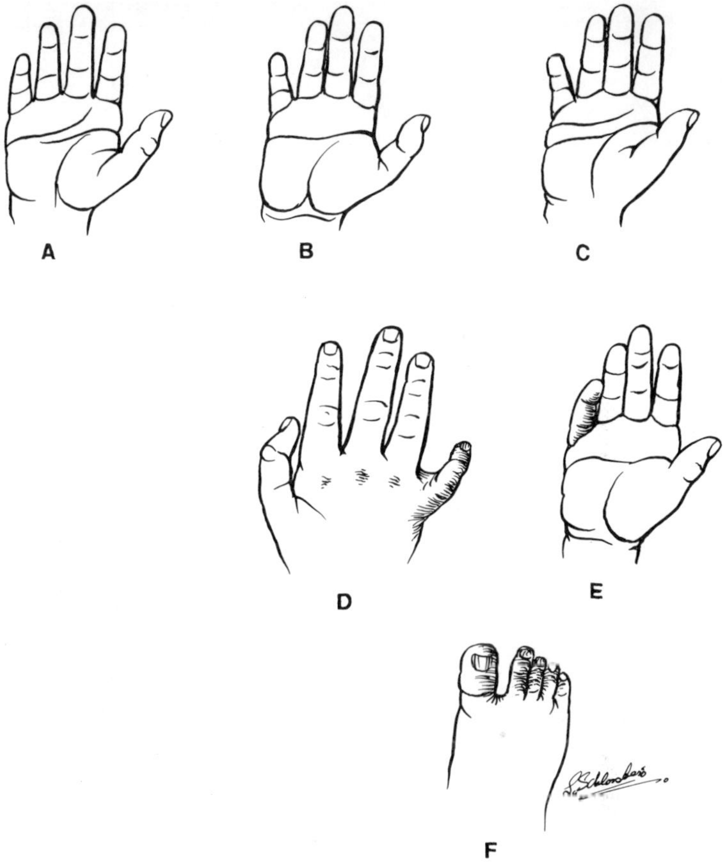

Figure 37. A single four-finger transverse palmar crease, Simian line (B), is distinct from the more usual double pattern (A) in normals. The Sydney line, an extended proximal transverse palmar crease (C), is a variant of the Simian line; they are both more common in Down syndrome and other types of retardation (Purvis-Smith, 1972).

Camptodactyly (D) is a flexion contracture of the digit; clinodactyly (E) is a radial incurvature of the digit. Broad separation of the first two toes (F), often associated with some degree of syndactyly of the other toes, can be familial but is also frequent in retardation. Very broad thumbs and toes should suggest the Rubinstein-Taybi syndrome.

38D) does not develop until late childhood, but white macules (Figure 38C), often with an ash-leaf shape, can be observed as early as the newborn period (Bundy, 1970; Gold and Freeman, 1965; Hurwitz and Braverman, 1970). An ultraviolet light source such as a Wood's lamp can be used to highlight these trunkal

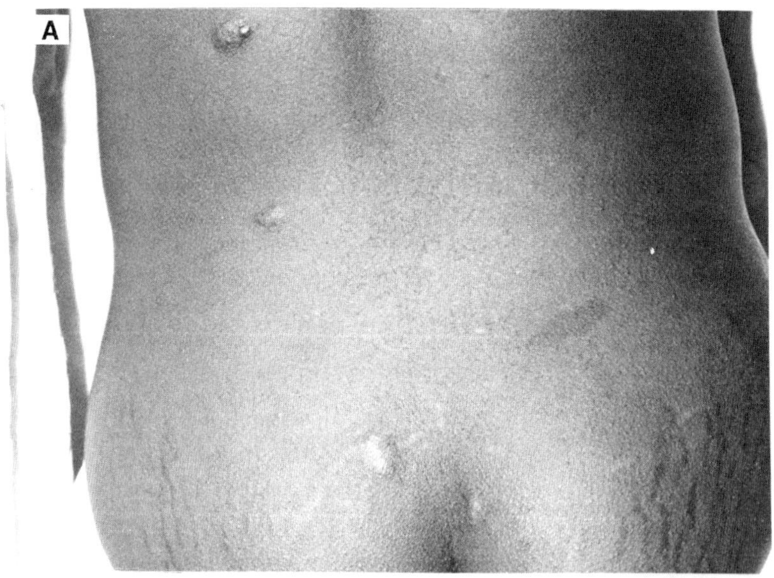

Figure 38. Neurofibromatosis demonstrates café au lait spots and fibromata (A) and axillary freckling (B). Hypopigmented macules (C) can be an early sign of tuberous sclerosis; later the more diagnostic adenoma sebaceum, or facial angiofibroma, appears in the nasolabial fold (D). Incontinentia pigmenti (Bloch-Sulzberger syndrome) presents a striking pigmentary pattern (E); this X-limited dominant condition is occasionally accompanied by mental retardation. Nevus sebaceus of Jadassohn (F, newborn) has also been associated with retardation. A, B, D, E, F, courtesy of Steven Passman, M.D. C, courtesy of Bruce K. Shapiro, M.D.

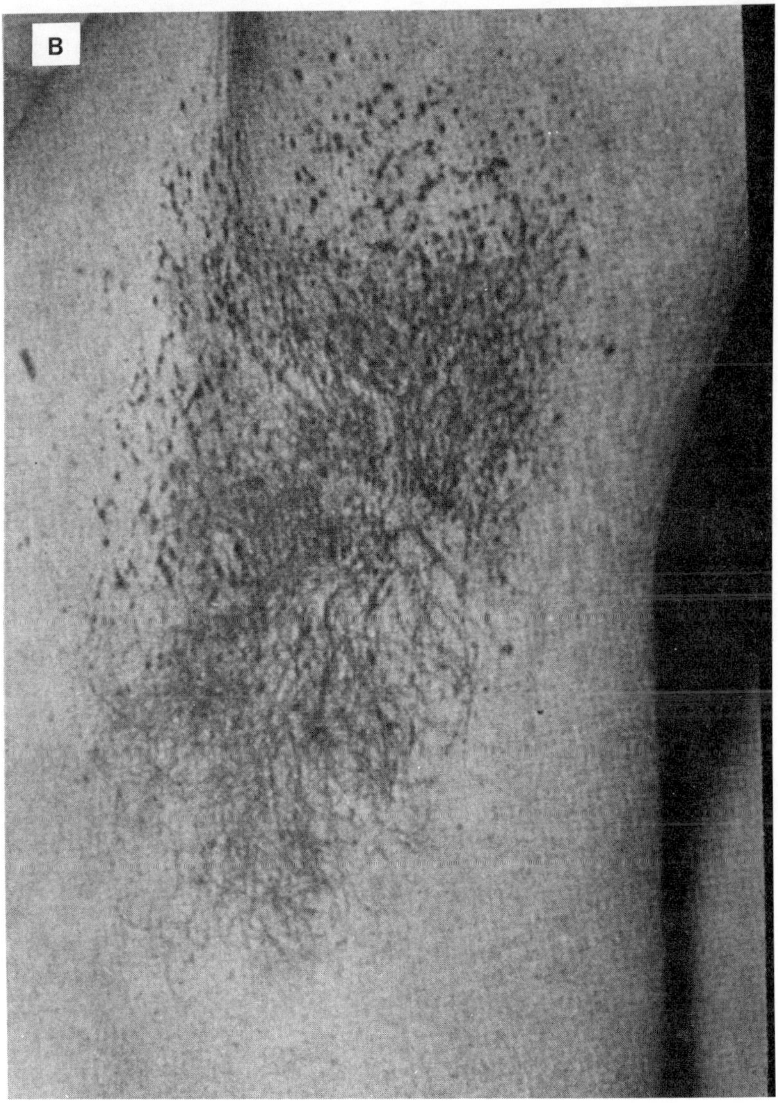

Figure 38B.

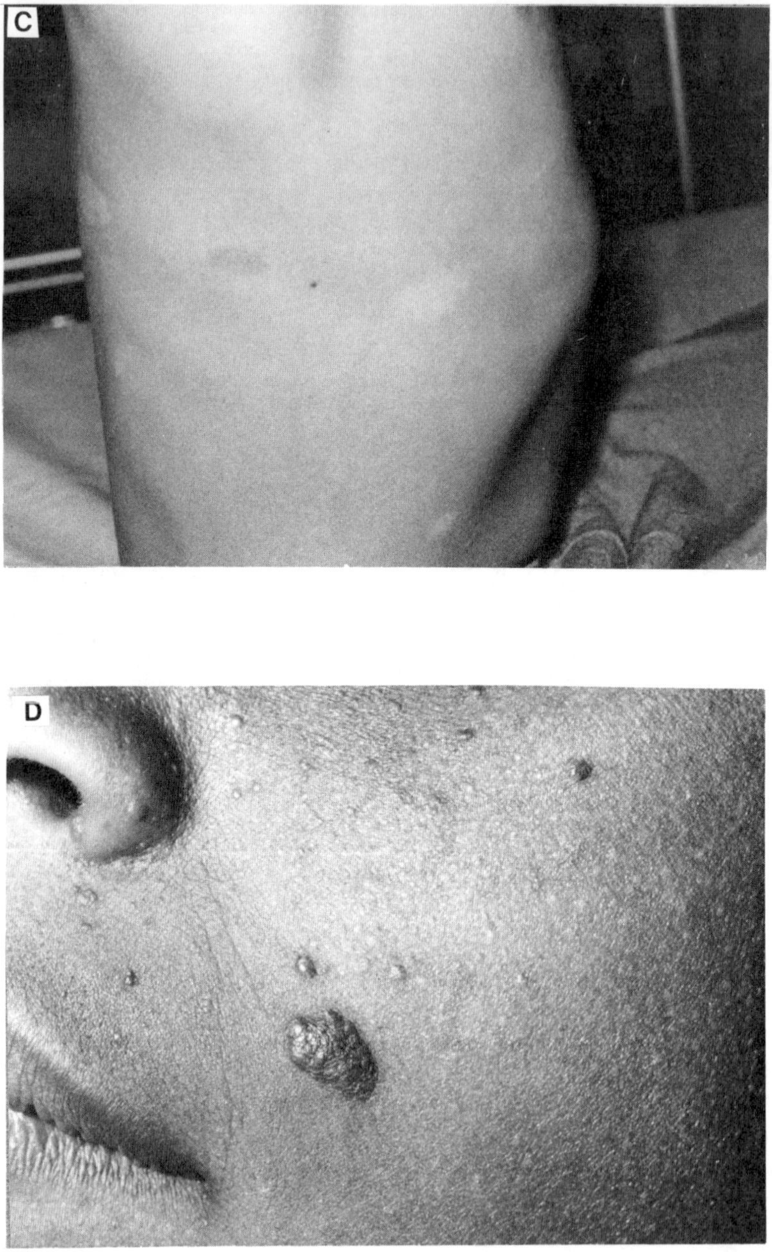

Figure 38C, D.

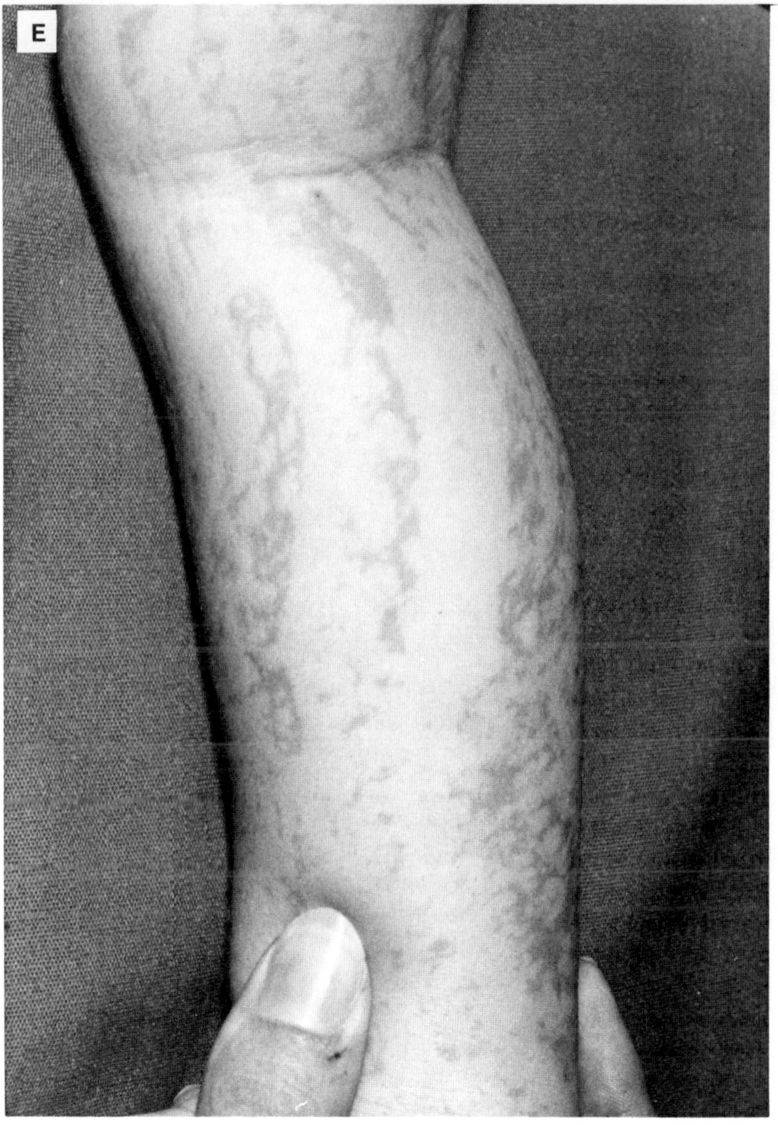

Figure 38E.

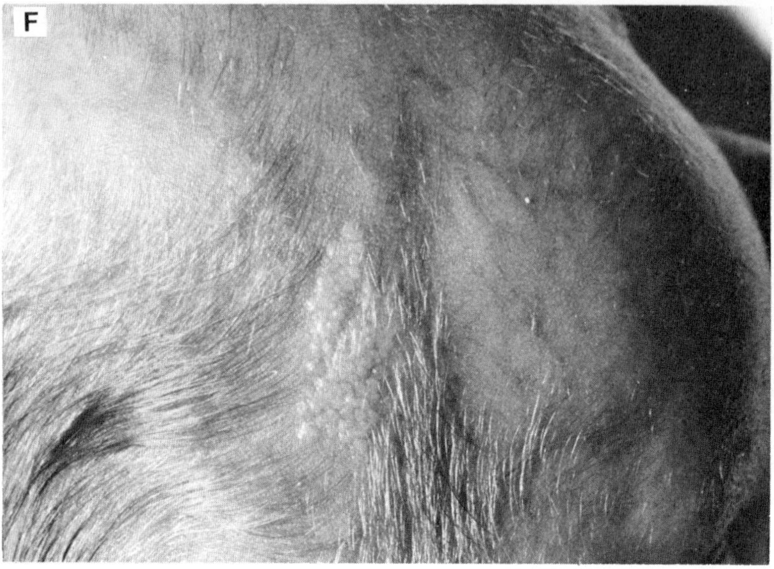

Figure 38F.

lesions. Another early sign is the shagreen patch, a raised flat plaque of skin in the lumbo-sacral area. The course for this disorder is progressive with the later development of intracranial calcifications.

The nevus sebaceus of Jadassohn (Figure 38F) is a linear raised scalp lesion with alopecia; it usually develops after the newborn period. Although it occurs in normals, it can also be part of a neurocutaneous syndrome with retardation and seizures. Cutis verticis gyrata (a deep sagittal infolding of the skin) is another scalp lesion that is seen in normals (males more than females, with an incidence that increases with age) but is also strongly associated with mental retardation, microcephaly, cerebral palsy, epilepsy, cataracts, neurofibromatosis, acromegaly, and other congenital anaomalies. It may be an autosomal recessive trait, and Iivanainen (1974) suggests that its role in mental retardation may be greater than expected: unless the head is shaved the lesion is easily overlooked. Other dermatologic findings associated with retardation include a pellagra-like rash in Hartnup's disease, a fair blond complexion in phenylketonuria, and ichthyosis in the Sjögren-Larsson syndrome. Any child with the combination of mental retardation and cerebellar signs should be carefully examined for telangiectasias.

Seizures are much more common and the control of seizures is much more difficult in the retarded than in the normal population. This has received surprisingly little recognition in the standard textbooks of epileptology: anticonvulsant management of the handicapped child is an area where many of the usual rules for seizure control encounter their exceptions.

Convulsions in the newborn period certainly place the child at increased risk for mental impairment: seizures before the fourth or after the eighth day of life are probably secondary to brain damage; those beginning between 5 and 8 days of life usually reflect underlying metabolic disturbances (Figure 39). Since the latter disorders are frequently treatable and transient, it is the brain damage convulsions that imply the worse prognosis (Brown, Cockburn, and Forfar, 1972).

Although the majority of patients with febrile seizures are simply more sensitive to high fevers in childhood, children with preexisting brain damage do demonstrate a lower seizure threshold in response to fever. Thus patients with febrile convulsions demonstrate an incidence of neurodevelopmental abnormalities almost 20 times that of patients without such convulsions (Nelson and Ellenberg, 1976). Thus, the febrile convulsion population is heterogeneous, and a careful neurodevelopmental examination is

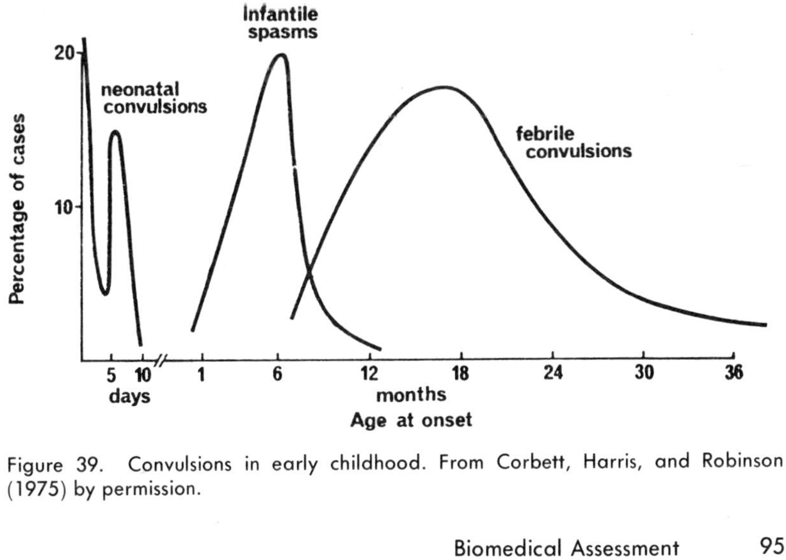

Figure 39. Convulsions in early childhood. From Corbett, Harris, and Robinson (1975) by permission.

necessary before venturing a prognosis. In the neurologically normal (and numerically larger) segment of this group, a higher risk for the development of temporal lobe seizures in later life has been documented. There is some evidence that mesial temporal sclerosis (of Ammon's horn) may result from repeated febrile convulsions (Falconer, 1974), but the related issue of treatment for febrile convulsions remains undecided.

In addition to the high incidence of seizures in the retarded, there is a still higher incidence of electroencephalographic (EEG) abnormalities without seizures. Disordered cerebral structure and function are reflected in abnormal electrical activity; the more severe the degree of retardation, the greater the likelihood of an abnormal electroencephalogram (Matthews and Manning, 1964). Thus, abnormal brain wave tracings in the retarded need to be interpreted with caution. The decision to treat a seizure disorder must rest on clinical evidence other than the EEG because the latter will frequently be abnormal in the absence of an active convulsive disorder. Treatment should be directed at the patient and not at the laboratory test. In other words, a decision to treat seizures should ideally precede the results of the EEG.

Although the EEG cannot diagnose a seizure disorder, there are several highly specific electroencephalographic patterns with distinct prognostic implications for cognitive functioning. One of the most striking of these is the West syndrome or infantile spasms. Children with this disorder frequently develop normally until about 6 months of age when they begin to demonstrate a severe mixed seizure disorder. The complex seizure pattern is composed mainly of three types of spells: flexion, extension, and lightning attacks. Many other colorful phrases have been employed in an attempt to describe a bizarre movement typology: oriental or salaam attacks, jackknife seizures, and head nodding spells. The episodes frequently occur in clusters similar to brief stretches of status; a quick cry heralds the onset of an attack. The disorder may be idiopathic (cryptogenic) or associated with multiple other processes: metabolic disorders (phenylketonuria, maple syrup urine disease, leucine-sensitive hypoglycemia), hypoxia, ischemia, head trauma, congenital brain malformations (such as porencephaly), rubella and other viral encephalidites, Sturge-Weber syndrome (trigeminal angiomatosis), tuberous sclerosis, and pertussis immunization. The cryptogenic (30%) and post-immunization (15%) groups have the best prognosis (Figure

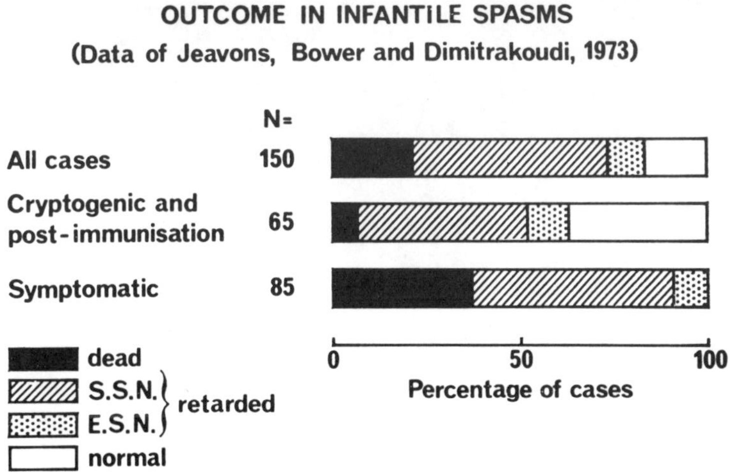

Figure 40. Outcome in infantile spasms. From Corbett, Harris, and Robinson (1975) by permission.

40); tuberous sclerosis is fairly common (approximately 20%) but frequently missed. One-fourth of the patients die and three-fourths of the survivors are severely retarded (Friedman and Pampiglione, 1971). The distinctive electroencephalographic pattern in infantile spasms is known as hypsarrhythmia ("mountainous waves"): there are bursts of high voltage spikes and sharp waves with intervening stretches of abrupt voltage depression (Figure 41). The seizures are very difficult to control, and resource is often had to adrenocorticotropic hormone (ACTH) and steroids, the ketogenic diet, and recently clonazepam. (Unfortunately, the last named drug may work for only a brief period.) By 3 years of age the seizure disorder burns out, the EEG abnormality improves, and the child is left severely retarded.

Many children with infantile spasms go on to develop the Lennox-Gastaut syndrome. This complex seizure disorder is characterized by multiple seizure types, especially atonic, akinetic, and myoclonic spells, which are very difficult to control. The typical patient is on high doses of three or more anticonvulsants with continued poor seizure control. The EEG pattern is specific: slow (1 to 2.5/sec) spike wave complexes (Figure 42); there is little temporal relationship between the EEG paroxysms and clinical seizures (Aicardi, 1973). The severity of the seizure disorder and the universally associated severe to profound mental

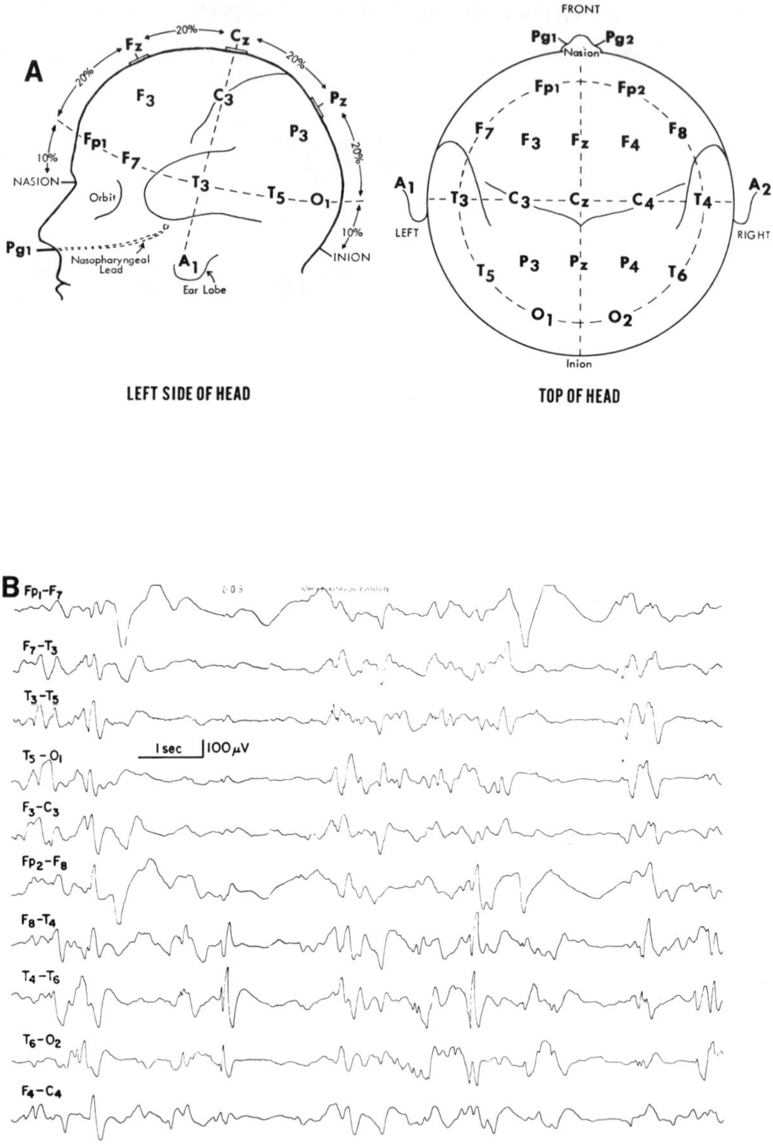

Figure 41. Electroencephalographic electrode placement (A): according to the International Electrode System for scalp recordings.

Hypsarrhythmia (B). EEG recorded in patient with infantile spasms demonstrating moderately well synchronized bursts of very high voltage activity, intermixed spikes, and brief stretches of voltage depression. From Niedermeyer (1974), courtesy of Charles C Thomas, Publisher, Springfield, Illinois.

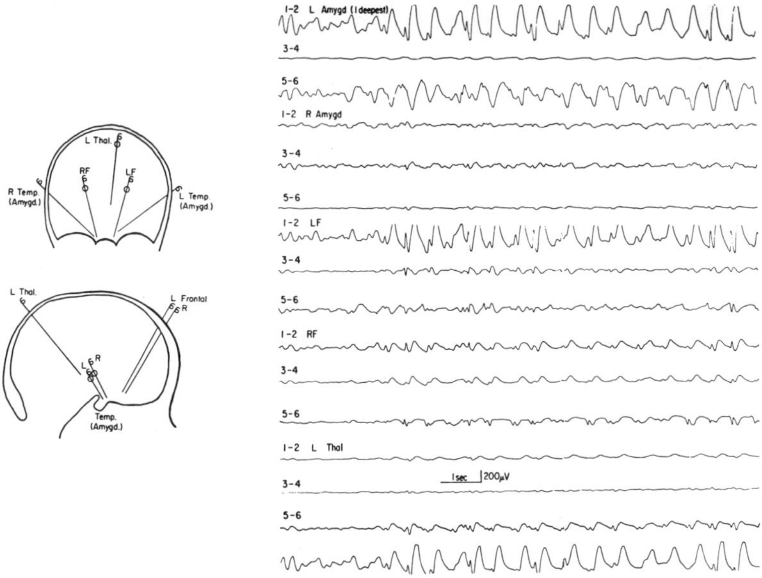

Figure 42. Lennox-Gastaut syndrome. Depth electrodes demonstrate widespread 1.5–2.5/sec spike wave activity. From Niedermeyer (1974), courtesy of Charles C Thomas, Publisher, Springfield, Illinois.

retardation is surprising considering that the 1 to 2.5/sec spike wave pattern ("petit mal variant") is so close to the 3/sec spike wave pattern diagnostic for petit mal epilepsy; the latter disorder is never seen in the retarded, is relatively easily to control with medication, and has a fairly benign prognosis.

Commonly employed anticonvulsants, their dosage ranges, and side effects are presented in Table 9. Unfortunately, anticonvulsant levels are becoming too routine; dosages are adjusted according to monitored blood concentrations rather than clinical efficacy and associated side effects. Dose-related toxicities respond to reductions in medication; Dilantin suspension is very difficult to titrate and is therefore not a recommended form of administration. A frequent complication of Dilantin therapy is gingival hyperplasia; once started, the process cannot be reversed but is slowed by a lowered dose or careful oral hygiene. Periodontal surgery (gingivectomy) will be necessary at periodic intervals as long as the drug is continued (Figure 43). Hydantoins, barbiturates, and combinations of the two have been associated with a rickets-like syndrome of osteoporosis, hypocalcemia, and

Table 9. Anticonvulsant medications

Trade name	Generic name	Class	Dosage range (mg/kg)	Therapeutic range (μg/ml)	Half life (hours) (T-½)	Dosage forms (mg)	Drug toxicity
Dilantin	Diphenylhydantoin	Hydantoin	4–7	5–20	22	tab. 50 cap. 30, 100	Gingival hyperplasia, nystagmus, ataxia, lymphadenopathy, lupus erythematosus, megaloblastic anemia (folate deficiency hypertrichosis), rickets
	Phenobarbital	Barbiturate	2–6	10–30	96	tab. 16, 32, 64	Drowsiness, paradoxical hyperactivity, allergic rash, rickets
Mysoline	Primidone	Barbiturate	10–25	4–15	7	tab. 50, 250	Transient: drowsiness, nausea and vomiting, disorientation, ataxia Dose related: drowsiness, dizziness, unsteadiness, nystagmus, diplopia, megaloblastic anemia (folate deficiency)
Tegretol	Carbamazepine	Iminostilbene	10–20	2–12	~40	tab. 200	Transient: fatigue, malaise, dizziness, lethargy Dose related: nystagmus, diplopia, drowsiness, ataxia, dysarthria Idiosyncratic: leukopenia, dermatoses, hematopoietic and hepatic dysfunction, decreased visual acuity
Clonopin	Clonazepam	Benzodiazepine	0.03–0.3	0.02–0.07	30	tab. 0.5, 1, 2	Ataxia, drowsiness, irritibility, weight gain, excessive bronchial secretions (infants), paradoxical hyperactivity

Adapted from Berman (1976), Dodson, et al. (1976a), Gomez and Klass (1972b), Hooshmand (1974), Singer and Freeman (1975).

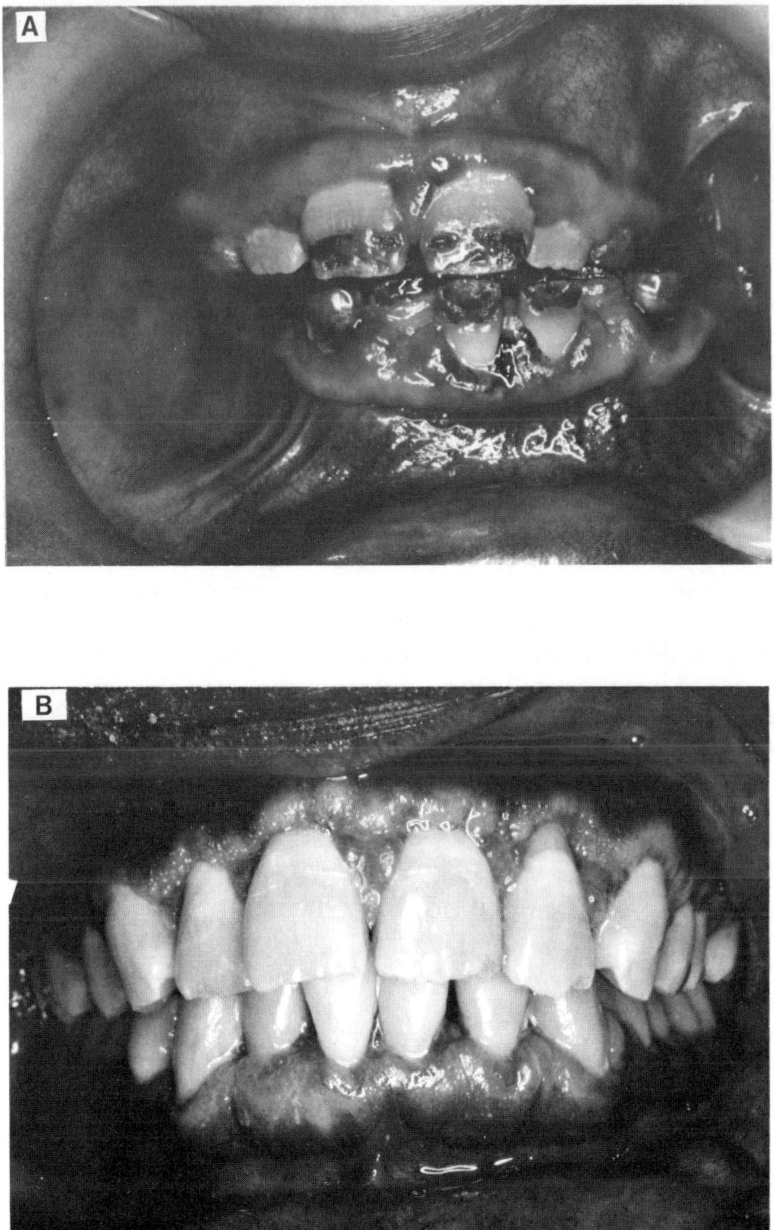

Figure 43. Gingival hyperplasia: preoperative (A) and status post-periodontal surgery (B). Courtesy of Seth B. Canion, D.D.S.

elevated alkaline phosphatase levels. Whether patients on long-term therapy with these medications should receive supplements of vitamin D as prophylaxis is still undecided (Churesigaew, Ruvalcaba, and Kelley, 1975; Silver et al., 1974; Winnacker et al., 1977). Cerebellar degeneration with Purkinje cell loss has been demonstrated in seizure patients on long-term hydantoin therapy. While Dam (1970) related this effect to the hypoxia occurring with seizures, Ghatak, Santoso, and McKinney (1976) found similar neuropathology in patients who were under good control and concluded that the tissue damage was caused by the medication. A new drug, sodium valproate (Depakene), appears useful in the more difficult generalized epilepsies and has relatively few side effects (Pinder et al., 1977). The development of safer and more effective anticonvulsant medications in the next few decades is a certainty that promises significant improvement in the life-style of the handicapped.

Holowach, Thurston, and O'Leary (1972) found that, if a child remained seizure-free for 4 years on anticonvulsants, there was only a 20% chance of seizure recurrence if medication were discontinued. Other variables, including seizure type, contributed little to this risk; but if the patient had a gross neurologic deficit (such as mental retardation), the recurrence rate almost doubled to 37%. Considering the side effects of long-term anticonvulsant therapy (proportionally multiplied when several drugs are used), even this higher rate warrants serious consideration, with parental cooperation and close monitoring.

BIBLIOGRAPHIC NOTE

Paine and Oppe (1966) is still the best introduction to pediatric neurology; principles of neurologic pathophysiology are covered by Eliasson, Prensky, and Hardin (1974). Degenerative disorders are reviewed in Freeman and McKhann (1969), Menkes, Andrews, and Cancilla (1971), and Rapin (1976); new concepts of adrenoleukodystrophy and subacute necrotizing encephalomyelopathy (Leigh's disease) are offered in Schaumberg et al. (1975) and Pincus (1972), respectively. The pitfalls of missing an organic neurologic disorder when the child presents with psychiatric symptomatology are cautioned against in Rivinus, Jamison, and Graham (1975).

One of the best introductions to syndromology is Gellis and Feingold's (1968) collection of color plates from the American Journal of Diseases of Children's Picture of the Month series. Smith's (1976) textbook is eminently readable and succeeds in imposing a semblance of order on the otherwise chaotic and hair splitting business of syndrome identification. Bergsma's (1973) compendium and McKusick's (1975) catalogue are comprehensive reference works. Syndromes of the head and neck are covered by Gorlin, Pindborg, and Cohen (1976), and syndromes associated with deafness are reviewed by Konigsmark (1969) and Konigsmark and Gorlin (1976). Some of the newer chromosomal disorders are indexed in Lewandowski and Yunis (1975) and in DeGrouchy and Turleau's (1977) atlas of clinically significant banding anomalies. Physical parameters useful in syndrome identification are found in Feingold and Bossert (1974); some of the complexities of analyzing the facies are discussed in Joseph and Dawbarn (1970). Standards for palatal measurements and indices are found in Redman, Shapiro, and Gorlin (1966). Penrose and Smith's (1966) monograph on Down syndrome is still worth reading. Scriver and Rosenberg (1973) on amino acid disorders and Stanbury, Wyngaarden, and Fredrickson (1978) on metabolic disorders are useful background sources; more clinically relevant for the laboratory diagnosis of genetic and metabolic disorders are Thomas and Howell (1973) and Thomas and Scott (1973). An approach to overwhelming metabolic disease in early infancy is outlined in Nyhan (1977). Centerwall and Centerwall (1972) briefly review phenylketonuria and its treatment. Shepard's (1973) *Catalogue of Teratogenic Agents* and Warkany's (1971) massive notebook on congenital malformations are both interesting compilations. Neurocutaneous syndromes are discussed by Chalhub (1976). For those with discriminating olfactory perception, unusual odor syndromes are listed in Thomas and Scott (1973) and Mace et al. (1976) (cf. also Lee et al., 1976.)

Dermatoglyphic nomenclature is defined in Penrose (1968); the genesis of dermatoglyphics is reviewed by Mulvihill and Smith (1969). The potential contributions of dermatoglyphics to clinical medicine are discussed in Davies (1976), Elbualy and Schindeler (1971), Holt (1961), Loesch (1973), and Schaumann and Alter (1976).

Gibbs and Gibbs (1964) contains a wealth of information on electroencephalographic patterns in the retarded; Niedermeyer

(1973) surveys the use of the EEG in clinical pediatric practice. Principles of anticonvulsant therapy are critically analyzed by Brett (1977).

The STYCAR tests of vision and hearing are available from NFER Publishing Co., Ltd., 2 Jennings Buildings, Thames Avenue, Windsor, Berks, England. The Chun gun is available from Radiation Measurements, Inc., P.O. Box 44, Middleton, Wisconsin 53562.

DEVELOPMENTAL ASSESSMENT

A smart mother makes often a better diagnosis than a poor doctor.

August Bier

Although some researchers have concluded that IQ scores obtained in the first year of life have no practical utility in predicting later intelligence, many other studies suggest that this may be true for an essentially normal population, but predictability within the retarded range of development is much more accurate. In other words, although degrees of normality are virtually impossible to predict, the IQs of dull to retarded children are much more constant than those of average to superior children. Defect is easier to predict than normality. The developmental component of the pediatric examination is better interpreted as a global indicator of the basic psychobiologic integrity of the infant organism than as an IQ test.

The present chapter is an introduction to the developmental assessment of the young child. Principles of comprehensive evaluation are stressed at the expense of briefer screening measures. The very concept of screening, the employment of "quickie" tests by minimally trained personnel, is in direct conflict with almost all current child development research. The theory behind such screening tools is purely metric and does nothing to foster a concept of development that would aid in understanding a particular child's developmental course.

The Denver Developmental Screening Test (DDST) (Frankenburg, Dodds, and Fandal, 1970) is the most widely used developmental screening test. Its correlation with Bayley Mental Development Indices (MDIs) at 1 year of age is strikingly poor (Frankenburg, Camp, and VanNatta, 1971). Assuming a 3% prevalence rate for retardation, out of 10,000 1-year-olds screened, 9700 should be normal and 300 delayed. Of the 9700 normal infants approximately 1164 will be called delayed by the DDST, and of the 300 retarded approximately 213 will be misclassified as normal (cf. Werner, 1972). As with other screening procedures, the DDST places too much reliance on history at the expense of direct observation.

The myth of the pediatrician's "built-in Gesell scale" has not been substantiated by research (Bierman et al., 1964; Korsch

Cobb, and Asher, 1961); pediatricians apparently tend to avoid the extremes of retardation and superiority by lumping children in an overly large average group. Carr and Stephen (1964) noted that physicians use condensations of the Gesell schedules or a selection of items from other standardized tests. The brevity of the resulting instrument bears a direct relationship to its unreliability. Accurate evaluation requires a definite time commitment; there can be no shortcut to precise developmental diagnosis. Although there is no single test or small group of items to assess development, it is still the pediatrician's responsibility to make a diagnosis without fragmenting the infant into neurologic and psychologic halves: "the physician has the responsibility for diagnosing developmental status, particularly in infancy, and he cannot delegate this responsibility to someone else" (Knobloch and Pasamanick, 1963). In other words, the pediatrician is responsible for the developmental evaluation of infants who pass their DDST as well as those who fail it.

Developmental histories are notoriously inaccurate. However, their inaccuracy and unreliability often correlate highly with the sloppiness with which they are performed. Vague general questions with regard to developmental milestones will rarely generate useful information. McGraw and Molloy (1941) documented that when questions about motor milestones were made specific (drawings illustrating the multiple stages of each milestone were used), parental histories demonstrated significantly fewer discrepancies. The affective content of developmental landmarks also helps them to be recalled with greater accuracy. Thus, the slow rate of progress in severely retarded children gives to their attainment of each milestone a significant emotional component and makes developmental history-taking in the retarded a much more reliable procedure than in the normal. The temporal pattern of developmental delay (Figure 22) can only be obtained from a careful developmental history; this pattern can contribute significantly to establishing an etiology as well as a diagnosis.

One of Gesell's major contributions was to stress the clinical usefulness of analyzing behavior along four major streams of development:

1. Motor { gross motor (lower extremity); fine motor (upper extremity) }
2. Problem solving (adaptive)

3. Language (communication)
4. Personal social (self-help)

Discrepancies between the age levels for these different developmental areas can contribute further to the process of medical diagnosis. A sample questionnaire to initially estimate functional levels is presented in Table 10.

Motor abilities have the weakest correlation with general function but nevertheless compose the common substrate for any evaluation of the preverbal child. Motor milestones come closest to the maturational ideal of an ordered sequence of behaviors that unfold like clockwork and seemingly depend only on myelination of the appropriate motor tracts (Dennis, 1940; Gesell and Amatruda, 1947). There remains a wide range for the achievement of various motor skills (e.g., walking may occur between 7 months and 2 years), and certain motoric patterns (such as crawling) may not occur in all infants. Caregiving behavior can influence the developmental timetable: British babies who are consistently placed supine in their cribs develop coordinated reaching schemata earlier than their American counterparts; the latter, who are almost universally put in prone positions, achieve ambulation earlier (Francis-Williams and Yule, 1967; Holt, 1960).

A careful motor assessment is an important part of the neurodevelopmental examination. It cannot diagnose mental retardation, but it does contribute to a diagnosis of the mild degrees of cerebral palsy that sometimes complicate retardation. More detailed functional evaluation of motor abilities can be carried out by physical and occupational therapists experienced in working with young handicapped children (Tables 11, 12, and 13). Depending on the child's mental age, an appropriate habilitation program can then be prescribed to facilitate the development of motor skills.

The dissociation between motor abilities and general cognitive functioning is most apparent in the observation that many profoundly retarded children will have essentially normal gross motor milestones (Shapiro, Accardo, and Capute, 1978); those severely retarded children with proportional motor delay can be considered to have their retardation complicated by some degree of cerebral palsy. It is unfortunate that despite their poor correlation with general developmental status, motor milestones receive the most stress in baby books and are among the best-remembered items

Table 10. Developmental questionnaire

Age	Posture and locomotion	Manipulation	Language	Social
3 months	A. Does he support himself on forearms when lying?	A. Are his hands usually open at rest?	A. Does he laugh or make happy noises?	A. Does he smile at you?
	B. Does he hold his head up steadily while on his stomach?	B. Does he pull at his clothing?	B. Does he turn his head to sounds?	B. Does he reach for familiar people or objects?
6 months	A. Does he lift his head when lying on his back?	A. Does he transfer a toy from one hand to the other?	A. Does he "babble," repeat sounds together (i.e., mum-mum-mum)?	A. Does he stretch his arms out to be picked up?
	B. Does he roll from back to front?	B. Does he pick up small objects?	B. Is he frightened by angry noise?	B. Does he show his likes and dislikes?
9 months	A. Does he sit for long periods without support?	A. Does he pick up objects with his thumb and one finger?	A. Does he understand "no-no," "bye-bye"?	A. Does he hold his own bottle?
	B. Does he pull up on furniture?	B. Does he finger-feed any foods?	B. Will he imitate any sounds or words if you make them first?	B. Does he play any nursery games ("peek-a-boo," "bye-bye")?
12 months	A. Is he walking (alone or with hand held)?	A. Does he throw toys (objects)?	A. Does he have at least one meaningful word other than "mama," "dada"?	A. Does he cooperate in dressing?
	B. Does he pivot when sitting?	B. Does he give you toys (let go) easily?	B. Does he shake his head for "no"?	B. Does he come when you call him?
18 months	A. Does he walk upstairs with help?	A. Does he turn book pages (two or three at a time)?	A. Does he have at least six real words besides his "jargon"?	A. Does he copy you in routine tasks (sweeping, dusting, etc.)?
	B. Can he throw a toy while standing without falling?	B. Does he fill spoon and feed self?	B. Does he point at what he wants?	B. Does he play in the company of other children?

Age								
2 years	A.	Does he run well without falling?	A.	Does he turn book pages one at a time?	A.	Does he talk in short (two- to three-word) sentences?	A.	Does he ask to be taken to the toilet?
	B.	Does he walk up and down stairs alone?	B.	Does he remove his own shoes, pants?	B.	Does he use pronouns ("me," "you," "mine")?	B.	Does he play in company of other children?
2½ years	A.	Does he jump, getting both feet off the floor?	A.	Does he unbutton any buttons?	A.	Does he use plurals or past tense?	A.	Does he tell his first and last name if asked?
	B.	Does he throw a ball overhand?	B.	Does he hold a pencil or crayon adult fashion?	B.	Does he use the word "I" correctly most of the time?	B.	Does he get himself a drink without help?
3 years	A.	Does he pedal a tricycle?	A.	Does he dry his hands (if reminded)?	A.	Does he tell little stories about his experiences?	A.	Does he share his toys?
	B.	Does he alternate feet (one stair per step) going upstairs?	B.	Does he dress and undress fully including front buttons?	B.	Does he know his sex?	B.	Does he play well with another child? Take turns?
4 years	A.	Does he attempt to hop or skip?	A.	Does he button clothes fully?	A.	Does he say a song or a poem from memory?	A.	Does he tell "tall tales" or "show off"?
	B.	Does he alternate feet going downstairs?	B.	Does he catch a ball?	B.	Does he know all his colors?	B.	Does he play cooperatively with a small group of children?
5 years	A.	Does he skip, alternating feet?	A.	Does he tie his own shoes?	A.	Can he print his first name?	A.	Is he a "mother's helper," likes to do things for you?
	B.	Does he jump rope or jump over low obstacles?	B.	Does he spread with a knife?	B.	Does he ever ask what a word means?	B.	Does he play competitive games and abide by the rules?

From Capute and Biehl (1973) by permission.

Table 11. Gross motor milestones

1–4 Months

Lifts head briefly and turns it to side P
Rolls partly to side SU
Rolls partly to side P
Lifts head recurrently P
Head compensates ventral suspension P
Head erect but bobbing SS
Lateral head righting SS

	R	L
flexion	____	____
rotation	____	____
both	____	____

Sustained lifting of head P
Supports self on forearms P
Legs extended P
Symmetrical head and arm posture predominates SU
Assists with head; no head lag PuS
Head steady but set slightly forward, upper back erect SS

Reciprocal kicking ____ ____

Landau:

head	____
trunk	____
UE	____
LE	____

5–8 Months

Rolls to supine P
Props self up on extended arms P
Rolls to prone SU
Head erect and steady SS
Brings knee up beside trunk, progresses forward in any manner P
Lifts head SU
Leans forward on hands, erect momentarily SI
Bears large fraction of weight ST

Equilibrium Reactions:

		R	L
P	head	____	____
	trunk	____	____
	UE	____	____
	LE	____	____

Supports on one arm P
Pivots P
Erect with support, 1 minute (unsteady) SI
Bounces when held ST
Sits up with rail SU
Steady without arm support, 10 minutes SI
Pulls to kneeling SI
Holds rail when placed, 1 minute ST

9–12 Months

Assumes hand-knee position with trunk elevated P
Comes to sit P
Sits up with assistance P or SU
Goes to prone SI
Pulls to stand L
Steady, maintains balance while turning to side SI
Holds with one hand ST
Creeps or crawls in any manner L
Cruises along furniture L
Pivots SI
Moves on hands and knees in reciprocal manner L
Comes to sit SU
Stands few seconds without support ST
Walks with one hand held L

13–16 Months

Stands with stability without support ST
Takes one or two independent steps L
Rises to standing independently L
Walks short distance; falls by collapse L
Kneels without support K
Walks with stability, full sole step; able to stop and start L
Walks carrying or pulling a toy L
Creeps to stairs L

SU	head	____	____
	trunk	____	____
	UE	____	____
	LE	____	____
SI	head	____	____
	trunk	____	____
	UE	____	____
	LE	____	____

Protective extension:
(parachute)

down	ST	____	____
ant	SI	____	____
lat	SI	____	____
post	SI	____	____

Table 11—*continued*

17–24 Months	
Runs stiffly without much knee motion	L
Hurls ball while standing, maintaining balance	L
Walks up stairs with one hand held	L
Creeps down stairs	L
Seats self in small chair	L
Climbs into adult chair	L
Assumes squatting position in play	L
Walks up stairs marking time (2 feet per step) with rail	L
Walks down stairs with one hand held	L
Walks with heel-toe gait	L
Runs well	L
Walks down stairs marking time (2 feet per step) with rail	L
Jumps from bottom step; one foot leading	L
Picks up object from floor without falling	L
Kicks large ball without demonstration	L
Reciprocal arm swing	L

KEY

P	Prone
SU	Supine
SI	Sitting
SS	Supported sitting
PS	Prone supported
PuS	Pulled to sitting
ST	Standing
K	Kneeling
L	Locomotion

Adapted from evaluation sheet currently used by the Division of Physical Therapy of The John F. Kennedy Institute. Courtesy of Susan Harryman, R.P.T.

Table 12. Fine motor milestones

0–4 Months

- Activates head, eyes, limbs in response to voice, noise
- Tends to lie in asymmetrical tonic neck reflex, eyes not focused on hand
- Tends to lie in asymmetrical tonic neck reflex, eyes fixate briefly on hand
- Maintains grasp of object (peg, rattle, for 5 sec)
- Tracks 180° with eyes (object at 2 feet)
- Swipes at object with hand fisted and object at side
- Holds and looks at object (rattle)
- Sustained hand regard
- Arms activate on sight of toy
- Head mostly in midline (75% of time)
- Hands mostly open (75% of time)
- Hands together at midline and clasped-finger play
- Both hands (clasped) raised
- Brings object to mouth when supine
- Mouthing of fingers
- Transfers object, uses mouth
- Moves head 180° to track moving object
- Primitive squeeze grasp: fingers only (ulnar), no thumb (use cube)
- Unilateral, indirect arm approach, watches hand as it approaches object (using hanging toy)

5–8 Months

- Grasps when hand comes in contact with object (hanging toy)
- Top level reaching: lifts hand out of visual field toward object and opens hand in anticipation of grasp
- Regards raisin
- Raking grasp: moves 1-inch block 3 inches across table top by raking
- Transfers object: pulling transfer
- Drops object—extends fingers from flexed position
- Bilateral reaching (hanging toy or round ring)
- Transfers object, direct
- Takes two 1-inch cubes, one in each hand
- Palmar squeeze grasp: picks up 1-inch dowel
- Unilateral reaching
- Attains raisin with raking grasp
- Radial palmar grasp: beginning thumb adduction to grasp 1-inch cube
- Pulls string to secure ring
- Bangs object on table top
- Inferior scissors grasp (lateral pinch): thumb adducted to index finger
- Mouths all objects
- Pulls ½-inch peg from hole
- Radial-digital or inferior forefinger grasp: radial digits provide pressure on object; thumb moves to opposition by pressing toward PIP of index finger
- Rotation of forearm to midposition from pronation
- Hand preference, six out of 10 trials

Table 12—*continued*

9–12 Months
Shakes bell
Inferior pincer grasp: thumb moves toward DIP of index finger with inhibition of other four digits
Isolation of index finger: pokes finger into a hole
Voluntary release of 1-inch cube against a surface (crude release)
Reach: oblique approach with supination to mid-position
Neat pincer grasp with slight wrist extension and overhand approach; forearm stabilized on table
Plays pat-a-cake
Removes cube from container in imitation
Holds crayon adaptively: projects from radial aspect of hand; one end up, one down, palmar grasp
Full supination from pronation
Puts cube into cup then removes it
Cooperates with dressing by extending arms and legs
Superior forefinger grasp: wrist extended and ulnarly deviated for grasp
Voluntary release smooth for 1-inch cube, clumsy for raisin
Attempts to stack two 1-inch cubes
Rolls ball imitatively
Releases ball with extensor thrust
Marks with crayon or pencil by banging (must have eye contact)
13–16 Months
Puts three or more cubes into cup
Builds a two-block tower
Picks up and places ½-inch bead or raisin into 2-inch bottle
Places ½-inch round peg into hole
Removes cover from small square box
Scribbles spontaneously
Places square peg into hole
Places circle into form board
Throws 3-inch ball with foreward extension in standing
17–20 Months
Points to three major body parts
Removes cotton socks by pulling from toes
Presses buttons
Turns pages two to three at a time; uses prehension and palmar grasp
Cylindrical grasp: all fingers in same place (turns pipe flange)
Builds a three-block tower
21–24 Months
Turns radio knob
Holds large crayon and manipulates with fingers
Hand preference, eight out of 10 trials
Imitates vertical scribble and circular scribble

Table 12—*continued*

Folds paper once, imitatively
Matches forms in three-piece formboard to corresponding holes
Throws ball (3 inches) inaccurately, shoulder-elbow movement
Puts lid on small square box
Builds a five-block tower
Strings 1-inch beads using both hands
Builds a six-block tower
Turns door knob
Turns one page at a time, uses prehension, ulnar twist, and individual finger action
Unscrews small jar lids
Builds three-block train without chimney
Imitates simple arm and hand movements
Removes shoes (tennis)
Removes pants from below hips

Adapted from evaluation forms currently used by the Division of Occupational Therapy of The John F. Kennedy Institute. Courtesy of Charlotte Exner, O.T.R. (cf. Pritkin, 1978).

Table 13. Oral motor/feeding milestones

0–4 Months

Up and down tongue and jaw movements in sucking
Rhythmic sucking
Lips usually closed
Suckling-protrusion/retraction in sucking
Slight tongue protrusion as nipple touches lips
Slight tongue protrusion in anticipation of feeding
Lateral lips used on nipple
Protrudes lips to surround nipple
Absence of rooting
Less suckling; less up and down jaw movements in sucking; tongue intrinsics and creation of negative pressure used part of the time
Opens mouth in anticipation of nipple
Involuntary tongue projection in feeding of solids
Purses lips at corners in swallowing and in moving food in mouth

5–8 Months

Draws in lower lip when spoon is removed
Protrudes tongue in imitation
Positions mouth for spoon insertion
Absence of bite reflex
Absence of suckling/swallowing reflex
Tongue held in grooved position for nipple
Draws in lower lip to remove food from it
Corner of food side of mouth drawn in

Table 13—*continued*

Lips active in eating
Lips closed tightly and corners drawn up during swallowing
Able to lateralize—not functional
Grasps spoon when being fed
Little choking on junior-ground foods
Clears spoon quickly and easily
Beginning chewing—mostly up and down movements
Finger feeds cracker

9–12 Months

Closes mouth on cup rim
Loses liquid from corners of mouth in drinking
Voluntary biting on objects
Munches cracker—does not suck
Beginning rotary chewing—improved lateralization and rotary jaw movements
Little mouthing
Voluntary tongue protrusion—play
Tongue retracted and depressed before feeding
Licks food off center of lower lip with tongue

13–16 Months

Absence of drooling except when concentrating on difficult task
Completes plate to mouth pattern with spoon—inversion of spoon before putting in mouth
Licks large area of lower lip with tongue
Lower lip clears upper lip
Upper lip drawn in to clear of food
Drinks with cup with two hands, hands to mother, drops; uses too much rotation and spills most of contents
Spits food purposefully
Completes plate to mouth pattern—inversion of spoon at mouth

17–24 Months

Able to chew most meats—improved rotary chewing
Scoops cereal from bowl
Drinks from cup with two hands—voluntary cup release
No inversion of spoon
Feeds self food from bowl, moderate spilling
Drinks from small glass—held in one hand, voluntary cup release
Licks center of upper lip

Adapted from evaluation forms currently used by the Division of Occupational Therapy of The John F. Kennedy Institute. Courtesy of Charlotte Exner, O.T.R.

when developmental histories are taken (Wenar and Coulter, 1962).

Next to language, *problem-solving* abilities are the best predictors of future intellectual endowment. Whereas the full range of language is rarely observed in an office setting (therefore necessitating a careful history), problem-solving skills are more easily assessed, mainly because children love to play with the toys used in the testing situation. Familiarity with the test instruments cannot be considered a significant variable, but discomfort with the pediatric office setting or poor rapport with the examiner may contribute to less than optimal performance.

There is much overlap between the assessment of fine motor skills (Table 12) and problem-solving items (Table 14, Figure 44). Indeed, Kopp (1974b) has demonstrated a significant association between the quality of fine motor behavior and the infant's performance on problem-solving tasks. Essentially the same item can be used to measure both areas, but the observer will interpret the child's behavior from two different perspectives. For example, the 10-month-old has a neat pincer grasp and shows a preference for picking up the smaller of two objects. A 2-year-old mentally retarded child may with much encouragement and repeated focusing of his attention smoothly pluck a pellet with a pincer grasp but distractedly and quickly lose interest so that he drops it almost immediately. A 2-year-old cerebral palsied child may never succeed in obtaining the pellet despite repeated overshooting attempts, but the examiner can observe the child's strong visual interest in the object. The first child passes the fine motor item but fails the same problem-solving item; the second child fails the motor while passing the problem-solving task. For the examiner experienced with young chidren such clinical appraisals should not be denigrated as "subjective." McGraw (1942) demonstrated the fallacies inherent in interpreting test solutions in too rigidly standardized a fashion; the qualitative aspects of behavior within the context of an evaluation of the whole child can contribute significantly to the predictive accuracy of infant testing (Escalona and Heider, 1959; Escalona and Moriarity, 1961). Failure to evaluate the infant's interest, alertness (especially visual), concentration, and degree of responsiveness implicitly reduces the assessment to a purely psychometric exercise.

In motor-impaired children it may be clinically useful to attempt to assign a motor or problem-solving age to each of the

Table 14. Problem-solving milestones

Behavior	Age (months)
Cube	
regards	3
attains	6
approaches second	6
takes second	7
attempts third	10
releases one in cup	12
releases three in cup	13
takes third	14
tower (two)	15
releases nine in cup	15
takes fourth	16
tower (three to four)	18
tower (five)	21
tower (six)	24
train	30
tower (nine)	36
bridge	36
gate	48
steps	60
Ring/string	
follows horizontally	1
vertically	2
circularly	3
approaches	4
attains	5
inspects	7
pulls string	8
Pellet	
regards	5
attains	6
inferior pincer	9
mature pincer	10
prefers pellet to bottle	10
Pellet in bottle	
finger bottle	14
imitates solution	14
solves spontaneously	16
Pegboard	
one out	7
fingers hole	10
one out and in	14
finishes round (A) urged	16

Table 14—*continued*

finishes round (A) spontaneously	18
finishes square (B) spontaneously	20
Three-hole formboard	
round form	16
round reversed	18
square form	20
solves	22
solves reversed	30
Miscellaneous	
visual threat	2
inspects bell	8
rings bell	9
looks for toy that disappears	9
uncovers toy	10
glass frustration	13
counts one	30

Adapted from Cattell (1940), Gesell (1940); Gesell and Amatruda, (1947), Illingworth (1962, 1967), and Sheridan (1968); for details of administration of the above items refer to the preceding references, especially Cattell (1940). Differences in the techniques of administration will be reflected in slightly different age norms for each item. The pediatrician should be able to define acceptable standards for his own patient population. Passing an item is always much easier to interpret than failure.

four extremities; when discrepancies are noted they may assist in the topographic and physiologic classification of cerebral palsy types.

Language is the common denominator in depicting the various developmental disabilities. In the absence of hearing impairment and communication disorders, language is the best predictor of future cognitive function. Children at all age levels give the impression of understanding more than they say (i.e., receptive language better than expressive). Language functioning must be carefully evaluated (see next chapter) to document the accuracy of these clinical impressions. It should be pointed out that even in nonlanguage areas, expressive abilities normally lag behind receptive ones: a child will perceptually discriminate sounds and shapes before he is able to correctly pronounce the sounds or copy the figures (Maccoby and Bee, 1965).

Perception, as Piaget (1954, 1963) has repeatedly stressed, is not so much a passive biologic substrate for knowledge as it is a

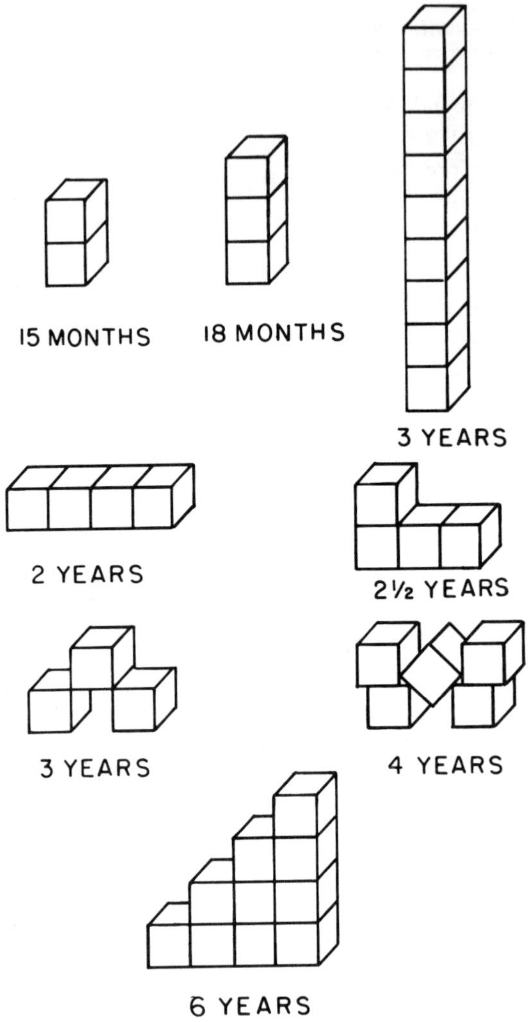

Figure 44. Age norms for block figure imitation. Add one-half year to the age levels for the train, bridge, and gate figures when copied (child shown finished figure) rather than imitated (child shown construction of figure). The steps are only presented for copying. Adapted from Taylor (1961) by permission.

type of cognitive behavior. The child needs to actively construct a world view of sufficient complexity (at least spatially; cf. Bower, 1974; Bryant, 1974) before he will demonstrate such obvious "perceptual" responses as blinking to a visual threat (2 months) and orienting to a bell (5 months). The older child who fails at these tasks may have a visual or auditory defect, or he may simply be functioning cognitively below the necessary developmental age. Perception is a particular type of cognition.

At the opposite extreme from motor milestones, which are relatively independent of environmental variations, *self-help* skills are sensitive to the effects of practice and teaching. One of the best examples of this dependence is the use of a cup. Neurologically an infant can sit, bring his hands to the midline, and raise objects to his mouth by 6 months of age; breast-feeding mothers often completely wean their infant to cup feedings at this age. Although the child can obtain all his fluid requirements in this manner, the mother must be prepared for a fair amount of spillage. It is thus the parents' tolerance for a certain degree of messiness as well as their enthusiasm to encourage the infant's skill acquisition that help determine the age for cup feeding. Without detailed sequential observations on childrearing practices, one cannot interpret bottle feeding at 2 or 3 years of age as a sign of developmental delay; passing an item has a unique significance as opposed to failure, which can have multiple determinants. This is perhaps even more obvious with the dressing skills of the pre- and early school age child when the mother dresses the dawdling child in the morning rush to get him off to school on time. Many parents of retarded children will volunteer that their children could succeed at certain tasks if only they, the overprotective parents, would allow the child sufficient opportunity. In reality, this is a method of denial that can easily confuse the inexperienced historian; it will be obvious that the child is still unable to perform the more basic component tasks on which these self-help skills depend.

Once these different streams of development have been evaluated the phenomenon of *dissociation* (i.e., differences between the child's motor, problem-solving, language, and self-help ages) may assist in formulating a diagnosis (Table 15). In mental retardation there is often no dissociation among the four major developmental areas; however, it is not uncommon to find a mild receptive-expressive language dissociation (receptive slightly better), and in the more severely retarded a cognitive-motor dissociation (motor skills almost normal) may be apparent. Any uncoupling of usually associated milestones may represent dissociation in a retarded child. In cerebral palsy there is a striking language-motor dissociation in the child with normal

Table 15. Dissociation phenomena in developmental disabilities

Developmental area	Mental retardation	Cerebral palsy	Deafness
Motor			
Gross	V[a]	D[b]	N[c]
Fine	V	D	N
Problem solving	D	V	N
Language			
Receptive	D	N	D
Expressive	D	V	D
Personal-Social	D	V	V

[a] V = variable.
[b] D = delayed.
[c] N = normal.

intelligence, but as the cerebral palsied child's IQ drops the lag becomes much less evident. Communicative disorders are marked by a language–problem-solving dissociation (with a higher problem-solving age). There may be a further receptive-expressive language dissociation.

An equally important developmental phenomenon is *deviancy.* Whereas dissociation refers to discrepant ages for the different streams of development, deviancy denotes a nonsequential appearance of skills within a single stream. For example, in the motor area, a child with cerebral palsy may roll from supine to prone by 2 months of age and before achieving head control (prone) or rolling from prone to supine. This inversion of the usual sequence is pathologic; the advanced milestone is a "splinter" skill which is rarely of functional use to the child. Such deviance contributes to an uneven developmental pattern and "scatter" on psychometric testing. Occasionally, experienced clinical judgment may consider a "splinter" skill to reflect a truer estimate of a child's potential; such individualized judgments are difficult to subsume under general rules (cf. Matheny, 1966). Both dissociation and deviance are more common in the acquired (brain damage) forms of mental retardation; the genetic types frequently demonstrate delays that are uniform, global, and sequential.

In infancy and early childhood, developmental assessment focuses on language, problem solving, perceptual-motor integration, self-help, and personal-social skills; in middle childhood attention shifts to academic performance. The pediatrician may then select assessment items from current educational test batteries or more directly from grade-appropriate tasks derived from local school curricula. Whereas the borderline to mildly retarded individual may not be noticed until school age, moderately to profoundly retarded children should be recognized within the first year of life. Indeed, except where careful developmental assessment is being routinely carried out, a child suspected of developmental delay within the first year of life is most probably severely retarded.

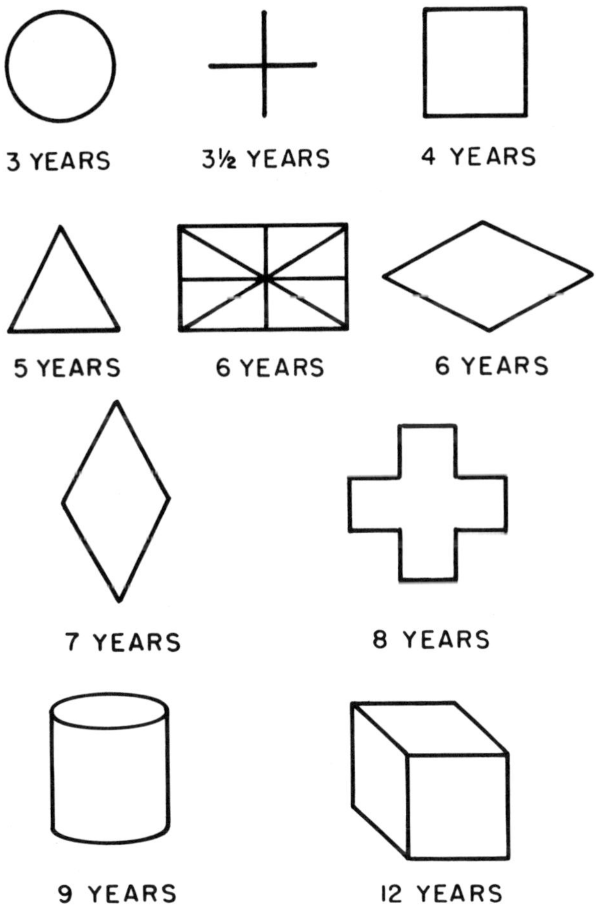

Figure 45. Age norms for figure copying. Adapted from Taylor (1961) by permission.

One of the most useful and interesting adjuncts to developmental assessment in the older child is the employment of various drawing tests. The Gesell drawings (Figure 45) demonstrate a rough association with mental age; the Goodenough (1926) Draw-A-Person Test presents a more refined correlation (Table 16, Figure 46). When the drawing age on this test appears well in advance of the mental age by other measures, a practice effect may be demonstrated by encouraging the child to draw a different person: the resulting picture will be a carbon copy of the first. More detailed scoring systems for human figure drawings have been developed by Koppitz (1968) and Harris (1963; Harris, Roberts, and Pinder, 1970). Although the Bender Gestalt Test (Figure 47) was designed as a projective psychiatric instrument, it can also be used to estimate children's perceptual-motor age; Koppitz (1963) has standardized a developmental scoring manual for this purpose.

The Complex Figure Drawing Test (Figure 48) was first developed as a memory test in adults recovering from severe head trauma. Osterrieth (1944) established age norms for the figure as a

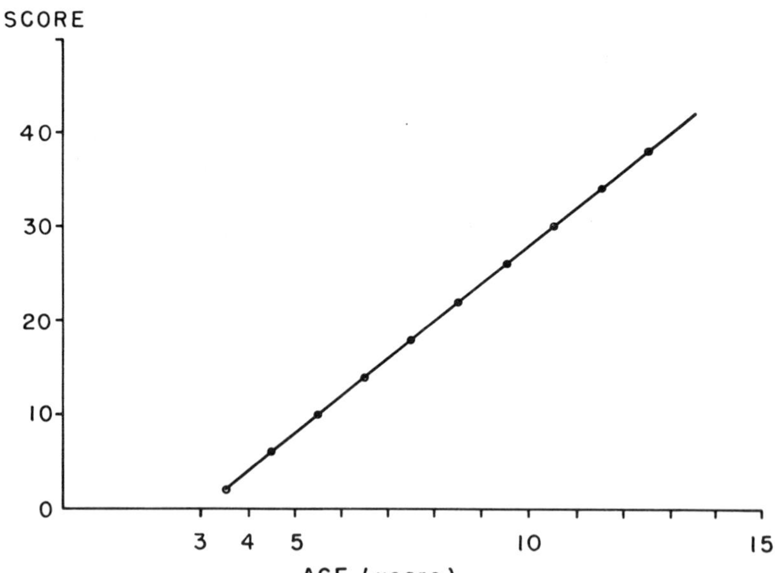

Figure 46. Age norms for Draw-A-Person Test. Adapted from Goodenough (1926) by permission.

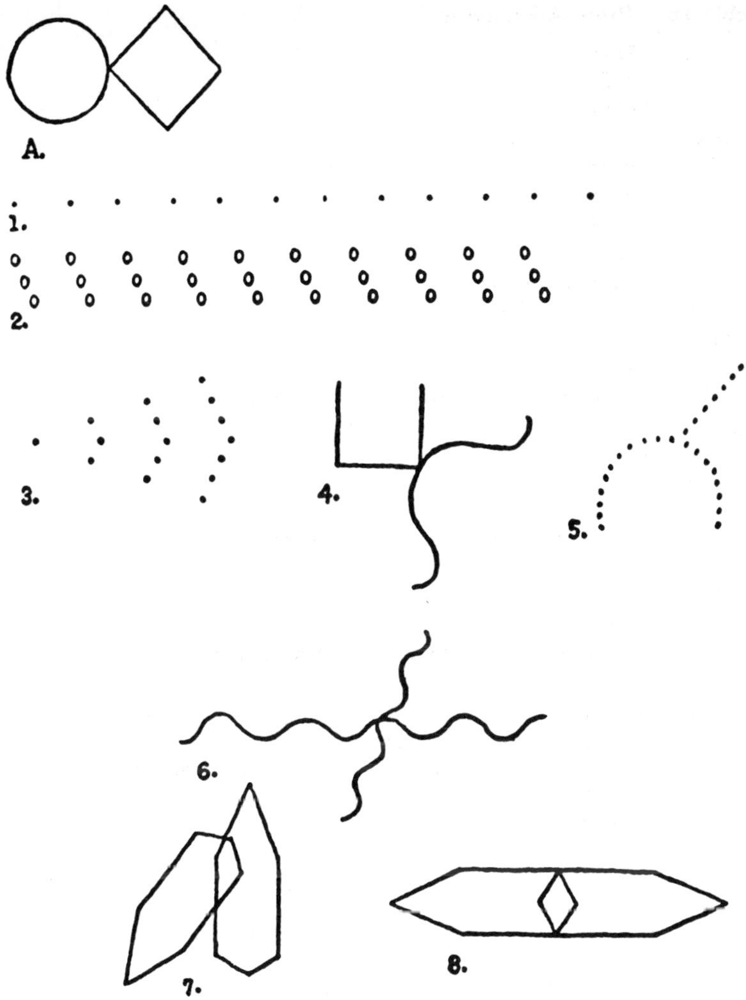

Figure 47. Bender Gestalt Test figures. From Bender (1938) by permission.

developmental copying task. Although more complex scoring procedures make the instrument valuable in describing perceptual disorders in the learning disabled, a simpler scale may be used to estimate mental age: for each of the 18 segments (Figure 49) of the drawing, two points are credited if the piece is fairly well drawn and correctly positioned, one point if some attempt is made to

Table 16. Draw-A-Person scale

1. HEAD
2. LEGS
3. ARMS

TRUNK

4. present
5. length greater than breadth
6. shoulders

ARMS AND LEGS

7. attached to trunk
8. at correct point

NECK

9. present
10. outline continuous with head, trunk, or both

FACE

11. eyes
12. nose
13. mouth
14. 12 and 13 in two dimensions; two lips
15. nostrils

HAIR

16. present
17. on more than circumference; nontransparent

CLOTHING

18. present
19. two articles; nontransparent
20. entire drawing nontransparent; sleeves and trousers
21. four articles
22. costume complete without incongruities

FINGERS

23. present
24. correct number
25. two dimensions; length $>$ breadth; subtended angle $< 180^\circ$
26. thumb opposition
27. hand distinct from fingers and arm

JOINTS

28. arm: elbow, shoulder, or both
29. leg: knee, hip, or both

PROPORTION

30. head: one-tenth to one-half of trunk area
31. arms: approximately same length as trunk
32. legs: Length 1 to 2 times trunk length; width $<$ trunk width
33. feet: one-tenth to one-third of leg length
34. arms and legs in two dimensions
35. HEEL

Table 16—*continued*

MOTOR COORDINATION

36. lines reasonably firm and well connected
37. lines firmly drawn with correct joining
38. head outline
39. trunk outline
40. outline of arms and legs
41. features

EARS

42. present
43. correct position and proportion

EYE DETAIL

44. brow or lashes
45. pupil
46. proportion
47. glance directed to front in profile drawing

CHIN

48. present; forehead
49. projection

PROFILE

50. not more than one error
51. correct

After Goodenough (1926) by permission.

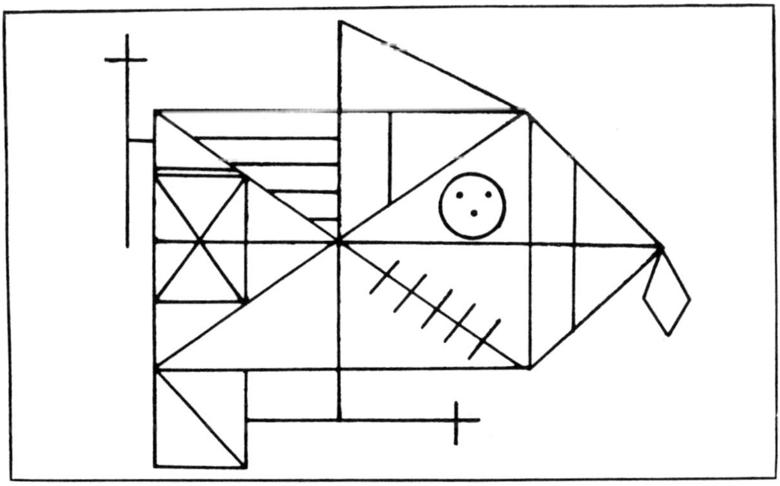

Figure 48. Rey-Osterrieth complex figure. From Osterrieth (1944) by pemission.

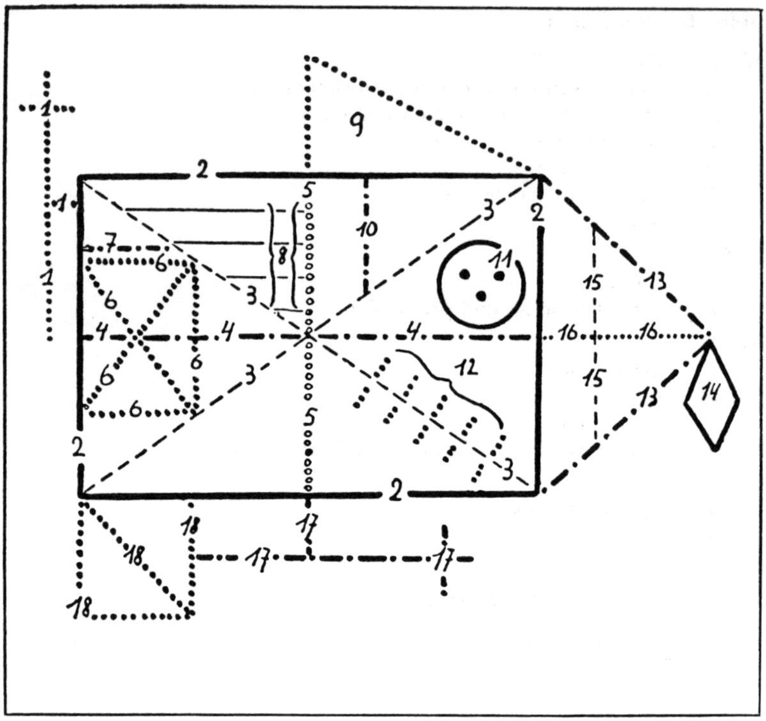

Figure 49. Scored items of Rey-Osterrieth complex figure. From Osterrieth (1944) by permission.

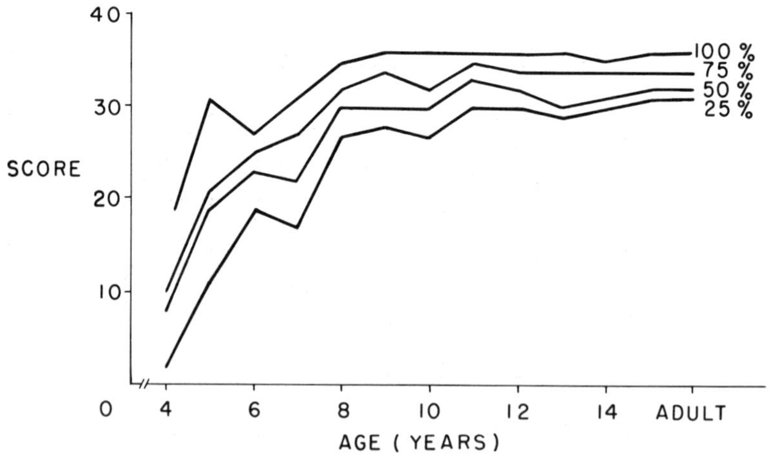

Figure 50. Age norms (percentiles) for Rey-Osterrieth complex figure drawing. Data from Osterrieth (1944) by permission.

represent the component, and no point if that part of the figure is completely left out. Age norms are depicted in Figure 50. It is critical for the interpretation of this and all the preceding drawing tests that the examiner observe the child while he draws; otherwise, significant deviances in performance may be missed.

BIBLIOGRAPHIC NOTE

Authors who have observed a useful predictive validity for infant tests include: Ames (1967), Bagdon (1973), Boothman, White, and Sweenie (1976), Drillien (1961), Erickson (1968), Fishler, Graliker, and Koch (1965), Holden (1972), Illingworth (1961b, 1967, 1971), Illingworth and Birch (1959), Knobloch and Pasamanick (1974), Koch et al. (1963), Share et al. (1964), and VanderVeer and Schweid (1974). A more negative evaluation of infant tests is expressed by Bayley (1933, 1970), Lewis (1976a), Lewis and McGurk (1972), McCall, Hogarty, and Hurlburt (1972), and Rutter (1970). Using refined statistical techniques on some of the Berkeley Growth Study data, Crano (1977) has suggested that the causal relationship between "mental" and behavioral development might well be opposite to that commonly supposed; i.e., cognitive development may be primary and qualitative behavioral characteristics may be purely derivative phenomena.

An abbreviated modification of the Gesell schedules, the Developmental Screening Inventory (DSI), is found in Knobloch, Pasamanick, and Sherard (1966) and Knobloch and Pasamanick (1974). An approach to pediatric developmental assessment (0 to 5 years) is presented in Egan, Illingworth, and MacKeith (1969). Some useful milestones for older children (2 to 9 years) are given in Hartlage and Lucas (1973). Abuses (sometimes political) of screening procedures are criticized in Thorpe and Werner (1974). Difficulties in evaluating the development of minority children are reviewed in Oakland (1977) and Wright and Isenstein (1977).

Nonquantitative assessment of children's drawings is illustrated in DiLeo (1970, 1973) and Burns and Kaufman (1970, 1972). Goodnow (1977) discusses the subject of children's drawings from a general psychologic perspective.

Principles of psychologic testing are discussed in Anastasi (1968) and Cronbach (1970). Psychometric instruments are reviewed briefly in Allen and Allen (1967) and in detail in Buros (1972) and Sattler (1974).

LANGUAGE ASSESSMENT

> Indeed, where no language is used, why should one speak of "thinking"? If this is done, it shows something about the *concept* of thinking.
>
> Wittgenstein

The most useful and most neglected index of infant development is language. Indeed, language is probably the best single indicator of developmental status, demonstrating the highest predictive correlation of all child behaviors with later intelligence.

As with all developmental phenomena, receptive aspects appear more advanced than productive (expressive) ones. Since one cannot expect a child to exhibit his full repertoire of verbal behavior in the atypical situation of the pediatric office setting, a careful parent interview is required for accurate language assessment in infancy. The range of variability in language acquisition is much more limited in the retarded than in the normal population; this makes a retrospective history of language milestones much more accurate in developmentally delayed children. For the assessment of language in normal children a prospective questionnaire seems most suitable. This chapter presents such an instrument and then discusses certain aspects of the differential diagnosis of the child who does not talk.

A 32-item scale of sequential and nonsequential language milestones is presented in Table 17; sample questions for the parents are given for the respective items in Table 18. When used longitudinally (serially at each well baby checkup), only several questions need be asked at each visit. It is helpful to describe to the parents the distinctions relevant to future items so that they can become more accurate observers.

Sequential Items

1. Alerting response to sound: Although many newborns demonstrate an overt response to sound, a number of infants will respond only with changes in heart rate, respiratory rate, or rate of sucking. Approximately 15% of parents will be uncertain whether their 2-week-old baby does hear. It is not until about 1 month of age that all babies produce a gross alerting response; the critical criterion at the 1-month level is that the response be visible.

Table 17. Linguistic and auditory milestones

Sequential	
Item	Month[a]
1. Alerting*	1
2. Social smile*	1½
3. Cooing	3
4. Orient to voice*	4
5. Orient to bell (I)*	5
6. "Ah-goo"	5
7. Razzing	5
8. Babbling	6½
9. Orient to bell (II)*	7
10. Gesture	7½
11. "Dada/mama" (inappropriate)	8
12. Orient to bell (III)*	9½
13. "Dada/mama" (appropriate)	10
14. One word	11
15. One-step command (with gesture)*	12
16. Two words	12
17. Three words	14
18. One-step command (without gesture)*	15
19. Four to six words	15
20. Immature jargon	15
21. Seven to 20 words	18
22. Mature jargon	18
23. One body part*	18
24. Three body parts*	21
25. Two-word combinations (N + N)	21
26. Five body parts*	23
27. Fifty words	24
28. Two-word sentences (S + P)	24
29. Pronouns (I, me, you; inapprop.)	24
Non-sequential	
30. Rooting reflex*	
31. Feeding/swallowing problems	
32. Percent articulation deficit	

From Capute and Accardo (in press) by permission. Attempt should be made to observe asterisked items; with an uncooperative child, parental observation may be recorded.

[a] Age levels are approximate and will need to be standardized on different normal populations.

2. Social smile: The social smile is a maturational phenomenon that unfolds at 46 post-conceptional weeks (6 weeks of age) (Bower, 1974). The true social smile is a response that can readily be elicited by the parent or examiner and needs to be distinguished from earlier spontaneous "smiles" in response to feeding, flatus, elimination, and other endogenous stimuli.
3. Cooing: Cooing is defined as long pure vowel sounds with variations other than those observed in crying or yawning. It needs to be distinguished from the earlier use of short vowels

Table 18. Sample questions for parental reporting of sequential items

1. When did your infant recognize the presence of sound by blinking, startling, moving any part of the body, etc.?
2. When did your infant smile at you when you talked to him or stroked his face?
3. When did your infant produce long vowel sounds in a musical fashion?
4. When you enter a room and the baby doesn't see you at first, does he turn immediately to the correct side when you speak to him or does he search for you, sometimes looking first in the right direction, and sometimes not?
6. Does the baby say "ah-goo"?
7. When did your baby first give you the "raspberry"?
8. When did your child first babble? (Demonstrate)
10. When did your child first wave bye-bye or play pat-a-cake?
11. When did your child say "dada" and "mama," but inappropriately?
13. When did your child begin to use "dada" and "mama" appropriately?
14. When did your child say his first word other than "dada" and "mama"?
15. When did your child begin to follow simple commands such as "Give me—" or "Bring me—" accompanied by a gesture?

16, 17, 19, 21, 27. How large is your child's vocabulary?

18. When was your child able to follow simple commands without an accompanying gesture?
20. When did your child begin to use jargon—to run unintelligible words together in an attempt to make a "sentence"?
22. When did your child's jargon begin to include several intelligible words?

23, 24, 25. How many body parts can your child point to when named? Which ones?

26. When did your child start to put two words together?
28. When did your child start to combine a noun or pronoun with a verb?
29. When did your child use three pronouns?

From Capute and Accardo (in press) by permission.

(ah, eh, uh), sighs, grunts, gurgles, belches, coughs, and other throaty noises. It is best characterized as being somewhat musical or playfully repetitive. In attempting to elicit information on the early stages of infant vocalization, the pediatrician may attempt to demonstrate the various distinctions and should always ask the parent to imitate the baby's actual sound productions. This reduces the incidence of misunderstanding and sensitizes the parent to a more careful observation of the succeeding stages.

Although abnormalities of infant cry (Karelitz and Fisichelli, 1962; Ostwald, Phibbs, and Fox, 1968; Prechtl et al., 1969; Weinberg, 1971) can provide clues to certain mental retardation syndromes such as the mewing cry of the cri-du-chat (5p−) syndrome, the growling of the de Lange syndrome, the seagull cry of trisomy E syndrome, the hoarse cry of congenital hypothyroidism, and the high-pitched, laughing cry of congenital microcephaly, analytic techniques are too complex for routine clinical use. It is interesting that Karelitz et al. (1964) were able to correlate a quantitative measure of crying in the newborn period with both intelligence and speech at 3 years of age; similarly, Cameron, Livson, and Bayley (1967) demonstrated a significant correlation between prespeech vocalizations in the first year of life and later intelligence. Although such associations are too rough for individual prediction, they do serve to highlight the essential continuity between infant vocalizations and later language development. The positive direction of such correlations probably reflects the limited communicative content of prespeech vocalizations (before 9 months of age communication is primarily visual, by expression and gesture) as well as the neural maturation of coupled speech and language centers (Lenneberg, 1964, 1967).

4. Orienting to voice: The infant should be able to turn immediately to the side of the room from which mother is speaking; the child who does not consistently look to the correct side first is not considered to orient to voice. If this is not observed during the examination, parental report needs to be carefully evaluated. There are actually three modalities of orienting responses in early infancy: 1) tactile orienting is present at birth in the form of the rooting reflex (cardinal points reflex), 2) visual orienting develops over the first 3

months; and 3) auditory orienting starts at 4 months with response to mother's voice and demonstrates an elaborate developmental sequence with regard to different stimuli over the next 20 months (Northern and Downs, 1974).

5. Orienting to bell (I): A bell is rung about 2 feet to one side of the infant's head and his ability to horizontally turn to the source of the sound is observed (see Figure 51). Repeat trials should randomize the side used until the examiner is certain that the response is not due to chance alone. Care should be taken that the infant does not receive any visual cues; this is best accomplished by bilateral confrontation, with the examiner's hands positioned symmetrically to each side of the infant's head.
6. "Ah-goo": "Ah-goo" is here considered a specific vocalization that has been described as appearing around 20 weeks of age. Although it can be considered to mark the transition between cooing and early babbling, about two-thirds of normal children will never use it.
7. Razzing: The child is able to place his tongue between his lips to produce a "raspberry" or "Bronx cheer." Approximately 50% of normal children will demonstrate this at 20 weeks; the remainder will learn to imitate it later.
8. Babbling: Mature babbling involves the playful repetition of consonant sounds (syllables including short vowels); the child's repertoire should consist of at least four different consonants that can be repeated in a string. It should be noted that the production of spontaneous vocalizations in the severely hearing impaired child usually progresses normally up to the stage of babbling, then plateaus, and within several months falls off. .
9. Orienting to bell (II): With the infant in a sitting position a bell is rung about 2 feet to one side of his head and at a 45° angle above the horizontal; the child looks first to the correct side (horizontally) and then localizes the bell by a secondary vertical gaze component (see Figure 51).
10. Gesture: The child either spontaneously (to verbal cues) or imitatively (to motor cues) engages in meaningful gestures such as waving bye-bye or playing pat-a-cake.
11. "Dada/mama" inappropriately: After babbling strings such as *dadadadada*, the baby begins to clip the sequence to produce "words" like *dada* fortuitously. A lack of compre-

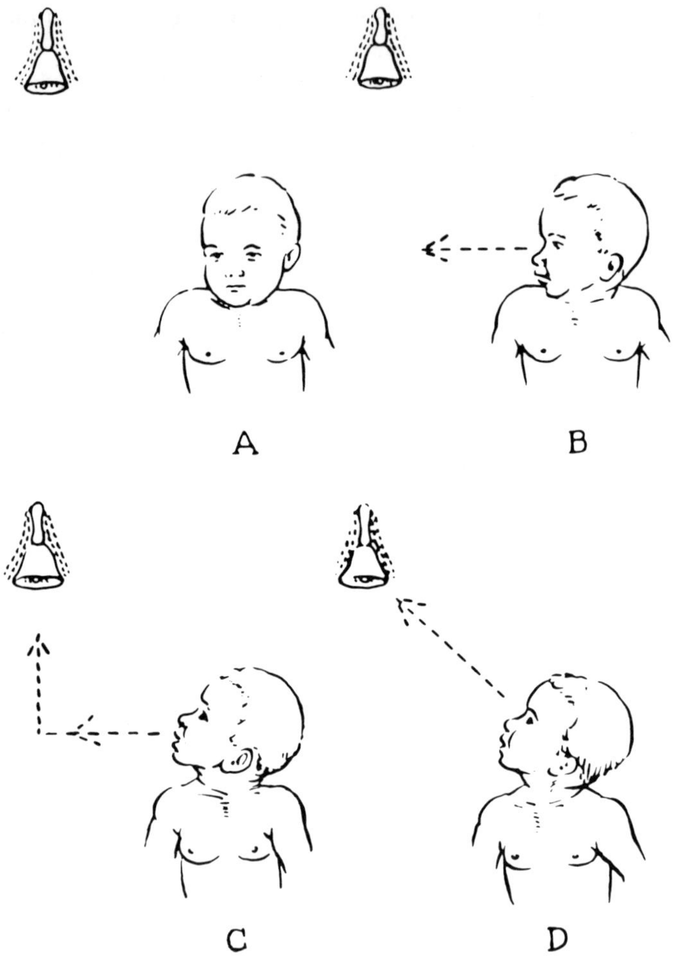

Figure 51. Orienting to bell. In the first stage (5 months) when a bell is rung to one side of the infant's head (A), the infant turns horizontally to the correct side (B). In the second stage (7 months) when a bell is rung to one side of the infant's head (A), the infant localizes the sound by a compound visual maneuver consisting of horizontal followed by a vertical component (C). In the third stage (9½ months) when a bell is rung to one side of the infant's head (A), the infant localizes the sound by a single visual movement (D). From Capute and Accardo (in press) by permission.

hension is demonstrated by the indiscriminate application of *dada* to persons of either sex as well as to inanimate objects or in a vacuum. This usage marks the evolution of the most mature end of the babbling spectrum ("babbling drift").

12. Orienting to bell (III): With the infant in a sitting position a bell is rung about 2 feet to one side of his head and at a 45° angle above the horizontal; the child immediately locates the bell by visually traversing the appropriate oblique vector path (see Figure 51).
13. "Dada/mama" appropriately: If his inappropriate vocalizations of *dada* and *mama* receive repeated reinforcement cues, by about 10 months of age the child begins to use them appropriately. *Dada* almost always precedes *mama*. The child's power of discrimination at this age is only slightly impaired by the presence of multiple caregivers (e.g., *mama* may be applied to both mother and grandmother or babysitter).

    Dada and *mama* used appropriately are the infant's first words. Sometimes a vocabulary of sibling and family names or other well-rehearsed words develops before *dada* or between *dada* and *mama*; this pattern should be considered highly suspect for developmental deviance.
14. One-word vocabulary: In estimating the size of a young child's spontaneous expressive vocabulary (items 14, 16, 17, 19, 21, 27), two rules need to be followed throughout: 1) *dada, mama*, and the proper names/nicknames of family members and pets do not count as words; 2) until the child's vocabulary exceeds two dozen words, the parents should be requested to list all the words that the child actually uses. Such an enumeration often reveals the first estimation of vocabulary size to be too large or too small.

    One must always be careful to assess the qualitative sequence of language development and not just several age-appropriate milestones. It is not uncommon for retarded children to begin to say single words around 12 months of age and, after infrequent usage, discontinue speech. When their earlier pattern of language development is examined, it will be found deviant—certain milestones skipped, first word other than *dada/mama*, etc.

    The usual order of acquisition of parts of speech is nouns, verbs, adjectives, and adverbs; pronouns and prepositions occur before the correct use of conjunctions. The discovery that everything has a name, the "naming mania," with its characteristic vocabulary explosion, usually occurs at the end of the second year of life.

15. One-step command (with gesture): By history the child is able to respond appropriately to simple commands such as "Give me—", "Bring me—"; these may need to be accompanied by a gesture for them to be understood. ("No" may be considered a simple command if it is obeyed even when spoken in a normal tone of voice).
18. One-step command (without gesture): The child follows simple one-step commands such as "Give me—" or "Bring me—" without an accompanying gesture.
20. Immature jargon: Jargon is vocalization with the rhythm and pattern of conversational speech except that the "words" that are run together are unintelligible—"pseudo-speech polysyllables"; it appears that the child is trying to speak a sentence using gibberish or is speaking some foreign language. Immature jargon does not include any genuine semantic items (true words). When the parents are questioned concerning the presence of jargon, it should be imitated for them and they should be requested to imitate the child's corresponding vocalizations.
22. Mature jargon: Mature jargon presents the same vocalization pattern as immature jargon except that several intelligible words are mixed in the child's otherwise unintelligible patois.
23. One body part: When one compares the normative data in different psychometric tests, there seems to be some differences between the ability to identify a body part on the subject, the examiner, a doll, or a picture. The pediatrician should try to corroborate parental report of body part identification by using the above testing variations.
25. Two-word combinations (N + N): Two-word combinations rarely occur before the child's vocabulary reaches 20 words. If the parent claims two-word combinations with a dictionary of less than 20 words, the child's entire vocabulary should be listed. The words in the two-word combinations (frequently both nouns) must refer to separate concepts; thus, combinations such as *bye-bye, all gone,* and *hot dog* are considered single words. The child who has at least a 50-word vocabu-

lary (item 27) is starting to put two words together. If the parent describes the child's dictionary as much greater than 50 words, with no two-word combinations, the child's vocabulary should be specifically enumerated.

28. Two-word sentences (S + P): At about 2 years of age, the child's two-word utterances begin to take on the grammatical structure of telegraphic sentences with a (noun or pronoun) subject and a (verb) predicate (e.g., *daddy go, me like*). The pronouns used are frequently reversed. Again, with a child at the 2-year level, the parent should be requested to list all of the child's two-word combinations.
29. Pronouns (I, me, you; inappropriately): The child is beginning to use three pronouns (I, me, you), but not necessarily with grammatical correctness.

In the normal population there seems to be less variability in the age at which the different items are passed in the first year of life; by the second year of life acceleration of language development becomes a more obvious indicator of superior intelligence. After the first 2 years of life some useful sequential milestones include:

2½ years	Uses pronouns appropriately
3 years	250+ word vocabulary; three- and four-word sentences; plurals; understands at least two prepositional commands (on, under, back of, front of, beside)
3½ years	Understands three prepositional commands
4 years	Uses complex syntax to tell stories and describe experiences
5 years	Can follow three-step commands in correct order; asks the meanings of words

This series of sequential language items demonstrates better than any other developmental milestones the phenomenon of coupling. Just as in medicine where no one physical finding stands alone, so in developmental pediatrics certain behavioral skills are typically coupled. Dissociation or uncoupling of these milestones should make one suspect either the accuracy of the history or the existence of deviant development in which certain language items are present in an isolated fashion. Such "splinter" skills are rarely functional and do not usually provide a reliable basis for developmental assessment; indeed, they are fairly reliable markers of developmental abnormality.

Coupling effects are noted at the 15- and 18-month levels where a 15-month-old has a minimum vocabulary of two to six words associated with immature jargon, whereas an 18-month-old has six to 12 words coupled with mature jargon. This is seen again at 2 years of age when the infant has a minimum vocabulary of 50 words along with two-word sentences; the 3-year-old has a minimum of 250 words along with three-word sentences, plurals, and pronouns. Should one of these language milestones be present by itself, an infant is high risk developmentally. For example, if a child had a 15-word vocabulary at 15 months but did not demonstrate immature jargon, one would question the quality of the vocabulary because this might well represent a splinter skill. If one were to list the child's vocabulary, one might find that it contained many names of siblings and relatives which are not of substantial or meaningful value; that is, this rote kind of learning would not reflect good underlying processes of conceptualization or abstraction.

The following three nonsequential items focus on early oral motor coordination. Although at first glance these oral motor skills seem to be related more to articulation than to language, Templin has shown that language has an "all-of-a-pieceness" and that children who make articulation errors are the same children who later demonstrate language-related disabilities (Templin, 1966). Conclusive longitudinal data are lacking, but there is a strong clinical impression that even transient abnormalities of rooting, feeding/swallowing, and disarticulation (out of proportion to age level) are all related to later language disfunction; disarticulation in the preschool child may be an indicator of later learning disability (Capute et al., 1977).

Nonsequential items

30. Persistence of the rooting reflex: The rooting reflex should be evaluated throughout the first half-year of life; parental report should also be obtained because the degree of response varies with the infant's state and the time since last feeding. Clinically, the reflex seems to be prolonged when reinforced by breast-feeding as opposed to bottle-feeding.

31. Feeding/swallowing problems: Poor suck and uncoordination of swallowing patterns can contribute to early feeding difficulties. Persistence of oral motor uncoordination has been hypothesized to correlate with later language and articulation problems.
32. Percent articulation deficit: As soon as the child begins to acquire a vocabulary, record should be kept as to approximately what percent (0, 25, 50, 75, 100) of the child's speech is intelligible a) to the family and b) to complete strangers.

    The development of articulation also follows a predictable timetable. Vowels are acquired before consonants, and consonants are mastered by the following age levels (Shank, 1964):

3½ years:	p, b, m, w; h
4½ years:	t, d, n, g, k, ng, y
5½ years:	f, v, s, z
6½ years:	sh, zh, l, th
Up to 8 years:	ch, r, wh

One may also monitor articulation using the Denver Articulation Screening Exam (DASE) (Drumwright, 1971). Spreen (1965a, 1965b) found a moderate correlation between speech sound development and intelligence; the incidence of articulation problems in the retarded was approximately 10 times that in the normal population. Retarded children with speech defects rarely demonstrate structural oral deficits. Speech pathologists are aware of the developmental character of articulation milestones and will not usually initiate formal speech therapy until the child has reached a mental age of about 5 to 6 years because it is at this neuromaturational stage that the child can benefit most from intervention. A more general language stimulation program to enhance communication skills can, of course, be implemented earlier. Reliable data on the incidence of oropharyngeal dysfunction, its relation to speech defects, and its response to various modalities of therapy in the noncerebral palsied retarded population are unfortunately lacking. Finally, with regard to dysarticulation, it needs to be repeated that a short lingual frenulum (the phenomenon of "tongue-tie") has no effect on language development and feeding, and the presence of problems in one of these areas is no indication for surgery.

The Child Who Does Not Talk

When a young child presents with delayed language, the assessment will have to evaluate nonlinguistic cognitive abilities as well as associated behavioral signs in order to reach a correct developmental diagnosis. The findings with the major entities that need to be considered are outlined in Table 19. The incidence breakdown for the subgroups (i.e., mental retardation, deafness, communication disorder, autism, and other categories) of the child who does not talk will vary tremendously depending on the population served and the nature of the referral center.

Mental Retardation

Growth and development take place in a sequential and orderly fashion with simple, less integrated tasks occurring before more complex ones. In the language area, a normal infant will smile by 6 weeks, coo by 3 months, babble by 6½ months, gesture by 7½ months, say "mama" and "dada" appropriately by 10 months, one word by 11 months, and have a 50-word vocabulary by 2 years of age. If the child is retarded, then sequential development will be altered proportionally. A moderately (trainably) retarded child functions at approximately 50% of normal (IQ 40–55) and his language milestones will likewise progress at half the normal rate: he will smile by 3 months, coo by 6 months, babble

Table 19. Differential diagnosis of delayed language

Behavioral signs	Mental retardation	Communication disorders and deafness	Autism
Global cognitive function	PD[a]	N[b]	D > N[c]
Verbal communication	PD	DD[d]	DD
Nonverbal comprehension	PD	N	DD
Problem solving (nonverbal)	PD	N	D > N
Motor perseveration	+, ++[e]	0[f]	+++[g]
Echolalia	+, ++	0	+++
Isolation	0	+, ++	+++

[a] PD = delay proportional to mental age.
[b] N = normal.
[c] D > N = frequently delayed, sometimes normal.
[d] DD = delay disproportional to mental age.
[e] + = infrequent; ++ = present.
[f] 0 = not present
[g] +++ = frequent and striking.

by 13 months, gesture by 15 months, say "mama" and "dada" appropriately by 20 months, one word by 22 months, and have a 50-word vocabulary by 4 years of age. Apart from the language delay, fine motor, adaptive (problem-solving), and personal-social skills are all delayed proportionally; i.e., testing these areas separately will yield similar estimates of the child's developmental age.

Echolalia is the repetition (inappropriate and nonfunctional) of words, phrases, or sentences immediately after they are heard. It occurs briefly in the normal child between 18 and 30 months and may be considered the extreme end of the spectrum of imitative behavior that began in early infancy. (It is usually so transient in normals that it may not be observed by parents at all.) During the third year of life, one can trick most children by offering them choices of different objects or responses ("yes" or "no") and always putting the less desirable alternative or incorrect answer last: they will tend to respond to a choice by repeating the last option heard. In retarded children the phase of echolalia begins closer to the mental age level of 30 months and may be prolonged out of proportion to the child's degree of retardation. This may occur secondary to specific brain damage patterns (as seen with the phenomenal auditory rate memory of some "idiots savants") or it may be the result of parental reinforcement of fragments of language behavior that superficially seem advanced for the child's functional level.

Certain types of brain damage produce characteristic language disorder patterns. Many children with hydrocephalus demonstrate the "chatterbox" or "cocktail talk" syndrome (Fraser, Agnew, and Grieve, 1975; Lawrence, 1969). They have a high verbal output with sophisticated syntax, but the content of their hyperverbal conversation can be described as shallow and tangential, inappropriate to the syntactical complexity and sometimes bizarre considering the circumstances. A good auditory memory and pleasant personality can combine to cause the casual observer to overestimate both the cognitive and the social abilities of these children.

An area of concern to parents of severely retarded children is the use of communication systems that do not depend on spoken language. Many parents feel that the use of symbols or manual communication (sign language) has the potential to delay their child's attainment of spoken language. The physician can reassure the parents that the use of alternative modes of communication enhances and often accelerates the acquisition of spoken language whenever this is a reasonable goal.

Communication Disorders and Deafness

In children with communication disorders, expressive language, receptive language, or both are delayed, but global intellectual functioning is normal. However, it is necessary to test their cognitive abilities using tests that do not depend on spoken language, such as the Hiskey Nebraska Test or the Arthur adaptation of the Leiter Scale. In early infancy children with communication disorders interact appropriately with others; as they get older their language deficit contributes to secondary psychologic and behavioral problems such as isolation.

The terminology for communicative disorders, including the various types of congenital and acquired aphasia, is still in a state of flux. These children all act as if they were deaf or hard of hearing because their disorders include degrees of central auditory imperception. Behaviorally there is little to distinguish the more severe cases from deafness without careful audiometric evaluation. Congenital aphasics usually reach the level of immature jargon ("scribble speech") with all the expressive intonational features appropriate to spoken language. Functionally this is the opposite of the echolalia observed in autistic children who correctly repeat words, phrases, and sentences in a mechanical monotone with stress and pitch out of context (Simon, 1975). Acquired aphasic syndromes may result from a focal encephalitis producing a seizure focus in the temporal lobe (Gascon et al., 1973, Shoumaker et al., 1974); anticonvulsant therapy and time tend to produce some degree of improvement.

Although thinking can certainly develop in the absence of language, language strongly influences the structure of developing thought. Nonretarded persons who are congenitally deaf have been found to be linguistically deficient with an average reading achievement under a fourth grade (functional literacy) level (Furth, 1971). Thus it would seem that severe hearing impairment from birth frequently implies cognitive as well as linguistic impairment.

Autism

Another group of children presenting with delayed language consists of autistic children, who may be considered to represent a type of mental retardation in which severe auditory perceptual deficiencies are the most prominent finding. The syndrome of early infantile autism was first described by Kanner (1943) as a disturbance of affective contact (Table 20). These children are noted to be different from earliest infancy and by the time they enter the third year of life the full symptom complex becomes apparent. Clancy, Dugdale, and Rendle-Short (1969) have proposed a screening list of 14 behavioral items useful in making a diagnosis of autism (Table 21); if seven of these items are present, the scale is considered positive for the disorder. Cox et al. (1975) and DeMyer (1975) have finally succeeded in debunking the myth that frigid, obsessive parents cause this peculiar psychiatric syndrome in their children; neuropsychologic studies (e.g., Bartak, Rutter, and Cox, 1975) now define autism as an innate cognitive deficit profoundly affecting receptive language. Indeed, the defect seems to involve "inner language" and so extends across all language modalities. Paradoxically, with their striking echolalia, these children give the impression of having expressive language skills in advance of receptive abilities—an obvious impossibility. This again emphasizes the importance of echolalia or "parrot talk" as an indicator for communication disorders, especially poor receptive language. The splinter skill of a good auditory rote memory helps explain the prominence of the echolalia; the echolalia is often delayed, with the child repeating a sentence verbatim and out of context a week or more after it is heard. One can observe such a child hear someone say "It's a beautiful day today, isn't it?", store it, and several days later repeat the same sentence while it is raining; these language fragments have not been comprehended. Because they are severely retarded in their ability to interpret auditory symbolization, autistic children are unable to use language functionally. This communicative difficulty is global in that the child relates inappropriately or dysfunctionally to all aspects of his environment, people, and things. The inability to

Table 20. Kanner's (1943) six key features of autism

1. Inability to relate to people
2. Failure to use language to communicate
3. Obsessive desire to maintain sameness
4. Fascination with inanimate objects
5. Good rote memory
6. Intelligent, obsessive, and cold parents

Table 21. Behavioral manifestations of autism

1. Great difficulty in mixing and playing with other children
2. Acts as if deaf
3. Strong resistence to any learning
4. Lack of fear about realistic dangers
5. Resists change in routine
6. Prefers to indicate needs by gestures
7. Laughing and giggling for no apparent reason
8. Not cuddly as a baby
9. Marked physical overactivity
10. No eye contact
11. Unusual attachment to a particular object or objects
12. Spins objects
13. Repetitive and sustained odd play
14. Standoffish manner

Adapted from Clancy, Dugdale, and Rendle-Short (1969) by permission.

communicate and relate to others results in the child's living in a world of his own ("isolation") and developing self-stimulatory activities such as rocking, head banging, spinning objects, and other repetitive behaviors.

The majority of autistic children are severely mentally retarded (Knobloch and Pasamanick, 1975). However, they are retarded children who demonstrate a disproportionate delay in language comprehension. The clinical picture can be further confused by the presence of splinter skills in the area of perceptual-motor abilities (for example, normal to outstanding performance on the Seguin formboard). Many obviously retarded children who do not fit the syndrome of autism nevertheless display many autistic mannerisms; these behaviors become more prevalent as the degree of mental retardation becomes more severe, particularly if brain damage is the etiology. Brain damage and some untreated metabolic disorders are frequently associated with uneven developmental delay and perceptual disorders.

The prognosis for the autistic child can be predicted from his overall intellectual functioning. Older psychiatric theories held out the promise of a cure; modern neurobiologic theories propose a maximization of function through the application of learning theory. A diagnosis of autism per se does not necessarily offer more hope than a diagnosis of mental retardation; both are located on the spectrum of chronic brain dysfunction and both are susceptible to varying degrees of severity.

BIBLIOGRAPHIC NOTE

The early language instrument (Capute and Accardo, 1978b) was derived from the following sources: Cattell (1940), Egan, Illingworth, and MacKeith (1969), Gesell and Amatruda (1947), Illingworth (1962, 1967), Knobloch, Pasamanick, and Sherard (1966), Lillywhite (1958); Lillywhite, Young and Olmsted, 1970), Mecham (1971), Northern and Downs (1974), Renfrew and Murphy (1964), Rutter and Martin (1972), and especially Sheridan (1964, 1968). Lenneberg and Lenneberg (1975) and Schiefelbusch and Lloyd (1974) provide good general introductions to normal and deviant language. The poor correlation between the Peabody Picture Vocabulary Test (PPVT), a nonverbal measure of receptive vocabulary, and general intelligence has been shown by Rice and Brown (1967) and Brown and Rice (1967). Similarities between autism and deafness were noted by Capute et al. (1975). Alternate modes of communication are presented by Fenn and Rowe (1975), Hollis and Carrier (1975), Richardson (1975), Topper (1975), and Vanderheiden et al. (1975). Little study has yet been done of oral motor mechanisms in the retarded (Massengill, 1969).

THERAPY

> The only way to cure or to prevent this habit is to pay no attention to it. No one likes to take useless trouble—not even children.
>
> Rousseau, *Emile*

In the more limited sense of cure for a disease, total eradication of an underlying pathology, there is little medical treatment for mental retardation beyond early therapy for metabolic disorders such as phenylketonuria, galactosemia, cretinism, maple syrup urine disease, and certain abnormalities of ammonia metabolism. Patients with selected other genetic and metabolic conditions can be prevented through genetic counseling, amniocentesis, and therapeutic abortion (Galjaard, 1976). But the list of diseases "treatable" in this fashion accounts for only a small fraction of the retarded population, and it would be unrealistic to expect an appreciable change in this situation in the near future.

Distinct from this kind of prevention, the treatment of retardation is actually the province of special education. It is only within a broader and somewhat older concept of treatment as caring rather than curing, as educating rather than medicating, that the pediatrician plays a role as member of the interdisciplinary team. Indeed, the very nature of his continuing relationship with the family of the handicapped child gives him a unique opportunity to engage in anticipatory guidance. He is the only professional who will follow the child from birth to 21 years (and perhaps longer); his advice will be sought on all major decisions in the life-span of the retarded child. Even if he denies any special competence in, for example, deciding on an appropriate school placement, parents will invest his slightest bias with disproportional significance.

The pediatrician will need to be thoroughly familiar with the exceptional child facilities in his community. When a diagnosis of mental retardation is made in the preschool period, concern is frequently expressed over the efficacy of various programs to stimulate the child to achieve his maximal potential. If the syllabus suggests the potential to cure mental retardation, it may be promising more than is reasonable to expect. Infant stimulation programs have not produced scientifically verifiable permanent results (cf. Cornell and Gottfried, 1976; Scarr-Salapatek and

Williams, 1973). This is not to say that children will not make progress in such programs—retarded children are not children who do not make progress—but without controls the interpretation of this progress will remain moot. In addition, all such programs achieve some striking "successes" (misdiagnoses?). Of course, when failure occurs, it is the parents' fault (as if their guilt were not great enough already) for not religiously following a rigid 25-hour day/8-day week schedule of exhausting perceptual-motor exercises designed (and usually documented in rat experiments) to stimulate the regeneration of damaged cortical structures. Other relevant variables such as time, expense, travel, waiting lists, and respite care need to receive serious consideration.

Although infant stimulation programs may reduce the incidence of sociocultural retardation (Heber and Garber, 1975; but cf. Page, 1975), it would be premature to generalize this conclusion to other types of retardation or other cultural milieus. "The enthusiasm of social scientists for the possibility of modifying early development has obscured the limitations of such intervention" (Gallagher, 1973). Although such intervention seems both easier and more effective the earlier it occurs (and thus the tremendous impetus toward early identification), parents need to be repeatedly assured that the degree and type of stimulation that is optimal for infants is unknown. In addition, there is a large body of data that indicates that any opportunity lost in early childhood is not irretrievable: human beings may have sensitive periods (optimal ages for skill acquisition) but they probably have no true critical periods (cf. Clarke and Clarke, 1976). Failure of the pediatrician to advise in this area will only contribute to the parental burden of guilt.

Many parents with a school age retarded child wage long and frustrating battles with the school system to get their child placed in classes for children with emotional disorders or learning disabilities rather than in a class for the retarded. Educators try to avoid this problem through several administrative tactics: they 1) change the labels of the special education classes to some more neutral term that parents will not find objectionable, 2) lump all categories of deviant children into one of these classes with a nondescript label, or 3) mainstream deviant children into regular classes. The movement toward mainstreaming and away from labeling has a certain justification. However, when the educator's attack on labeling exceeds reasonable bounds by implying that accurate diagnosis and prognosis are impossible (the myth of the infinite plasticity of human nature in the hands of the social engineer), then his idealistic hope is certainly not in the best interests of the child. Although a few of the higher functioning children at each level of retardation may perform well (especially in the acquisition of social competence) in a class geared to the next higher level, one cannot ultimately hope to successfully mix children needing basic instruction in self-help skills with those who have already achieved competence at this level and have advanced to early academic skills. In this regard, some educational programs tend to lose contact with developmental reality.

The educational and life goals for the different degrees of retardation were outlined in an earlier chapter. For example, with the trainable mentally retarded the curriculum would focus on self-help skills (such as dressing, eating, grooming, and toileting), social skills (such as cooperation, orderliness, table manners, and behavior in public), communication skills (such as the use of gestures and the tone of voice), and some functional academics (such as printing one's name, survival words, and the counting of objects). Strength and coordination would also be enhanced by a variety of gross and fine motor exercises. Although there are many competing philosophies of special education, perhaps, as is often the case with normal children, the interest and dedication of the individual teacher will far outweigh differences in or inadequacies of training. Parents will praise or blame the attitude and interest of teachers much more than the content or level of programs. Penrose (1963) best summarized the human achievement of special education: "The most important work carried out in the field of training defectives is unspectacular. It is not highly technical but requires unlimited patience, good will and common sense. The reward is to be expected not so much in scholastic improvement of the patient as in his personal adjustment to social life."

Although teachers' lobbies often support legal restrictions against it, the most appropriate teacher for many severely and profoundly retarded children is often not a teacher at all, but rather an occupational or physical therapist. These professionals have the requisite expertise to facilitate in mentally and physically handicapped individuals the basic fine and gross motor skills in the relevant areas of upper and lower extremity functioning, respectively. With increased funding for the educational needs of the severely and profoundly handicapped and retarded (SPH/

SPR), such therapists are being employed as school consultants and resource persons; they are also taking a more active role in the training of special education teachers. Their contribution to the interdisciplinary habilitation of handicapped children should not be viewed as limited to the management of the child with severe physical impairment. In their turn, physical and occupational therapists make use of the findings of behavioral psychology.

In some older and a few younger retarded children behavior is the major obstacle to the child's acceptance by the school and family. At the root of many such behavioral problems there is frequently a failure to adjust expectations to the child's level of maturation. With children whose functional profile demonstrates a significant scatter of abilities, it is an easy trap for the school or parents to expect the child to behave consistently at the level of his highest abilities; this leads to a vicious cycle characterized by increasing frustration and deteriorating behavior on the part of the child. The help necessary often resembles common sense advice—not because the parents lack common snese, but because they have become so entangled in the in-fighting, like front line combatants, that they are unable to see the problem in perspective. In such a situation, a skilled neutral observer can be effective.

Successful methods for handling such problems have been delineated by the school of behavioral psychology, also known as learning theory. An important fact for the pediatrician to keep in mind is that the successful application of behavior modification techniques is completely independent of an extreme behaviorist viewpoint. Before Watson and Skinner, Rousseau (1899) advocated a behavioral treatment for temper tantrums that is still in use: ignore them. In other words, the use of operant conditioning techniques—analytically focusing on the simpler components of complex behaviors with a careful observation of the frequency of these component behaviors as well as of the nature of the reward inherent in the situation in which the behaviors occur in order to extinguish undesired and shape desired outcomes—does not imply an acceptance of the underlying nondevelopmental philosophy.

There is no single route to learning. Normal children frequently use verbal mediators, but even retarded children who have expressive language tend to utilize internal verbalizations much less. They depend instead on the accumulation of stimulus-response associations. Thus normal children achieve toileting close to 3 years of age when their imitative ability and capacity to internalize social demands are sufficiently matured so that they almost seem to master the behavior overnight. With retarded children toileting is acquired slowly and late, usually when the child reaches a mental age between 12 and 18 months (Figure 52). The norm-referenced problem-solving age of 18 months equates easily with criterion-referenced requirements of 1) ambulation, 2) motor skills for dressing/undressing, and 3) sufficient expressive language to follow one-step commands (Foxx and Azrin, 1973). Either of these approaches can help select children who are ready for an intensive behavioral program. In institutionalized retardates, territoriality (population density and associated visible boundaries) may affect frequency of urinary and fecal incontinence (Hereford, Cleland, and Fellner, 1973).

Even in the twentieth century one rarely encounters parents of children with severe behavior disorders who are averse to new methods of discipline; the usual complaint is that all the punishments they have tried have failed. When, on the other hand, it is suggested that they carefully observe the child for good behavior, reinforce such behavior when it occurs, and attempt to shape it when absent, then parents often will refuse to have any part of such bribery. They forget that bribery is a reward for immoral conduct, behavior in conflict with recognized standards. Even Aristotle considered habits of moral conduct as prerequisite to any rational analysis of such behavioral ethics; the habit must be

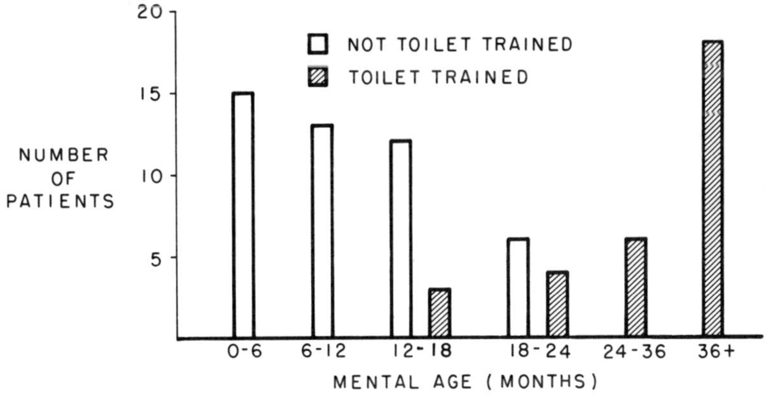

Figure 52. Mental age for toileting. All subjects had IQs below 55. No child with a mental age below 1 year was toilet trained; no child with a mental age above 2 years was not toilet trained. A mental age of 12 to 18 months seems to be necessary for independent toileting.

deeply ingrained first. The search for acceptable nonfood rewards for the profoundly retarded can indeed be a challenge. Another common source of misunderstanding is the distinction between cuing and nagging: a cue is a helpful reminder (often needing frequent repetition with the distractible retardate); nagging is the same reminder in a negative, scolding, sometimes hostile tone. The former requires much patience and, if not carefully timed, can actually serve as an attentional reward for not performing the desired behavior; the latter is self-defeating.

When such simple guidelines are applied to a detailed description of the child's day, improvement is frequently forthcoming. Indeed, even during a baseline period of data collection, the very process of observation acts as a stimulus for behavioral change (Johnson and Katz, 1973) or at least makes the parents aware that the situation was not quite as bad as they had thought. (Perhaps it forces them to notice some good behavior.) Further improvement is achieved by focusing on discrete, observable problem behaviors and identifying the factors that precipitate or subsequently reward them. When by successive approximations the problem is reduced to more manageable proportions, the parents will have been educated to function as effective therapists. All too often instead of being made to see themselves as an integral part of the solution, parents are made to feel totally responsible for the problem—the child is the way he is because of their mishandling. They need to be reinforced with the perception that brain damaged children can make almost impossible demands on their caregivers and that to seek professional guidance is not a sign of failure on their part but rather a reflection of their continuing concern.

Child psychiatrists estimate that 50% of retardates have psychotic manifestations characterized by poor eye contact and self-stimulatory, repetitive mannerisms such as head banging, rocking, and body rolling, with occasional hallucinations (Menolascino, 1969, 1970; Philips and Williams, 1975). The developmental pediatrician, on the other hand, interprets this behavioral complex as reflecting an "expanded Strauss syndrome," amenable to behavior modification, psychotropic drug therapy, or a combination of both. The Strauss syndrome, manifested by attentional peculiarities such as short attention span, perseveration, emotional instability, easy distractability, hyperactivity, and fidgetiness, is seen in the child with minimal cerebral dysfunction and is usually associated with a learning disability. Because this behavioral pattern becomes more pronounced as the degree of brain damage increases, the expanded Strauss syndrome occurs most often in those retardates who are trainable or below and have organicity as a major component of their disorder.

There is no generally accepted explanation for the stereotypies (rhythmic habit patterns such as head banging, rocking, or self-mutilation) that are frequently seen in profoundly retarded or brain damaged individuals (Mitchell and Etches, 1977). Many of these behaviors occur transiently in a much milder form in normal infants (cf. DeLissovoy, 1962); their exaggeration and prolongation may be a type of self-stimulatory behavior or a way of relieving tension. Klaber and Butterfield (1968) found that such behavior decreased with general improvement in the quality of institutional care, so that these stereotyped patterns may also be a reaction to boredom. One occasionally observes idiosyncratic time cycles with the above behaviors demonstrating an almost regular periodicity (e.g., a worsening of the behavior every third week); this may reflect the release of a brainstem biorhythm for irritibility in the more brain damaged patients.

Particularly with such brain damaged retardates, behavior techniques, although helpful, may not be sufficient to control aggression, organically driven hyperactivity, short attention span, and other stimulus-bound behavior. Psychotropic drugs offer a necessary adjunct, with the caution that these never be employed in the absence of a careful overview of the whole patient and in association with an ongoing behavioral therapy program. The stimulants, dextroamphetamine (Dexedrine) and methylphenidate (Ritalin), which produce excellent results in controlling the hyperactivity syndrome in children of normal intelligence, rarely have this positive effect in retarded individuals. Such neuroanaleptics have a very limited role in retardation.

Among the phenothiazine major tranquilizers, thioridazine (Mellaril) has been found most effective in treating behavior disorders in severely retarded children at a dosage of between 0.5 and 3.0 mg/kg/day divided into three to four doses. In addition to tablet form (10, 15, 25, 50, 100, 150, 200 mg), it is available in a 30 mg/ml elixir. It should be started at a dose of 10 to 25 mg t.i.d. and increased according to its effect on behavior. The commonest side effects include weight gain and constipation; dystonic reactions are treatable with diphenhydramine (Benadryl). Other possible side effects include hepatotoxicity, nasal stuffiness, dry mouth, hypotension, and retinitis pigmentosa; skin reactions such as urticaria, photosensitivity, and pigmentary changes can occur. Male ejaculation may be inhibited. In general, the incidence of untoward side reactions common to the phenothiazine group (such as jaundice and extrapyramidal symptoms) is lowest with thioridazine. An initially positive response can wear off after a few weeks, and this may necessitate one or more dose increases. Children on long-term medication may demonstrate a worsening of behavior; this may be secondary to a weight gain that effectively lowers their mg/kg dose, but they will sometimes respond to a withdrawal of medication. Periodic trials off psychotropic drugs need to be a routine part of the therapeutic regimen. It is also not unusual to see a profoundly retarded child whose difficult behavior is nicely responsive to a dosage somewhat higher than the range recommended here. Less commonly, damaged brains may respond to homeopathic doses and may even be exquisitely sensitive to these very low doses. The drug is not approved for use in children under 2 years of age.

Treatment obviously needs to be individualized. The ethics of psychopharmacology requires that such a drug not be used to produce sedation (an overdose effect) but rather that it should decrease aggressive and hyperactive behavior sufficiently for the child to learn more easily and interact with his environment more appropriately; it should contribute to the child's moral autonomy. Both parent and teacher observations need to be monitored closely to ensure that these goals are being met; many "drug failures" actually reflect poor communication between involved professionals.

Chlorpromazine (Thorazine) is another useful phenothiazine. It comes in tablets (10, 25, 50, 100, 200 mg) and liquid concentrate (30, 100 mg/ml). Its list of potential side effects is similar to thioridazine, but hypotension, cholestatic jaundice, and extrapyramidal symptoms such as ataxia and choreoathetosis are more common. In addition, corneal opacities, tardive dyskinesias, electrocardiographic changes, menstrual irregularities, galactorrhea, and breast enlargement are also seen. Blood dyscrasias occur as sensitivity reactions. Effective dosages are in the same range as thioridazine; the drug is not approved for use in children under 6 months of age.

Trifluoperazine (Stelazine) also belongs to the phenothiazine group. It is available in tablet (1, 2, 4, 10 mg) and liquid (10 mg/ml) forms with a dose range of 1 to 10 mg per day in children between 6 and 12 years of age. It demonstrates the entire gamut of phenothiazine side effects (with extrapyramidal symptoms being prominent) except that it is one of the least sedating in this group. Because it is something more of a stimulant, it is especially useful in the child who is withdrawn as well as hyperactive or aggressive. The drug is not approved for use in children under 6 years of age.

The phenothiazines do not lower seizure threshholds and are not contraindicated in patients on anticonvulsant therapy. Other major tranquilizers include prochlorperazine (Compazine) and the butyrophenone haloperidol (Haldol). The latter is not approved for pediatric usage but is the drug of choice for the peculiar Gilles de la Tourette syndrome of multiple tics, barking, and coprolalia. Because of the high incidence of extrapyramidal side effects with haloperidol, the anti-Parkinsonian agent benztropine mesylate (Cogentin) is often administered concomitantly.

Minor tranquilizers are of more limited use with the retarded. Diphenhydramine (Benadryl) is frequently used for sleep problems but it exhibits marked tachyphylaxis; the dose needs to be increased every few weeks until the medication has little effect at any dose. The drug is most effective when it supplements a short-term behavioral program. Hydroxyzine (Vistaril, Atarax) has an additional antihistaminic property; diazepam (Valium) can function as a muscle relaxant when the retardation is complicated by cerebral palsy. Meprobamate (Miltown, Equinil) is of doubtful efficacy in retardates or normals. Imipramine (Tofranil) is a tricyclic antidepressant that is sometimes effective in the treatment of nocturnal enuresis in normals; it is rarely of benefit with incontinence in retardates.

The most useful drug in the sedative/hypnotic class is chloral hydrate (Noctec). It is available as capsules (250, 500 mg) and syrup (500 mg/5 cc). Except for some gastric irritation, it is relatively free of side effects and can be used as a safe nighttime sedative over long periods. The effective dose is 50 mg/kg. Although phenobarbital is frequently employed as a sedative and an anticonvulsant, a paradoxical hyperactivity may complicate its use in the brain damaged population. In particularly intractable cases of severe behavioral disturbances, the use of lithium carbonate may be considered in children over 12 years of age if blood levels are available. Toxicity does not occur with lithium concentrations below 1.5 mEq/liter; the drug comes in capsules and tablets (both 300 mg).

Medication should never be employed as a shortcut to replace rather than supplement behavioral therapy. Drugs are to be used reluctantly, monitored closely, and, when indicated, titrated to tolerance levels. The goal is not to sedate retarded children into passive conformity but to make them more receptive to teaching and to improve their social interaction. Finally, it should always be kept in mind that older retardates are not dissimilar to very young children who cannot tell the pediatrician what is wrong: not infrequently sudden inexplicable changes in behavior are secondary to occult physical disease, which must always be searched for diligently.

BIBLIOGRAPHIC NOTE

Some of the basic principles of behavioral psychology are reviewed in Bry (1975). Many practical handbooks for both parent and practitioner are available: Becker (1971), Deibert and Harmon (1973), Krumboltz and Krumboltz (1972), Madsen and Madsen (1974), Patterson (1975), and Patterson and Gullion (1971). Thompson and Grabowski (1972) is a more advanced text applying specifically to the retarded. A model trainable curriculum is described in Bender and Valletutti (1976). Feeding problems in the retarded are best approached by a combination of learning theory and neurodevelopmental principles (Holser-Buehler, 1966; Sholl and Scherzer, 1974; *Feeding the Child with a Handicap,* 1973). A surgical approach to drooling is presented by Townsend, Morimoto, and Kralemann (1973). The debate over sensorimotor patterning is argued in Newman (1975), Newman et al. (1975), and Zigler and Seitz (1975). Psychopharmacology is surveyed in Freeman (1970) and White (1977).

PARENT COUNSELING

All happy families resemble one another; every unhappy family is unhappy in its own way.

Tolstoy

The counseling of parents of retarded children implicitly involves a long-term commitment that many physicians are unwilling to make. Yet here where the art of medicine faces one of its most difficult challenges lies some of its greatest potential for service to others.

After Lain Entralgo (1969) one may characterize every doctor-patient interaction ("medical event") as being constructed of four major aspects (Table 22). In the cognitive aspect the physician communicates a diagnosis; in the operative aspect he attempts to engage the patient's participation in a treatment program. Psychiatry has usually analyzed the affective aspect in terms of the phenomenon of transference from patient to doctor. However, Korsch in a number of studies (Francis, Korsch, and Morris, 1969; Freemon et al., 1971; Korsch, Gozzi, and Francis, 1968; Korsch and Negrete, 1972) has demonstrated physicians' insensitivity to the psychological content of routine doctor-patient interactions. Problems in this third sphere have repercussions in the first two areas: when the pediatrician fails to address himself to the mother's underlying concerns, even though he makes a correct diagnosis and prescribes appropriate therapy, he has markedly increased the probability that his evaluation will be neutralized (i.e., that the prescription will not be filled, that the mother will present the child to an emergency room late at night, etc.). If impaired psychologic insight can have such disastrous effects on the treatment of acute minor illnesses of childhood, how much greater impact must such amblyopia have on the physician's ability to counsel parents of retarded children. (The possi-

Table 22. Aspects of doctor-patient interaction

Encounter	Medical event
1. Cognitive	Diagnosis
2. Operative	Treatment
3. Affective	Transference
4. Ethico-religious	

ble contribution of the fourth, ethico-religious, factor is considered at the conclusion of this chapter.)

The imparting of a diagnosis of mental retardation needs to be individualized to each specific situation. Nevertheless an attempt may be made to offer some general guidelines (Table 23); most of these have their origin in parental criticisms of such initial counseling sessions:

> "He was very abrupt. When I went there, I went alone. And he rang a few bells and then he measured his head and did a few, I guess, standard tests. And I think it took about fifteen minutes, and then he said 'Would you take your son into my office?' And so we went, and I sat down. And then he said 'I'm sure you're aware that your child is severely retarded . . .' That was the opening comment. I guess I was aware that something was wrong with my child, but I wasn't prepared for him to say that . . . I didn't really know that much about retardation. I really didn't know what to say. I think I said, 'What does that mean?' And he said, 'Well, that means that he probably will never walk or talk, and you can keep him at home or you can put him into an institution.' And then he said, 'Well, do you have any questions?' And I had to get out of there; at that point I just had to run."

When imparting a diagnosis of mental retardation, following certain guidelines will result in the parents' feeling more comfortable and in a better understanding of the diagnosis:

1. It is extremely important that both parents be present so as to relieve the one parent of the overwhelming burden of attempting to explain the results of such an evaluation to the absent spouse (or, as is often the case, from either deliberately or subconsciously distorting the findings to protect the other parent).

Table 23. Parent counseling: Guidelines for the initial session

1. Both parents present
2. Unlimited time
3. Questions expected
4. Restatement of problem
5. Description of child's behavior
6. MA Range
7. Etiology
8. Consultation offered
9. Present situation
10. Open-door policy

2. Watches, clocks, and other time pieces need to be outlawed from the room where the counseling is held; interruptions must be placed under absolute prohibition—the parents must in no way feel the usual rush and pressure that is part of the doctor's daily routine.
3. Questions are to be not only allowed but encouraged; they should in no way be considered as delaying the progress of the session, but rather their absence must be considered to signal a breakdown in communication. Technical language should be avoided as much as possible; diagrams of the brain localizing potential lesions often impress the speaker with his own status and hinder free communication, reducing the parents to silent bewilderment.

> "The terms that he used, moderately, mildly retarded, were unfamiliar to me. I didn't know that there was any difference; retarded was retarded. I knew that there were children who couldn't do anything and they were the worst, and then children who could do better, but I didn't have any kind of classification at all for it. So I remember I kept asking him over and over what were the terms that he was using."

4. Rather than open the session with a diagnostic label or a psychometric number, a more successful approach is to let the parents review their own perception of the child's development. It will be a frequent source of amazement how accurately parents (even of only children and often with little or no familiarity with popular child-rearing literature) can assess their child's mental age when queried, "How old a child would you say he acts like?" Indeed, they are even successful in picking up discrepancies between different areas of development.
5. When they have successfully depicted the child's actual behavior with its implicit level of functioning, this picture can be interpreted back to them utilizing the results of the pediatric and psychological evalutions. The parents are thus made to play an *active* role in the diagnostic process itself, a mode that needs to be fostered in all future interactive processes.
6. A mental age range is often much more intelligible than an IQ score.
7. When etiology is discussed, extreme caution in phraseology must be exercised if any of the possible diagnoses referred to

can in any way be interpreted as assigning responsibility to either parent. Feelings of guilt and inadequacy are to a certain extent inevitable and should not be fueled by careless reference to the possible contribution of, for example, a suspected history of mental defect in a distant relative on the maternal or paternal side of the family. Marriages burdened with retarded children show a significantly higher rate of disintegration, and therefore any means that can be employed to shore up the family's strengths need to be utilized.

8. Regardless of the certitude of the diagnostic evaluation, the results should be qualified so as to allow the parents to hope—even in the face of imminent death, hope is fostered. One of the most effective means to avoid "doctor shopping" is to offer at the beginning a referral to (other) competent specialists for confirmation; if openly volunteered, this gesture will often solidify parental confidence in the pediatrician, and if the parents do decide to seek elsewhere, the physician will have helped to guarantee that their search will be directed toward a reputable resource. The need for such confirmation is easily recognized with other serious and even life-threatening nonacute conditions.
9. The conclusion of a counseling session focuses on the present situation—how the child is currently functioning and what are the most appropriate means available to attain immediate short-term habilitation goals. In the initial counseling session it is unwise to plot out one's predictions for the child's entire life cycle; no matter how accurate these may be, they will probably overload the parents' information processing abilities. (The greatest difficulty in sketching the life history of a retarded child rests in the marked potential variation in future social attitudes determining the role to be imposed on deviant individuals.) One should attempt to answer specific questions concerning behaviors such as reading, toileting, speech, and ambulation. The positive—the humanness of the handicapped child—must be stressed throughout. The most frequent misunderstanding caused by a diagnosis of mental retardation is that the child will remain static and never develop; therefore, one of the points that needs repetition is that retardation refers to a slower than normal *rate* of development. All children demonstrate change with time—

even the most profoundly handicapped children will show some progression along the various substages of Piagetian sensorimotor schemas. Compared to normal children, with their seemingly rapid rates of development, retarded children may seem to plateau, but compared to themselves they demonstrate a steady, if predictably slow, progress.

> "I really try to think back on what my immediate reaction was at the time, and I think I was fairly numb. And I'm not really sure that I heard that much of what he actually said."
>
> "I don't think I would have taken in that much more at the time, but I think what I really wanted was just some more time to talk to him."
>
> "I can't say that enough. You can tell somebody exactly what they need to do, but you have to be willing to wait for them to get to the point where they can do it."

10. Finally, the pediatrician who undertakes to involve himself in this therapeutic process needs to maintain an open-door policy—ready availability to answer questions, to review the patient's status, and to assess the appropriateness of major changes in placement.

> "I'm not sure that anybody is ever going to get up from a conference like that and feel that everything has been said satisfactorily, or that you feel comfortable about the situation. And that's probably one thing that a doctor going into this for the first time should be ready to deal with. No matter how kind he is. . . . even if he says everything exactly right, that parent is not going to thank him because of what he has to say. No matter how nicely you say that your child is retarded, you're still saying that to a parent. I think that's something the doctor has to work out his feelings about so that he is not put on the defensive by whatever the parent says to him, so that he's not turned off if the parent gets up and walks out of the room."
>
> "I wasn't as angry at my pediatrician as I was at the neurologist, because the pediatrician never said the words. So I had to transfer all my anger onto the guy who told me."
>
> "I can compare it only to somebody who's lost a child, except that people who have lost children would disagree, I'm sure. It's the same kind of grieving, but it doesn't even end, it just goes on and on as long as the child is living."

The pediatrician must demonstrate sensitivity to the successive emotional stages through which the family evolves (Table

24). The reaction to the initial diagnosis of retardation has been compared to grief upon the death of a child, the death of the hoped-for normal child who has inexplicably been replaced by this changeling (Solnit and Stark, 1961). Perhaps the stage of "acceptance" is never really reached, but rather there is a continuing process of "chronic sorrow," an intelligible, healthy response to a tragic and irreversible fact. Complicating the doctor-patient relationship is the emotional reaction (frequently hostility) toward the physician who first imparts the diagnosis. In the ancient world, the messenger who delivered bad news was often slain for his reward; in the modern world, the physician who makes the diagnosis loses the patient. The anger that many parents of retarded children feel toward certain physicians is intense, deep seated, and frequently with cause; fragments of it often persist well into the "acceptance" stage. Since retarded children have a high incidence of chronic medical disability, the source of this hostility should be treated prophylactically by sensitive and considerate management from the beginning.

The concept of stages can be overemphasized. Parents are almost never exclusively at a single stage. Much has been written of the difficulty of getting parents of retarded children to *accept* their child's diagnosis—as if the diagnostic label were some kind of magic pill that when swallowed would suddenly make all things well. It is often overlooked that parental resistance to poorly presented and inadequately documented findings may reflect an attitude that is both appropriate and healthy. There is rarely any need to ram the word "retarded" down the parents' throats—they have already begun to accept the fact of the child's slowness by bringing him in for diagnostic evaluation. Nevertheless, the word "retarded" ought to be used during the counseling: no number of cautious euphemisms will protect the parents from hearing this

Table 24. Stages of parental adjustment

Denial Anger	Stage I: Shock, disorganization, denial
Bargaining Depression	Stage II: Adjustment, chronic sorrow, anger
Acceptance	Stage III: Reintegration, acceptance

The first column is from Kubler-Ross (1969), the second from Miller (1968). There are significant similarities among the processes of accepting one's own death, the death of one's child, and mental retardation in one's child.

word in the community. True acceptance is as much a product of time and patience as the counseling skill of the physician; it is doubtful that its achievement can be accelerated, although mismanagement can certainly retard it.

At first glance, an intensive psychiatric experience would seem necessary to respond to the subtle cues presented by these different emotional stages. As a matter of fact, only one basic skill is essential: the art of listening. When one is mentally reviewing the long list of points to be covered during a counseling session, it is best to discard all but a few of the most significant, leaving the remainder to be considered in later sessions. The better part of the time should be spent in listening—this is itself as significant a part of the practice of medicine as the imparting of technical information. It is important to remember that even with the most common problems of pediatric practice, the most frequent parental complaint is that the physician never heard *their* concerns, but rather addressed himself to some area of technical expertise where he felt most comfortable and least ill at ease.

Battle's (1975) questions for the parents of a child with chronic physical disease (Table 25) present a useful outline of the areas that need to be covered during succeeding counseling sessions. The importance of this information for patient management by the primary care physician cannot be overestimated.

The parents of retarded children are frequently maligned as relying on neurotic mechanisms and demonstrating both overprotective and rejecting behavior. These psychiatric formulations assume guilt to be the principal reaction but in actuality have little data to support this interpretation (Hewett, 1976; Matheny and Vernick, 1969). Even indirect evidence is inconclusive: Tew, Payne, and Lawrence (1974), working with meningomyelocele children, found that the quality of the marital relationships deteriorated and the divorce rate doubled, but Anderson and Spain (1977), working with a similar population, concluded that the impact of a handicapped child on a marriage was just as likely to be beneficial as detrimental—the greatest stress occurred immediately after the child's birth; with time the child brought the parents closer together. Again, stereotypes must be avoided and family management individualized. Careful evaluation of what seems to be deviant parental behavior will often demonstrate its source to be a failure of anticipatory guidance (or downright misinformation) by involved professionals. Finally, it must be

Table 25. Questions for the parents of a child with a chronic handicap

Ask in any way you can, how the parents feel about their child. Do not fear to cause any damage by gentle questioning.

Was this child a planned baby?
When did you first find out there was something wrong?
What did the doctor say at first? Did you understand what the doctor said at the beginning?
How long after the birth of the baby did you see your child? (if there is a birth defect)
What did you think about your child's problem?
How did your husband feel about it?
What did your mother say?
Did anyone suggest institutionalizing your child?
Did you ever think it would have been better if the baby had died?
Did you feel uneasy about showing your baby to relatives and friends?
Were your friends helpful at this time? Did they come around, or stay away?
Was the baby difficult to care for in the first few months?
Do you and your husband feel the same about your child's condition?
What do you disagree about?
Do you agree about seeking treatment for the child?
Do you feel uncomfortable now about taking your child out in public?
Do you and your husband share in the care of your child?
Do you ever get the opportunity to be away from the home to do something you would like for yourself?
Does anyone ever babysit for your child?
How often do you and your husband go out together?
Do you feel that this child takes most of your time?
Do you think your other normal children resent the time that you spend with your child?
Have you discussed the chronic disease and related issues, such as heredity and possibility of marriage, with your child?
Does your child take any responsibility for his health or treatment needs?
What are your worries about the future of your child?
What are your plans for the future of your child?

From Battle (1975) by permission.

remembered that families are especially liable to decompensate under the stress of major turning points in the child's life, such as a change of schools or the onset of puberty.

Numerous attitude studies have attempted to analyze the variables contributing to parental acceptance of retarded children (Graliker, Parmelee, and Koch, 1959; Koch et al., 1959). Parental religion seems to be a significant variable, with the more religious parents tending to be more accepting of retarded children and with Catholics tending to be the most religious (Hoffman, 1965; Zuk et al., 1961). The researchers attempted to explain these findings by reference to sectarian beliefs about guilt and suffering. Allport's (1968) studies of the relationship between prejudice and religion achieve relevance here when one remembers that retardation and other handicapping conditions are deviancy roles subject to prejudice. Perhaps the extent to which medicine neglects the ethical dimension is reflected in the physician's frequent failure to explore the possibly positive contribution of the family's religious faith.

Community attitudes toward the retarded are at best ambiguous; there is no reason to suspect that physician attitudes are less so. A comparison of research findings on the desirability of home rearing for Down syndrome children (Birch and Belmont, 1961; Cornwell and Birch, 1969; Golden and Davis, 1974) with physicians' actual recommendations (Centerwall, 1971) is even more discouraging: one-half the general practitioners and one-fourth of the pediatricians surveyed favored early institutionalization.

> "He was so much trouble, and why burden myself with the, you know, with this problem. And I always seemed to have to justify why I was keeping my own child. I thought that was unnecessary. I shouldn't have to justify that."

As deinstitutionalization progresses, more severely and profoundly handicapped persons will be depending on their families and various community support services. In addition to direct medical care and involvement with parent and sibling groups, the pediatrician needs to be fully aware of the ever widening range of available services along with some critical knowledge of their quality and appropriateness for the individual child. His decision in these areas will never be final but rather the considered judgment of someone concerned with the total child; it will be weighed with the opinions of the other professionals involved with the child's management, and all of these in turn will be discussed with the parents. There can be no final common pathway in such complex issues; different disciplines will carry different weights depending on the individual case. Parents are always encouraged to actively participate in the process, but in some cases they may want to deliberately retreat into a more passive role. Depending on the particular stresses on the family, this need not be pathologic. One of the physician's key roles is to support the parents when facilities are inadequate; as a child advocate he needs to work with the parents to reorder community priorities and help sensitize service delivery systems to their inadequacies.

In reviewing profession attitudes toward counseling parents of retarded children, the most uniform finding (Fishler et al., 1968; Harth, 1973; Lipton and Svarstad, 1977; Olshansky and Kettell, 1963; Olshansky and Sternfeld, 1962) is that both a positive attitude and the ability to effectively communicate are directly related to the extent of formal experience with developmental disabilities. In the absence of such training the physician feels uncomfortable, fails to counsel appropriately, and may actually become a source of increased parental anxiety or misinformation. Most pediatric training programs have yet to give adequate representation to the spectrum of developmental disabilities.

Thus, not all pediatricians have the training or inclination to work with the families of severely handicapped patients. When the physician and the parents have contrasting value systems, the influence of the fourth aspect of the doctor-patient interaction, the ethico-religious, may be felt. The question needs to be asked whether the physician who sincerely believes in active euthanasia for the profoundly retarded can function effectively as a primary health care provider for such defective children. With a normal child it can be assumed that both the pediatrician and the parents place a high value on the child's well-being and that both will tend to interpret that well-being in a similar fashion. With a retarded child such an assumption may be premature, and an added burden will be placed upon the parents to find a physician who will clearly distinguish that advice dictated by medical practice from that reflecting a more personal opinion of the child's worth.

BIBLIOGRAPHIC NOTE

The unascribed quotations in this chapter are from an educational tape on parent counseling made by Pasquale J. Accardo. Wolfensberger and Kurtz (1969) have edited a useful sourcebook on family management. The vulnerable child syndrome (Green, 1967; Green and Solnit, 1964) provides a reasonable introduction to parental psychodynamics. Sweedler and Kraushaar (1975) offer a novel approach to working with siblings of retarded children.

An annotated bibliography of literature for parents of handicapped children (Moore and Morton, 1976) is a helpful resource.

SOCIAL POLICY AND ETHICAL ISSUES

> To what degree can the therapeutic state invade a person's bodily and personal integrity? . . . . Where are these limits to be drawn and by whom?
>
> Kittrie (1971)

The most critical ethical question in the area of mental retardation concerns the definition of humanhood, since it is from this concept that restrictions on rights and duties will flow. Fletcher's (1972, 1974b) approach in reducing his 20 indicators of humanhood to four, of which the base is minimal intelligence, would essentially resolve the dilemma of physicians working with retarded children: patients with IQs less than 20 are not human—and may therefore be treated accordingly. A more skeptical approach to the definition of human nature would be more in keeping with an independent realm of values. Unfortunately, much of the debate on a definition of death has focused on describing the essence of humanhood as residing in the neocortex and its functions. This development tends to give pseudoscientific support to Fletcher's IQ criterion and may have disastrous repercussions on attempts at refining society's moral role toward the handicapped. In opposition to Fletcher's utilitarianism, recent trends in the ethics of the handicapped stress a legal philosophy that can best be described as civil libertarian.

The impetus of the civil rights movement over the past decade has extended to various oppressed minorities a legal status previously denied them. The latest of these groups encompasses both children and the retarded. One of the problematic areas opened to discussion concerns human sexuality in the mentally and physically handicapped. With various movements to foster the sexual rights of the retarded, multiple cross-purposes are pursued which have the effect of clouding certain basic concepts. Sex can be viewed as a predominantly cerebral activity: as intelligence decreases, so does sexual drive. The myth of the hypersexuality of the retarded was based on the frequency with which masturbation and indecent exposure were observed in institutionalized retardates. In reality, these attention-getting behaviors were appropriate both to these patients' mental age and to their state of enforced boredom.

Although an attitude of general acceptance toward sex prevails, there is appropriate concern over limitations for the protection of society. The complexity of the issues involved can easily be realized if one considers the absence of a general consensus on sex education for normal children and of standards for acceptable sexual behavior in normal adults. Unfortunately, discussions of sex education for the retarded frequently focus on the limited and negative aspect of birth control—how society can ensure that the retarded make use of effective contraception—rather than the more positive aspect of sexual activity as part of an expression of human personality through the development of interpersonal relationships.

The right to marriage has traditionally been subject to both legal and canonical restrictions, many of which are currently waning. As more retarded persons become normalized into the community, it becomes a question of to what degree acceptance by the community will depend on their marriages remaining childless. Does marriage entail a right to have children or is the latter a privilege to be earned or to qualify for? Society seems to be increasingly wary of considering procreation an inalienable right, especially for persons unable to accept full responsibility for their actions. The concerns as to who will raise the children of the retarded or who will bear the expense for special intervention programs are in some ways strongly reminiscent of the fear during the eugenic scare that the unfit would swamp the normal population. In his famous pro-sterilization decision, Justice Holmes complained that three generations of imbeciles were enough. The third generation imbecile was a little girl diagnosed as retarded at 1 month of age; by the second grade this child was described by her teachers as "quite bright." (As a rule, embarrassing facts like this have little impact on the principles of the law; the potential for such error certainly ought to be given greater consideration.) The contribution of classical genetics to mental retardation is problematic, but neo-Malthusian misconceptions can be reinforced by conditions of economic unrest.

A quarter of a century ago Kanner (1949) observed that he had seen percentwise at least as many intelligent adults as retardates who were unfit to rear their offspring. He concluded that, to a large extent, fitness for parenthood was independent of IQ and was determined by emotional involvements and relationships. More recently, Wolfensberger (1972) noted the existence of "many nonretarded, physically healthy people who are sex-driven, shallow, incompetent, unstable, and incapable of deep and perhaps even of sustained relationships; yet our political system accords them the constitutional right to enter a legal marriage." The key moral and legal issues revolve around the fact that the label of mental retardation leads to discrimination: standards are applied to the retarded that one would not think of applying to someone not so labeled. In other words, fitness for parenthood has never been a routine criterion for either marriage or childbearing for persons of normal intelligence. The illusion of omniscience with regard to the prerequisites for parenting is indirectly fostered by current publications on the importance of bonding behavior and maternal-infant interaction—all of which reflect only the limited beginnings of a new branch of experimental investigation, with rather limited practical consequences. We can only conclude with Price and Burt (1976) that "fiscal irresponsibility and 'bad parenting' are reasons to *choose* contraception. They may not be reasons to *mandate* it or to mandate it for a stigmatized class, such as mentally retarded persons." To mandate sterilization under the cloak of deinstitutionalization does nothing to resolve the ethical dilemma.

With the adolescent retardate, sexual acting out is a frequent parental concern. Oral contraception is relatively ineffective in the female because of poor compliance; however, irreversible surgical procedures pose serious legal and ethical questions. Contraception of any sort cannot be considered a substitute for adequate supervised activity, appropriate sex education, and protection from sexual abuse by the more intelligent deviates in the community.

Effective medical sterilization of females is one of the triumphs of twentieth-century technology. Applied involuntarily, such irreversible procedures require medical and not merely social indications. Otherwise, hysterectomy becomes another item in a long list of dehumanizing scientific advances. As Nichtern (1974, p. 227) has observed, the concept of sterilization

> destroys both the sterilized and the sterilizer. It robs each of his rights to relatedness and his responsibilities to the other for meaning and fulfillment. Compulsory sterilization laws have not altered the incidence of retardation nor have they eased the task of caring for the retarded. They have contributed to the depersonalization and institutionalization of so many of our attitudes and procedures.

Not infrequently, hysterectomy will be recommended for "hygienic" reasons, despite the fact that with minimal nursing supervision, the care of menstrual flow is less complicated than toileting. (A problem-solving age of approximately 18 months suffices for toileting in older retardates.) Paralleling the strategies devised for toilet training the retarded, behavior modification techniques have been successfully employed to teach moderately to profoundly retarded females the essentials of menstrual hygiene (Table 26). In terms of social acceptability, cleanliness may be next to godliness, but in view of the existence of a less invasive alternative to achieve the same end, surgical intervention can hardly be countenanced. The employment of surgery as a shortcut to replace more time-consuming social and behavioral services seems counterproductive to the realization of a true normalization.

By reason of his intellectual deficiency, a retarded person cannot give true informed consent to sterilization. Do there nevertheless exist certain "hard cases," identifiable exceptions, where the fiction of third-party consent can be justified? In an adversary legal system, it is assumed that a person will stand up for his rights in court if necessary. In the past, the retarded have been considered legal infants, and the power to make decisions for them has been delegated to parents and to the state. Due process of law has thus been denied, on the grounds that whatever the parents or the state may decide will be in the best interest of the child—i.e., that it will be in the nature of therapy for this diseased state, mental retardation—and therefore, not subject to due process. Current concepts of child advocacy have stressed the

Table 26. Procedures for training menstrual hygiene to the retarded

1. Check sanitary napkin at the correct time
2. Change napkin only in the appropriate place (i.e., in bathroom with the door closed)
3. Pull underpants down
4. Remove soiled napkin
5. Place soiled napkin in paper bag
6. Pull tab off napkin with self-adhesive strip
7. Put sticky side of napkin next to underpants
8. Pull underpants up
9. Throw bag away
10. Check for clean clothes at increasing time periods from 10 to 120 minutes

Courtesy of Michael F. Cataldo, Ph.D. (Cf. Shapiro et al., 1977.)

danger of uncritically allowing parents the final say in all health matters for normal children. With respect to the state, Goldstein, Freud, and Solnit (1973) have documented the tragic irony implicit in the court's use of the phrase "in the best interests of the child." The situation of parents requesting surgical sterilization for a retarded adolescent is in some ways analogous to that of parents requesting needless and risky surgery—such as tonsillectomy—in the absence of medical indications. Examples could easily be multiplied—parents who insist on a penicillin shot for a child's cold, parents who want the child's normo-active behavior modified by drugs—examples of children being subjected to medical procedures for the primary purpose of relieving parental anxiety. The pediatrician as educator usually finds safer means to achieve parental peace of mind. The child or the retardate is the patient, not the parent or society; the expectations of the latter may simply have to be changed. Medical authority should not be employed to further victimize the helpless. The most powerless, by the very nature of their handicap, demand the greatest protection from misguided "therapies."

Involuntary sterilization cannot be subject to abuses, because it is itself an abuse—a violation of the nature of both participants in the doctor-patient relationship. The attitude and behavior of the gynecologist who performs hysterectomies on retarded females often reveal his real patient to be a social abstraction residing elsewhere than in the flesh and blood reality on the operating room table. The surgeon as pure technician is a dangerous tool.

To some, the coexistence of a problem and the technology to resolve the problem cancels out any moral consideration, so strong is the lure of technology. The difficulty in defining limits to unwarranted therapeutic intrusion becomes obscured by the ethical dilemma of our time: our power to do, our technology, the means at our disposal, have all far outstripped our moral and social conscience. To escape the consequences of our own retardation in these areas, we grasp at forms of committee ethics—with all its avoidance of personal commitment and responsibility—and this is the same as no ethics at all.

Over a century ago Seguin (1971) voiced the philosophy that even after therapeutic modalities had reached their limits, the doctor still had an ethical responsibility. A civil libertarian position, which places the rights of individuals above social (albeit disguised as medical) concerns, demands that meticulous legal restrictions surround the involuntary invasion of another human being's person—"no man is good enough to cure another without his consent"—and opposes the *medicalization* of *behavioral* problems out of expediency. A basic right of the retarded is not to be sterilized involuntarily.

BIBLIOGRAPHIC NOTE

Children's rights are reviewed in Foster (1974), Marker and Friedman (1973), and *The Rights of Children* (1974). Legal aspects of mental retardation are discussed in Brakel and Rock (1971), Elmes and Herrmann (1976), Kindred et al., (1976), *Mental Health Law Project* (1973), and Murdock (1973). Ethical aspects of mental retardation are elaborated in Cooke (1973) and Crocker and Cushna (1972); ethical guidelines for behavioral procedures are presented in Twardosz (1976). Cost-benefit analysis has been applied to PKU screening (Steiner and Smith, 1973) and to special education (Conley, 1973). De La Cruz and LaVeck (1973) debunk the previous myths concerning retardate sexuality but provide little concrete data on which to base social policy. Perrin et al. (1976) offer an alternative approach to sterilization of the retarded.

Shaw, Randolph, and Manard (1977) and Todres et al. (1977) have used questionnaires to study the impact of several variables on ethical decision making. Religion, age, and degree of specialization seemed to significantly affect how pediatricians approached life and death decisions when the "quality of life" was less than optimal. But when Crane (1975) tried to check the results of ethics questionnaire surveys with actual practice reflected by medical records, she found poor correlations: there was a significant discrepancy between what was said and what was done.

At the negative end of the spectrum one finds articles advocating active euthanasia for hydrocephalics (Lachs, 1976; the editor had neglected to correct this to hydranencephalics) and eugenics primers (Fletcher, 1974a) suggesting that medical care is responsible for spreading the genetic defect of mongolism. Moric-Petrovic and Garzicic (1970) provide data to place this latter theological speculation in the realm of fantasy. But then those who prefer to generalize on broad social issues have always considered factual data and firsthand experience as unwarranted constraints on their liberty to assault the rights to life and bodily integrity of others.

REFERENCES

Abt, I. A., Adler, H. M., and Bartelme, P. 1929. The relationship between the onset of speech and intelligence. JAMA 93:1351–1355.

Achenbach, T. M. 1970. Comparison of Stanford-Binet performance of non retarded and retarded persons matched for MA and sex. Am. J. Ment. Defic. 74:488–498.

Adams, J. 1973. Adaptive behavior and measured intelligence in the classification of mental retardation. Am. J. Ment. Defic. 78:77–81.

Aicardi, J. 1973. The problem of the Lennox syndrome. Dev. Med. Child. Neurol. 15:77–80.

Aladjem, S., Perrin, E., and Fanaroff, A. 1972. Placental score and neonatal outcome. Obstet. Gynecol. 39:591–602.

Alexander, F. G., and Selesnick, S. T. 1968. The History of Psychiatry. New American Library, New York.

Allen, R. M., and Allen, S. P. 1967. Intellectual Evaluation of the Mentally Retarded Child: A Handbook. Western Psychological Services, Los Angeles.

Allport, G. W. 1968. The Person in Psychology. Beacon Press, Boston.

Alpern, G. D., and Boll, T. J. 1972. Developmental Profile Manual. Psychological Development Publications, Indianapolis.

Alter, M. 1966. Dermatoglyphic analysis as a diagnostic tool. Medicine 46:35–56.

Ambrose, A. (ed.). 1969. Stimulation in Early Infancy. Academic Press, New York.

Ames, L. B. 1967. Predictive value of infant behavior examinations. In J. Hellmuth (ed.), Exceptional Infant, Vol. 1, The Normal Infant, pp. 207–240. Brunner/Mazel, New York.

Anastasi, A. 1968. Psychological Testing. Macmillan Publishing Company, New York.

Anderson, E. M., and Spain, B. 1977. The Child with Spina Bifida. Methuen & Co., London.

Anderson, J. M., Milner, R. D. G., and Stritch, S. S. 1966. Pathological changes in the nervous system in severe neonatal hypoglycaemia. Lancet ii:372–375.

Angeli, E., and Kirman, B. 1975. Genetic prognosis in severe mental handicaps. J. Ment. Defic. Res. 19:173–193.

Apley, J., and MacKeith, R. 1968. The Child and His Symptoms. F. A. Davis Company, Philadelphia.

Aries, P. 1962. Centuries of Childhood. Vintage, New York.

Armstrong, D., and Norman, M. G. 1974. Periventricular leucomalacia in neonates: Complications and sequelae. Arch. Dis. Child. 49:367–375.

Astrup, C., Sersen, E. A., and Wortis, J. 1967. Conditional reflex studies in mental retardation: A review. Am. J. Ment. Defic. 71:513–530.

Avery, G. B., Meneses, L., and Lodge, A. 1972. The clinical significance of "measurement microcephaly." Am. J. Dis. Child. 123:214–217.

Azrin, N. H., Bugle, C., and O'Brien, F. 1971. Behavioral engineering: Two apparatuses for toilet training retarded children. J. Appl. Behav. Anal. 4:249–253.

Azrin, N. H., and Foxx, R. M. 1971. A rapid method of toilet training the institutionalized retarded. J. Appl. Behav. Anal. 4:89–99.

Azrin, N. H., Kaplan, S. J., and Foxx, R. M. 1973. Autism reversal: Eliminating stereotyped self-stimulation of retarded individuals. Am. J. Ment. Defic. 78:241–248.

Babad, E. Y. 1977. Pygmalion in reverse. J. Spec. Educ. 11:81–90.

Babbitt, D. P., Tang, T., Dobbs, J., and Berk, R. 1969. Idiopathic familial cerebrovascular ferrocalcinosis (Fahr's disease) and review of differential diagnosis of intracranial calcification in children. Am. J. Roentgenol. 105:352–358.

Bagdon, L. 1973. Developmental evaluation of the pre-school child. Ped. Conf. 16:1–13.

Baker, B. L., and Ward, M. H. 1971. Reinforcement therapy for behavior problems in severely retarded children. Am. J. Orthopsychiatry 41:124–135.

Baldwin, A. L., and Baldwin, C. P. 1973. The study of mother-child interaction. Am. Sci. 61:714–721.

Ball, T. S. 1973. Bobath's facilitation training and Seguin's physiological method related to escape-avoidance conditioning. In G. Tarjan, R. K. Eyman, and C. E. Meyers (eds.), Sociobehavioral Studies in Mental Retardation, pp. 186–196. Monogr. Am. Assoc. Ment. Defic. No. 1.

Barclay, A. 1969. Longitudinal changes in intellectual and social development of non-institutionalized retardates. Am. J. Ment. Defic. 73:831–837.

Baroff, G. S. 1959. WISC patterning in endogenous mental deficiency. Am. J. Ment. Defic. 64:482–485.

Bartak, L., Rutter, M., and Cox, A. 1975. A comparative study of infantile autism and specific developmental receptive language disorder. I. The Children. Br. J. Psychiatry 126:127–145.

Battle, C. U. 1975. Chronic physical disease: Behavioral aspects. Pediatr. Clin. North Am. 22:525–531.

Bayley, N. 1933. Mental growth during the first three years. Genet. Psychol. Monogr. 14.

Bayley, N. 1969. Bayley Scales of Infant Development. The Psychological Corporation, New York.

Bayley, N. 1970. Development of mental abilities. In P. Mussen (ed.), Carmichael's Manual of Child Psychology, Vol. 1, pp. 1163–1210. John Wiley & Sons, New York.

Beaudet, A. L. 1978. Genetic diagnostic studies for mental retardation. Curr. Probl. Pediatr. 8(5).

Becker, W. C. 1971. Parents Are Teachers: A Child Management Program. Research Press, Champaign.

Bender, L. 1938. A Visual Motor Gestalt Test and Its Clinical Use. Research Monograph No. 3. American Orthopsychiatric Association, New York.

Bender, M., and Valletutti, P. J. 1976. Teaching the Moderately and Severely Handicapped: Curriculum, Objectives, Strategies, and Activities, 3 vols. University Park Press, Baltimore.

Bensberg, G. J., Colwell, C. N., and Cassell, R. H. 1965. Teaching the profoundly retarded self-help activities by behavior shaping techniques. Am. J. Ment. Defic. 69:674–679.

Bergsma, D. (ed.). 1973a. Birth Defects: Atlas and Compendium. Williams & Wilkins, Baltimore.

Bergsma, D. (ed.). 1973b. Contemporary Genetic Counseling. Birth Defects: Original Article Series 9 (4):1–48.

Berkowitz, S., Sherry, P. J., and Davis, B. A. 1971. Teaching self-feeding skills to pröfound retardates using reinforcement and fading procedures. Behav. Ther. 2:62–67.

Berkson, G., and Landesman-Dwyer, S. 1977. Behavioral research on severe and profound mental retardation (1955–1974). Am. J. Ment. Defic. 81:428–454.

Berman, P. H. 1976. Management of seizure disorders with anticonvulsant drugs: Current concepts. Pediatr. Clin. North Am. 23:443–459.

Bierman, J. M., Connor, A., Vaage, M., and Honzik, M. P. 1964. Pediatricians' assessment of intelligence of two year olds and their mental test scores. Pediatrics 34:680–690.

Bill of Rights for Foster Children. 1973. Child. Today 2(4):21.

Binding, K., and Hoche, A. 1975. The Release of the Destruction of Life Devoid of Value. R. L. Sassone, Santa Ana.

Birch, H, G., and Belmont, L. 1961. The problem of comparing home-reared versus foster-home-rearing in defective children. Pediatrics 28:956–961.

Birch, H. G., and Demb, H. 1959. The formation and extinction of conditioned reflexes in "brain-damaged" and mongoloid children. J. Nerv. Ment. Dis. 129:162–170.

Blanchard, I. 1964. Speech pattern and etiology in mental retardation. Am. J. Ment. Defic. 68:612–617.

Bloom, B. S. 1964. Stability and Change in Human Characteristics. John Wiley & Sons, New York.

Bogdan, R., and Taylor, S. 1976. The judged, not the judges: An insider's view of mental retardation. Am. Psychol. 31:47–52.

Boothman, R., White, E. M., and Sweenie S. 1976. Predictive value of early developmental examination. Arch. Dis. Child. 51:430–434.

Bortner, M., and Birch, H. G. 1970. Cognitive capacity and cognitive competence. Am. J. Ment. Defic. 74:735–744.

Bower, T. G. R. 1974. Development in Infancy. W. H. Freeman & Company, San Francisco.

Bower, T. G. R. 1976. Repetitive processes in child development. Sci. Am. 235(5):38–47.

Bower, T. G. R. 1977. A Primer of Infant Development. W. H. Freeman & Company, San Francisco.

Bradley, R. H., and Caldwell, B. M. 1976. The relation of infants' home environments to mental test performance at fifty-four months: A follow-up study. Child. Dev. 47:1172–1174.

Brady, R. O., and Kolodny, E. H. 1972. Disorders of ganglioside metabolism. In A. G. Steinberg and A. G. Bearn (eds.), Progress in Medical Genetics, Vol VIII, pp. 225–241. Grune & Stratton, New York.

Brakel, S. J., and Rock, R. S. (eds.). 1971. The Mentally Disabled and the Law. University of Chicago Press, Chicago.

Braun, F. H. T., Jones, K. L., and Smith, D. W. 1975. Breech presentation as an indicator of fetal abnormality. J. Pediatr. 86:419–421.

Brazelton, T. B., Parker, W. B., and Zuckerman, B. 1976. Importance of behavioral assessment of the neonate. Curr. Prob. Pediatr. 7(2).

Brazelton, T. B., Scholl, M. L., and Robey, J. S. 1966. Visual responses in the newborn. Pediatrics 37:284–290.

Brett, E. 1977. Implications of measuring anticonvulsant blood levels in epilepsy. Dev. Med. Child. Neurol. 19:245–251.

Brody, H. 1976. Ethical Decisions in Medicine. Little, Brown & Company, Boston.

Broman, S. H., Nichols, P. L., and Kennedy, W. A. 1975. Preschool IQ: Prenatal and Early Developmental Correlates. Lawrence Erlbaum Associates, Hillsdale.

Bronfenbrenner, U. 1975. Is early intervention effective? In B. Z. Friendlander, G. M. Sterritt, and G. E. Kirk (eds.), Exceptional Infant, Vol. 3, Assessment and Intervention, pp. 449–475. Brunner/Mazel, New York.

Brooks, J., and Weinraub, M. 1976. A history of infant intelligence testing. In M. Lewis (ed.), Origins of Intelligence, pp. 19–58. Plenum Press, New York.

Brown, J. K., Cockburn, F., and Forfar, J. O. 1972. Clinical and chemical correlates in convulsions of the newborn. Lancet i:135–139.

Brown, L. F., and Rice, J. A. 1967. The Peabody Picture Vocabulary Test: Validity for EMR's. Am. J. Ment. Defic. 71:901–903.

Brown, S. F. 1955. A note on speech retardation in mental deficiency. Pediatrics 16:272–273.

Brunner, J. S. 1973. Beyond the Information Given. W. W. Norton & Company, New York.

Bry, A. 1975. A Primer of Behavioral Psychology. New American Library, New York.

Bryant, P. 1974. Perception and Understanding in Young Children. Basic Books, New York.

Bugiani, O., Toso, V., and Gatti, R. 1975. Primary immunodeficiency with encephalopathy in two siblings. Eur. Neurol. 13:405–417.

Bundy, S. 1970. The significance of a white macule on the skin of a child. Dev. Med. Child. Neurol. 12:805–806.

Bundy, S., and Carter, C. O. 1974. Recurrence risks in severe undiagnosed mental deficiency. J. Ment. Defic. Res. 18:115–134.

Burns, R. C., and Kaufman, S. H. 1970. Kinetic Family Drawings (K-F-D): An Introduction to Understanding Children Through Kinetic Drawings. Brunner/Mazel, New York.

Burns, R. C., and Kaufman, S. H. 1972. Actions, Styles and Symbols in Kinetic Family Drawings (K-F-D): An Interpretative Manual. Brunner/Mazel, New York.

Buros, O. K. (ed.). 1972. The Seventh Mental Measurements Yearbook. 2 Vols. Gryphon Press, Highland Park.

Butterfield, E. C., and Zigler, E. 1965. The influence of differing institutional social climates on the effectiveness of social reinforcement in the mentally retarded. Am. J. Ment. Defic. 70:48–56.

Byrd, C., and Springfield, L. 1969. A note on the Draw-A-Person test with adolescent retardates. Am. J. Ment. Defic. 73:578–579.

Caffey, J. 1972. Pediatric X-Ray Diagnosis. 2 Vols. Year Book Medical Publishers, Chicago.

Caldwell, B. M., Bradley, R. H., and Elardo, R. 1975. Early stimulation. In J. Wortis (ed.), Mental Retardation VII, pp. 152–194. Brunner/Mazel, New York.

Caldwell, B., and Drachman, R. 1964. Comparability of three methods of assessing the developmental level of young infants. Pediatrics 34:51–57.

Caldwell, B. M., Heider, J., and Kaplan, B. The inventory of home stimulation. Center for Early Development and Education. Little Rock. Mimeographed.

Cameron, J., Livson, N., and Bayley, N. 1967. Infant vocalizations and their relationship to mature intelligence. Science 157:331–333.

Capute, A. J. 1974. Developmental disabilities: An overview. Dent. Clin. North Am. 18:557–577.

Capute, A. J. 1975. Mental retardation. In R. H. A. Haslam and P. J. Valletutti (eds.), Medical Problems in the Classroom, pp. 217–233. University Park Press, Baltimore.

Capute, A. J., and Accardo, P. J. 1978a. Mental retardation. In S. Gellis and B. M. Kagan (eds.), Current Pediatric Therapy, pp. 13–19. W. B. Saunders Company, Philadelphia.

Capute, A. J., and Accardo, P. J. Linguistic and auditory milestones in the first two years of life: A language inventory for the practicing pediatrician. Clin. Pediatr. In press.

Capute, A. J., Accardo, P. J., Bender, M., and Ross, A. 1977. Reading Retardation. Unpublished manuscript.

Capute, A. J., Accardo, P. J., Vining, E. P. G., Rubenstein, J. E., and Harryman, S. 1978. Primitive Reflex Profile. University Park Press, Baltimore.

Capute, A. J., and Biehl, R. F. 1973. Functional developmental evaluation: Prerequisite to habilitation. Pediatr. Clin. North Am. 20:3–26.

Capute, A. J., Derivan, A. T., Chauvel, P. J., and Rodriguez, A. 1975. Infantile autism I: A prospective study of the diagnosis. Dev. Med. Child. Neurol. 17:58–62.

Carey, W. B. 1973. Measurement of Infant Temperament in Pediatric Practice. In J. C. Westman (ed.), Individual Differences in Children, pp. 293–306. John Wiley & Sons, New York.

Carr, D. H. 1965. Chromosome studies in spontaneous abortions. Obstet. Gynecol. 26:308–326.

Carr, J., and Stephen, E. 1964. Paediatricians and developmental tests. Dev. Med. Child Neurol. 6:614–620.

Castner, B. M. 1932. The development of fine prehension in infancy. Genet. Psychol. Monogr. 12.

Cattell, P. 1940. The Measurement of Intelligence of Infants and Young Children. The Psychological Corporation, New York.

Centerwall, S. A. 1971. The mentally retarded and the family physician: Results of a survey of Michigan doctors. Mich. Med. 70:597–602.

Centerwall, W. R., and Centerwall, S. A. 1972. Phenylketonuria. U.S. Government Printing Office, Washington, D.C.

Chalhub, E. G. 1976. Neurocutaneous syndromes in children. Pediatr. Clin. North Am. 23:499–516.

Chamberlin, R. W. 1977. Can we identify a group of children at age 2 who are at high risk for the development of behavior or emotional problems in kindergarten and first grade? Pediatrics 59:971–981.

Charles, D. C. 1957. Adult adjustment of some deficient American children. Am. J. Ment. Defic. 62:300–304.

Chase, A. 1977. The Legacy of Malthus: The Social Costs of the New Scientific Racism. Alfred A. Knopf, New York.

Cheldelin, L. V., Davis, P. C., Jr., and Grant, W. W. 1975. Normal values for transillumination of skull using a new light source. J. Pediatr. 87:937–938.

Chen, A. T. L., Sergovich, F. R., McKim, J. S., Barr, M. L., and Gruber, D. 1970. Chromosome studies in full-term, low-birth-weight, mentally retarded patients. J. Pediatr. 76:393–398.

Chess, S. 1966. Individuality in children, its importance to the pediatrician. J. Pediatr. 69:676–684.

Chess, S., Thomas A., and Birch, H. G. 1972. Your Child Is a Person. Viking Press, New York.

Chik, L., Sokol, R. J., Rosen, M. G., Regula, G. A., and Borgstedt, A. D. 1977. Computer interpreted fetal monitoring data: Discriminant analysis of perinatal data as a model for prediction of neurologic status at one year of age. J. Pediatr. 90:985–989.

Christian, J. C., Johnson, V. P., and Biegel, A. A. 1971. Sisters with low birth weight, dwarfism, congenital anomalies and dysgammaglobulinemia. Am. J. Dis. Child. 122:529–534.

Churesigaew, S., Ruvalcaba, R. H. A., and Kelley, V. C. 1975. Epilepsy and abnormal calcium metabolism in institutionalized mentally retarded patients. Am. J. Ment. Defic. 79:738–741.

Cicchetti, D., and Stroufe, L. A. 1976. The relationship between affective and cognitive development in Down's syndrome infants. Child. Dev. 47:920–929.

Clancy, H., Dugdale, A., and Rendle-Short, J. 1969. The diagnosis of infantile autism. Dev. Med. Child. Neurol. 11:432–442.

Clarke, A. D. B., and Clarke, A. M. 1977. Prospects for prevention and amelioration of mental retardation. Am. J. Ment. Defic. 81:523–533.

Clarke, A. M., and Clarke, A. D. B. (eds.). 1976. Early Experience; Myth and Evidence. The Free Press, New York.

Clausen, J. 1967. Mental deficiency—development of a concept. Am. J. Ment. Defic. 71:727–745.

Cohen, H. J., and Diner, H. 1970. The significance of developmental dental, enamel defects in neurological diagnosis. Pediatrics 46:737–747.

Cohen, H. J., Taft, L. T., Mahadeviah, M. S., and Birch, H. G. 1967. Developmental changes in overflow in normal and aberrantly functioning children. J. Pediatr. 71:39–47.

Committee on Children with Handicaps. 1971. The Pediatrician and the Child with Mental Retardation. American Academy of Pediatrics, Evanston.

Conley, R. W. 1973. The Economics of Mental Retardation. The Johns Hopkins University Press, Baltimore.

Cooke, R. E. 1973. Ethics and law on behalf of the mentally retarded. Pediatr. Clin. North Am. 20:259–268.

Cooke, R. E. 1975. The role of ethics in pediatrics. Am. J. Dis. Child. 129:1157–1161.

Corbett, J. A., Harris, R., and Robinson, R. G. 1975. Epilepsy. In J. Wortis (ed.), Mental Retardation and Developmental

Disabilities: An Annual Review VII, pp. 79–111. Brunner/Mazel, New York.

Corey, M. J., Tischler, B., and Sandercock, J. 1971. Structural aberrations of autosomes in a mentally retarded population. Am. J. Ment. Defic. 75:487–498.

Cornell, E. H., and Gottfried, A. W. 1976. Intervention with premature infants. Child. Dev. 47:32–39.

Cornwell, A. C., and Birch, H. G. 1969. Psychological and social development in home-reared children with Down's Syndrome (Mongolism). Am. J. Ment. Defic. 74:341–350.

Cox, A., Rutter, M., Newman, S., and Bartak, L. 1975. A comparative study of infantile autism and specific developmental receptive language disorder. II. Parental characteristics. Br. J. Psychiatry 126:146–159.

Crane, D. 1975. The Sanctity of Life: Physicians' Treatment of Critically Ill Patients. Russell Sage Foundation, New York.

Crano, W. D. 1977. What do infant mental tests test? A cross-lagged panel analysis of selected data from the Berkeley Growth Study. Child. Dev. 48:144–151.

Crocker, A. C., and Cushna, B. 1972. Pediatric decisions in children with serious mental retardation. Pediatr. Clin. North Am. 19:413–421.

Cromer, R. F. 1974. The development of language and cognition: The cognition hypothesis. In B. Foss (ed.), New Perspectives in Child Development, pp. 184–252. Penguin Books, Baltimore.

Cronbach, L. J. 1970. Essentials of Psychological Testing. Harper & Row Publishers, New York.

Cronbach, L. J. 1975. Five decades of public controversy over mental testing. Am. Psychol. 30:1–14.

Crowe, F. W., Schull, W. J., and Neel, J. V. 1956. A Clinical, Pathological, and Genetic Study of Multiple Neurofibromatosis. Charles C Thomas Publisher, Springfield.

Dacou-Voutetakis, C., Karpathios, T., Logothetis, N., Constantinidis, M., Matsaniotis, N., and Michalopoulou, E. 1974. Defective growth hormone secretion in primary microcephaly. J. Pediatr. 85:498–502.

Daly, R. F. 1970. Chromosome aberrations in 50 patients with idiopathic mental retardation and in 50 control subjects. J. Pediatr. 77:444–453.

Dam, M. 1970. Number of Purkinje cells in patients with grand mal epilepsy treated with diphenylhydantoin. Epilepsia 11:313–320.

Dangel, H. 1972. Biasing effect of pretest referral information on WISC scores of mentally retarded children. Am. J. Ment. Defic. 77:354–359.

Davies, J. S. 1976. Dermatoglyphics. In W. L. Nyhan and N. O. Sakati, Genetic and Malformation Syndromes in Clinical Medicine, pp. 351–363. Year Book Medical Publishers, Chicago.

Davies, P. A., and Davis, P. J. 1970. Very low birth weight and subsequent head growth. Lancet ii:1216–1219.

Davis, K. V., Sprague, R. L., and Werry, J. S. 1969. Stereotyped behavior and activity level in severe retardates: The effect of drugs. Am. J. Ment. Defic. 73:721–727.

DeGrouchy, J., and Turleau, C. 1977. Clinical Atlas of Human Chromosomes. John Wiley & Sons, New York.

Deibert, A. N., and Harmon, A. J. 1973. New Tools for Changing Behavior. Research Press, Champaign.

De La Cruz, F. F., and LaVeck, G. D. (eds.). 1973. Human Sexuality and the Mentally Retarded. Brunner/Mazel, New York.

DeLissovoy, V. 1962. Head banging in early childhood. Child. Dev. 33:43–56.

DeMause, L. 1974. The evolution of childhood. Hist. Child. Quart. 1:503–575.

DeMeyer, M. K. 1975. Research in infantile autism: A strategy and its results. Biol. Psychiatry 10:433–452.

DeMyer, W. 1972. Megalencephaly in children: Clinical syndromes, genetic patterns, and differential diagnosis from other causes of megalocephaly. Neurology 22:634–643.

DeMyer, W., Zeman, W., and Palmer, C. G. 1964. The face predicts the brain: Diagnostic significance of median facial anomalies for holoprosencephaly. (Arhinencephaly). Pediatrics 34:256–263.

Dennis, W. 1940. The effect of cradling practices upon the onset of walking in Hopi children. J. Genet. Psychol. 56:77–86.

Dennis, W. (ed.). 1972. Historical Readings in Developmental Psychology. Appleton-Century-Crofts, New York.

DeSouza, S. W., and Milner, R. D. G. 1974. Clinical and CSF studies in newborn infants with neurological abnormalities. Arch. Dis. Child. 49:351–358.

Despert, J. L. 1970. The Emotionally Disturbed Child. Anchor Books, Garden City.

DeVries, R. 1974. Relationships among Piagetian, I.Q., and achievement assessments. Child. Dev. 45:746–756.

DiLeo, J. H. 1967. Developmental evaluation of very young infants. In J. Hellmuth (ed.), Exceptional Infant, The Normal Infant, Vol. 1, pp. 121–142. Brunner/Mazel, New York.

DiLeo, J. H. 1970. Young Children and Their Drawings. Brunner/Mazel, New York.

DiLeo, J. H. 1973. Children's Drawings as Diagnostic Aids. Brunner/Mazel, New York.

Dobbing, J., and Sands, J. 1973. Quantitative growth and development of human brain. Arch. Dis. Child. 48:757–767.

Dodson, W. E., Prensky, A. L., DeVivo, D. C., Goldring, S., and Dodge, P. R. 1976a. Management of seizure disorders: Selected aspects. Part I. J. Pediatr. 89:527–540.

Dodson, W. E., Prensky, A. L., DeVivo, D. C., Goldring, S., and Dodge, P. R. 1976b. Management of seizure disorders: Selected aspects. Part II. J. Pediatr. 89:695–703.

Doll, E. E. (ed.). 1967. Historical review of mental retardation. Am. J. Ment. Defic. 72:165–189.

Doll, E. E. 1972. A historical survey of research and management of mental retardation in the United States. In E. P. Trapp and P. Himelstein (eds.), Readings on the Exceptional Child: Research and Theory, pp. 47–97. Appleton-Century-Crofts, New York.

Doman, R. J., Spitz, E. B., Zucman, E., Delacato, C. H., and Doman, G., 1960. Children with severe brain injuries. JAMA 174:257–262.

Donovan, D. E., Coues, P., and Paine, R. S. 1962. The prognostic implications of neurologic abnormalities in the neonatal period. Neurology 12:910–914.

Donovan, F. R. 1968. Raising Your Children. Thomas Y. Crowell, New York.

Doust, J. W. L., and Podnieks, I. 1973. Cerebral haemodynamic factors in mentally retarded children. J. Ment. Defic. Res. 17:123–128.

Doyle, M., and Holland, J. J. 1973. Prophylaxis and immunization in mice by use of virus-free defective T particles to protect against intracerebral infection by vesicular stomatitis virus. Proc. Natl. Acad. Sci. USA. 70:2105–2108.

Drage, J. S., Kennedy, C., Berendes, H., Schwarz, B. K., and Weiss, W. 1966. The Apgar score as an index of infant morbidity: A report from the collaborative study of cerebral palsy. Dev. Med. Child. Neurol. 8:141–148.

Drake, M. E., and Ober, G. 1963. Parental medical histories of mental retardates as compared and evaluated against newborn and hospitalization records. Am. J. Ment. Defic. 67:688–690.

Drillien, C. M. 1961. A longitudinal study of the growth and development of prematurely and maturely born children. Arch. Dis. Child. 36:233–240.

Drillien, C. M. 1972. Abnormal neurologic signs in the first year of life in low birth weight infants: Possible prognostic significance. Dev. Med. Child. Neurol. 14:575–584.

Drumwright, A. F. 1971. The Denver Articulation Screening Exam. University of Colorado Medical Center.

Dubowitz, V. 1977. Fetal movements in utero. Dev. Med. Child. Neurol. 19:239–240.

Dudek, S. Z., Lester, E. P., Goldberg, J. S., and Dyer, G. B. 1969. Relationship of Piaget measures to standard intelligence and motor scales. Percept. Mot. Skills 28:351–362.

Dunn, L. M. 1963. Educable mentally retarded children. In L. M. Dunn (ed.), Exceptional Children in the Schools, pp. 53–127. Holt, Rinehart & Winston, New York.

Egan, D. F., Illingworth, R. S., and MacKeith, R. C. 1969. Developmental Screening 0–5 Years. Clinics in Developmental Medicine No. 30. Spastics Society/William Heinemann Medical Books, Ltd., London.

Elbualy, M. S., and Schindeler, J. D. 1971. Handbook of Clinical Dermatoglyphics. University of Miami Press, Miami.

Eliasson, S. G., Prensky, A. L., and Hardin, W. B. 1974. Neurological Pathophysiology. Oxford University Press, New York.

Elkind, D. 1973. Infant intelligence. Am. J. Dis. Child. 126:143–144.

Elkind, D. 1974. Children and Adolescents: Interpretive Essays on Jean Piaget. Oxford University Press, New York.

Ellis, N. R. (ed.). 1963. Handbook of Mental Deficiency. McGraw-Hill, New York.

Ellis, N. R. 1969. A behavioral research strategy in mental retardation: Defense and critique. Am. J. Ment. Defic. 73:557–566.

Elmes, D., and Herrmann, T. 1976. Handbook on the Legal Rights of Handicapped People. U.S. Government Printing Office, Washington, D.C.

Environment, Heredity, and Intelligence. 1969. Harvard Educational Review. Reprint No. 2.

Erbe, R. W. 1976a. Principles of medical genetics. Part I. N. Engl. J. Med. 294:381–383.

Erbe, R. W. 1976b. Principles of medical genetics. Part 2. N. Engl. J. Med. 294:480–482.

Erhardt, P. P. 1974. Sequential levels in development of prehension. Am. J. Occup. Ther. 28:592–596.

Erikson, E. H. 1963. Childhood and Society. W. W. Norton & Company, New York.

Erickson, M. 1968. The predictive validity of the CIIS for young mentally retarded children. Am. J. Ment. Defic. 72:728–733.

Erickson, M., Johnson, N. M., and Campbell, F. A. 1970. Relationships among scores on infant tests for children with developmental problems. Am. J. Ment. Defic. 75:102–104.

Erlenmeyer-Kimling, L., and Jarvik, L. F. 1963. Genetics and intelligence: A review. Science 142:1477–1479.

Escalona, S. K. 1968. The Roots of Individuality. Aldine Publishing Company, Chicago.

Escalona, S. K., and Heider, G. M. 1959. Prediction and Outcome. Basic Books, New York.

Escalona, S. K., and Moriarity, A. 1961. Prediction of school age intelligence from infant tests. Child. Dev. 32:597–605.

Eyman, R. K., Dingman, H. F., and Sabagh, G. 1966. Association of characteristics of retarded patients and their families with speed of institutionalization. Am. J. Ment. Defic. 71:93–99.

Falconer, M. A. 1974. Mesial temporal (Ammon's horn) sclerosis as a common cause of epilepsy. Lancet ii:767–770.

Feeding the Child with a Handicap. 1973. U.S. Government Printing Office, Washington, D.C.

Feingold, M., and Bossert, W. H. 1974. Normal values for selected physical parameters: An aid to syndrome delineation. Birth Defects 10(13):1–15.

Fenn, G., and Rowe, J. A. 1975. An experiment in manual communication. Br. J. Disord. Commun. 10:3–16.

Field, T. M., Dabiri, C., Hallock, N., and Shuman, H. H. 1977. Developmental effects of prolonged pregnancy and the postmaturity syndrome. J. Pediatr. 90:836–839.

Fisher, M. A., and Zeaman, D. 1970. Growth and decline of retardate intelligence. In N. R. Ellis (ed.), International Review of Research in Mental Retardation, Vol. 4, pp. 151–191. Academic Press, New York.

Fishler, K., Graliker, B. V., and Koch, R. 1965. The predictability of intelligence with Gesell development scales in mentally retarded infants and young children. Am. J. Ment. Defic. 69:515–525.

Fishler, K., Koch, R., Sands, R., and Bills, J. 1968. Attitudes of medical students toward mental retardation: A preliminary study. J. Med. Educ. 43:64–68.

Fitzhardinge, P. M., and Steven, E. M. 1972. The small-for-date infant. II. Neurological and intellectual sequelae. Pediatrics 50:50–57.

Fletcher, J. 1975. Moral and ethical problems of pre-natal diagnosis. Clin. Genet. 8:251–257.

Fletcher, J. F. 1972. Indicators of humanhood: A tentative profile of man. Hastings Cent. Rep. 2:(5)1–4.

Fletcher, J. F. 1974a. The Ethics of Genetic Control: Ending Reproductive Roulette. Anchor Press, Garden City.

Fletcher, J. F. 1974b. Four indicators of humanhood—the inquiry matures. Hastings Cent. Rep. 4:(6)4–7.

Ford, F. R. 1973. Diseases of the Nervous System in Infancy, Childhood and Adolescence. Charles C Thomas Publisher, Springfield.

Ford, L. J. 1975. Teaching dressing skills to a severely retarded child. Am. J. Occup. Ther. 29:87–92.

Foster, H. H., Jr. 1974. A "Bill of Rights" for Children. Charles C Thomas Publisher, Springfield.

Fotheringham, J. B., and Morrison, M. 1976. Prevention of Mental Retardation. National Institute on Mental Retardation, Toronto.

Foxx, R. M., and Azrin, N. H. 1973. Toilet Training the Retarded: A Rapid Program for Day and Nighttime Independent Toileting. Research Press, Champaign.

Francis, V., Korsch, B. M., and Morris, M. J. 1969. Gaps in doctor-patient communication: Patients' response to medical advice. N. Engl. J. Med. 280:535–540.

Francis-Williams, J., and Yule, W. 1967. The Bayley Infant Scales of Mental and Motor Development: An exploratory study with an English sample. Dev. Med. Child Neurol. 9:391–401.

Frankenburg, W. K., and Camp, B. W. (eds.). 1975. Pediatric Screening Tests. Charles C Thomas Publisher, Springfield.

Frankenburg, W. K., Camp, B. W., and VanNatta, P. A. 1971. Validity of the Denver Developmental Screening Test. Child. Dev. 42:475–485.

Frankenburg, W. K., Dodds, J. B., and Fandal, A. W. 1970. Manual: Denver Developmental Screening Test. University of Colorado Medical Center.

Frankenburg, W. K., Goldstein, A. D., and Camp, B. W. 1971. The revised Denver Developmental Screening Test: Its accuracy as a screening instrument. J. Pediatr. 79:988–995.

Fraser, W. I., Agnew, J., and Grieve, R. 1975. The linguistic behavior of the hydrocephalic mentally handicapped adult. Br. J. Subnormal. 21:38–42.

Freeman, J. M., and Borkowf, S. 1962. Craniostenosis. Pediatrics 30:57–70.

Freeman, J. M., and McKhann, G. M. 1969. Degenerative disease of the central nervous system. In I. Schulman (ed.), Advances in Pediatrics, Vol. 16, pp. 121–175. Year Book Medical Publishers, Chicago.

Freeman, R. D. 1970. Psychopharmacology and the retarded child. In F. J. Menolascino (ed.), Psychiatric Approaches to Mental Retardation, pp. 294–368. Basic Books, New York.

Freemon, B., Negrete, V. F., Davis, M., and Korsch, B. M. 1971. Gaps in doctor-patient communication: Doctor-patient interaction analysis. Pediatr. Res. 5:298–311.

Freytag, E., and Lindenberg, R. 1967. Neuropathologic findings in patients of a hospital for the mentally deficient: A survey of 359 cases. Johns Hopkins Med. J. 121:379–392.

Friedman, E., and Pampiglione, G. 1971. Prognostic implications of electroencephalographic findings of hypsarrhythmia in first year of life. Br. Med. J. 4:323–325.

Fujikura, T., and Klionsky, B. 1975. The significance of meconium staining. Am. J. Obstet. Gynecol. 212:45–50.

Funderburk, S. J., Spence, M. A., and Sparkes, R. S. 1977. Mental retardation associated with "balanced" chromosome rearrangements. Am. J. Hum. Genet. 29:136–141.

Furth, H. G. 1971. Linguistic deficiency and thinking: Research with deaf subjects 1964–1969. Psychol. Bull. 76:58–72.

Galjaard, H. 1976. European experience with prenatal diagnosis of congenital disease: A survey of 6121 cases. Cytogenet. Cell. Genet. 16:453–467.

Gallagher, J. 1973. Preventive intervention. Pediatr. Clin. North Am. 20:681–693.

Gardner, G. E., Tarjan, G., and Richmond, J. B. (eds.). 1965. Mental Retardation, A Handbook for the Primary Physician. Report of the American Medical Association Conference on Mental Retardation, April 9–11, Chicago.

Garrard, S. D. 1968. On the diagnosis of syndromes in mental retardation. Pediatr. Clin. North Am. 15:925–942.

Garrison, F. H. 1923. History of Pediatrics. In I. A. Abt (ed.), Pediatrics, Vol. 1, pp. 1–170. W. B. Saunders Company, Philadelphia.

Gascon, G., Victor, D., Lombroso, C. T., and Goodglass, H. 1973. Language disorder, convulsive disorder, and electroenchephalographic abnormalities. Arch. Neurol. 28:156–162.

Gellis, S. S., and Feingold, M. 1968. Atlas of Mental Retardation Syndromes: Visual Diagnosis of Facies and Physical Findings. U.S. Government Printing Office, Washington, D.C.

Gerald, P. S. 1976. Sex chromosome disorders. N. Engl. J. Med. 294:706–708.

Gesell, A. 1940. The stability of mental-growth careers. 39th Yearbook Nat. Soc. Stud. Educ. Part II: 149–159.

Gesell, A. 1945. The Embryology of Behavior. Harper & Brothers, New York.

Gesell, A., and Amatruda, C. S. 1947. Developmental Diagnosis: Normal and Abnormal Child Development. Paul B. Hoeber, New York.

Gesell, A., and Halverson, H. M. 1936. The development of thumb opposition in the human infant. J. Genet. Psychol. 48:339–361.

Gesell, A., Halverson, H. M., Thompson, H., Ilg, F. L., Castner, B. M., Ames, L. B., and Amatruda, C. S. 1940. The First Five Years of Life. Harper & Row, New York.

Gesell, A., and Ilg, F. L. 1943. Infant and Child in the Culture of Today. Harper & Brothers, New York.

Gesell, A., and Thompson, H. 1943. Learning and maturation in identical infant twins: An experimental analysis by the method of co-twin control. In R. G. Barber, J. S. Kounin, and H. F. Wright (eds.), Child Behavior and Development, pp. 209–227. McGraw-Hill Book Company, New York.

Ghatak, N. K., Santoso, R. A., and McKinney, W. M. 1976. Cerebellar degeneration following long-term phenytoin therapy. Neurology 26:818–820.

Gibbs, F. A., and Gibbs, E. L. 1964. Atlas of Electroencephalography. 3 Vols. Addison-Wesley, Reading.

Glaser, H. H., Heagarty, M. C., Bullard, D. M., Jr., and Pivchik, E. C. 1968. Physical and psychological development of children with early failure to thrive. J. Pediatr. 73:690–698.

Gold, A. P., and Freeman, J. M. 1965. Depigmented nevi: The earliest sign of tuberous sclerosis. Pediatrics 35:1003–1005.

Golden, D. A., and Davis, J. G. 1974. Counseling parents after the birth of an infant with Down's syndrome. Child. Today 3(2):7–11, 36, 37.

Goldie, L. 1966. The psychiatry of the handicapped family. Dev. Med. Child. Neurol. 8:456–462.

Goldstein, J., Freud, A., and Solnit, A. J. 1973. Beyond the Best Interests of the Child. Free Press, New York.

Goldstein, K. 1942–1943. Concerning rigidity. Character Person. 11:209–226.

Gomez, M. R., and Klass, D. W. 1972a. Seizures and other paroxysmal disorders in infants and children. Part I. Curr. Prob. Pediatr. 2(6).

Gomez, M. R., and Klass, D. W. 1972b. Seizures and other paroxysmal disorders in infants and children. Part II. Curr. Prob. Pediatr. 2(7).

Gomez, M. R., and Reese, D. F. 1976. Computed tomography of the head in infants and children. Pediatr. Clin. North Am. 23:473–498.

Goodenough, F. L. 1926. Measurement of Intelligence by Drawings. Harcourt, Brace & World, New York.

Goodnow, J. 1977. Children Drawing. Harvard University Press, Cambridge.

Goodwin, W. C., and Erickson, M. T. 1973. Developmental problems and dental morphology. Am. J. Ment. Defic. 78:199–204.

Gordon, E. J., and Rosenstein, S. N. 1965. A study of the enamel of primary teeth in cerebral palsied children. New York State Dent. J. 31:245–249.

Gordon, N. 1976. Paediatric Neurology for the Clinician. Clinics in Developmental Medicine Nos. 59/60. Spastics International Medical Publications in association with William Heinemann Medical Books, Ltd., London.

Gorlin, R. J., Pindborg, J. J., and Cohen, M. M. 1976. Syndromes of the Head and Neck. McGraw-Hill Book Company, New York.

Gottesman, I. 1963. Genetic aspects of intelligent behavior. In N. R. Ellis (ed.), Handbook of Mental Deficiency, pp. 253–296. McGraw-Hill Book Company, New York.

Gottfried, A. W. 1973. Intellectual consequences of perinatal anoxia. Psychol. Bull. 80:231–242.

Gottlieb, J. 1974. Attitudes toward retarded children: Effects of labeling and academic performance. Am. J. Ment. Defic. 79:268–273.

Goulet, L. R., and Barclay, A. 1963. The Vineland Social Maturity Scale: Utility in assessment of Binet M. A. Am. J. Ment. Defic. 67:916–921.

Graliker, B. V., Parmelee, A. H., Sr., and Koch, R. 1959. Attitude study of parents of mentally retarded children II. Initial reactions and concerns of parents to a diagnosis of mental retardation. Pediatrics 24:819–821.

Green, M. 1967. Care of the child with a long-term, life-threatening illness: Some principles of management. Pediatrics 39:441–445.

Green, M., and Solnit, A. J. 1964. Reactions to the threatened loss of a child: A vulnerable child syndrome. Pediatrics 34:58–66.

Griffiths, M. I. (ed.). 1973. The Young Retarded Child: Medical Aspects of Care. Williams & Wilkins, Baltimore.

Grossman, H. J. 1973. Manual on Terminology and Classification in Mental Retardation. American Association on Mental Deficiency Special Publication No. 2.

Gruber, H. E., and Voneche, J. J. (eds.). 1977. The Essential Piaget. Basic Books, New York.

Guilford, J. P. 1967. The Nature of Human Intelligence. McGraw-Hill Book Company, New York.

Gustafson, J. M. 1973. Mongolism, parental desires, and the right to life. Perspect. Biol. Med. 16:529–557.

Gustavson, K. H., and Jorulf, H. 1976. Recurrence risks in a consecutive series of congenitally malformed children dying in the perinatal period. Clin. Genet. 9:307–314.

Haffter, C. 1968. The changeling: History and psychodynamics of attitudes to handicapped children in European folklore. J. Hist. Behav. Sci. 4:55–61.

Hahn, T. J., Hendin, B. A., Scharp, C. R., Boisseau, V. C., and Haddad, J. G., Jr. 1975. Serum 25—hydroxycalciferol levels and bone mass in children on chronic anticonvulsant therapy. N. Engl. J. Med. 292:550–554.

Hall, B. 1966. Mongolism in newborn infants. Clin. Pediatr. 5:4–12.

Halsey, J. H., Allen, N., and Chamberlin, H. R. 1968. Chronic decerebrate state in infancy. Arch. Neurol. 19:339–346.

Halverson, C. F., Jr., and Victor, J. B. 1976. Minor physical anomalies and problem behavior in elementary school children. Child. Dev. 47:281–285.

Halverson, H. M. 1931. An experimental study of prehension in infants by means of systematic cinema records. Genet. Psychol. Monogr. 10:109–285.

Hamerton, J. L., Canning, H., Ray, M., and Smith, S. 1975. A cytogenetic survey of 14,069 newborn infants. 1. Incidence of chromosome abnormalities. Clin. Genet. 8:223–243.

Hanshaw, J. B., Scheiner, A. P., Moxley, A. W., Gaev, L., Abel, V., and Scheiner, B. 1976. School failure and deafness after "silent" congenital cytomegalovirus infection. N. Engl. J. Med. 295:468–470.

Harris, D. B. 1963. Children's Drawings as Measures of Intellectual Maturity: A Revision and Extension of the Goodenough Draw-A-Man Test. Harcourt, Brace & World, New York.

Harris, D. B., Roberts, J., and Pinder, G. D. 1970. Intellectual Maturity of Children as Measured by the Goodenough-Harris Drawing Test. Public Health Service Publication No. 1000—Series 11—No. 105.

Harth, R. 1973. Attitudes and Mental Retardation. Review of the Literature. Train. School Bull. 69:150–164.

Hartlage, L. C., and Lucas, D. G. 1973. Mental Development Evaluation of the Pediatric Patient. Charles C Thomas Publishers, Springfield.

Harwood-Nash, D. C., and Breckbill, D. L. 1976. Computed tomography in children: A new diagnostic technique. J. Pediatr. 89:343–357.

Heber, R., and Garber, H. 1975. The Milwaukee Project: A study of the use of family intervention to prevent cultural-familial mental retardation. In B. Z. Friedlander, G. M. Sterritt, and G.

E. Kirk (eds.), Exceptional Infant, Vol. 3, Assessment and Intervention, pp. 399–433. Brunner/Mazel, New York.

Hemple, D. J., Harris, L. E., Svien, H. J., and Holman, C. B. 1961. Craniosynostosis involving the sagittal suture only: Guilt by association? J. Pediatr. 58:342–355.

Henderson, A. G. 1975. Electrophysiological tests of hearing. Dev. Med. Child. Neurol. 17:96–99.

Herbst, A. L., Poskanzer, D. C., Robboy, S. J., Friedlander, L., and Scully, R. E. 1975. Prenatal exposure to stilbestrol. A prospective comparison of exposed female offspring with unexposed controls. N. Engl. J. Med. 292:334–339.

Hereford, S. M., Cleland, C. C., and Fellner, M. 1973. Territoriality and scent-marking: A study of profoundly retarded enuretics and encopretics. Am. J. Ment. Defic. 77:426–430.

Hewett, S. 1976. Research on families with handicapped children—an aid or an impediment to understanding. Birth Defects 12(4):35–46.

Himelstein, P. 1968. Use of the Stanford-Binet, Form LM with retardates: A review of recent research. Am. J. Ment. Defic. 72:691–699.

Hingtgen, J. N., and Bryson, C. Q. 1972. Recent developments in the study of early childhood psychoses: Infantile autism, childhood schizophrenia and related disorders. Schizophren. Bull. 5:8–53.

Hobel, C. J., Hyvarinen, M. A., Okada, D. M., and Oh, W. 1973. Prenatal and intrapartum high-risk screening. 1. Prediction of the high-risk neonate. Am. J. Obstet. Gynecol. 117:1–9.

Hoffman, J. L. 1965. Mental retardation, religious values and psychiatric universals. Am. J. Psychiatry 121:885–889.

Hoffman, M. L. 1970. Moral Development. In P. H. Mussen (ed.), Carmichael's Manual of Child Psychology, pp. 261–359. John Wiley & Sons, New York.

Holden, R. 1972. Prediction of mental retardation in infancy. Ment. Retard. 10(1):28–30.

Holden, R., and Willerman, L. 1972. Neurological abnormality in infancy, preschool intelligence, and social class. In P. Trapp and P. Himmelstein (eds.), Readings on the Exceptional Child, pp. 501–513. Prentice-Hall, Englewood Cliffs.

Holland, J. J. 1974. Slow, inapparent and recurrent viruses. Sci. Am. 230(2):32–40.

Hollis, J. H., and Carrier, J. K., Jr. 1975. Research implications for communication deficiencies. Except. Child. 41:405–412.

Holmes, L. B. 1976. Congenital malformations. N. Engl. J. Med. 295:204–207.

Holmes, L. B., Moser, H. W., Halldorsson, S., Mack, C., Pant, S. S., and Matzilevich, B. 1972. Mental Retardation: An Atlas of Diseases with Associated Physical Abnormalities. The Macmillan Publishing Company, New York.

Holowach, J., Thurston, D. L., and O'Leary, J. 1972. Prognosis in childhood epilepsy: Follow-up study of 148 cases in which therapy had been suspended after prolonged anticonvulsant control. N. Engl. J. Med. 286:169–174.

Holser-Buehler, P. 1966. The Blanchard Method of Feeding the Cerebral Palsied. Am. J. Occup. Ther. 20:31–34.

Holt, K. S. 1960. Early motor development. J. Pediatr. 57:571–575.

Holt, S. B. 1961. Palm-prints and their uses in medical biology. Cerebral Palsy Bull. 3:333–347.

Honzik, M. P. 1976. Value and limitations of infant tests: An overview. In M. Lewis (ed.), Origins of Intelligence, pp. 59–95. Plenum Press, New York.

Hook, E. B., and Porter, I. H. (eds.). 1977. Population Cytogenetics: Studies in Humans. Academic Press, New York.

Hooshmand, H. 1974. Toxic effects of anticonvulsants: General principles. Pediatrics 53:551–557.

Hunt, J. McV. 1961. Intelligence and Experience. Ronald Press, New York.

Hunt, J. V., and Rhodes, L. 1977. Mental development of preterm infants during the first year. Child. Dev. 48:204–210.

Hurwitz, S., and Braverman, I. M. 1970. White spots in tuberous sclerosis. J. Pediatr. 77:587–594.

Iivanainen, M. 1974. A Study on the Origins of Mental Retardation. Clinics in Developmental Medicine No. 51. Spastics International Medical Publications. William Heinemann Medical Books, Ltd., London.

Illingworth, R. S. 1961a. Delayed maturation in development. J. Pediatr. 58:761–770.

Illingworth, R. S. 1961b. The predictive value of developmental tests in the first year, with special reference to the diagnosis of mental subnormality. J. Child. Psychol. Psychiatry 2:210–215.

Illingworth, R. S. 1962. An Introduction to Developmental Assessment in the First Year. Little Club Clinics in Developmental Medicine No. 3. The National Spastics Society Medical Education and Information Unit in association with William Heinemann Medical Books, Ltd., London.

Illingworth, R. S. 1967. The Development of the Infant and Young Child: Normal and Abnormal. 3rd Ed. Williams & Wilkins, Baltimore.

Illingworth, R. S. 1968. The Normal Child. J. & A. Churchill, Ltd., London.

Illingworth, R. S. 1971. The predictive value of developmental assessment in infancy. Dev. Med. Child. Neurol. 13:721–725.

Illingworth, R. S., and Birch, L. B. 1959. The diagnosis of mental retardation in infancy: A follow-up study. Arch. Dis. Child. 34:269–273.

Ingram, T. T. S. 1962. Clinical significance of the infantile feeding reflexes. Dev. Med. Child. Neurol. 4:159–169.

Ingram, T. T. S. 1969. The new approach to early diagnosis of handicaps in childhood. Dev. Med. Child. Neurol. 11:279–290.

Inhelder, B. 1966. Cognitive development and its contribution to the diagnosis of some phenomena of mental deficiency. Merrill-Palmer Quart. 12(4):299–321.

Inhelder, B. 1968. The Diagnosis of Reasoning in the Mentally Retarded. John Day, New York.

Inhelder, B., Sinclair, H., and Bovet, M. 1974. Learning and the Development of Cognition. Harvard University Press, Cambridge.

Ireland, W. W. 1877. On Idiocy and Imbecility. J. & A. Churchill, Ltd., London.

Itard, J. M. G. 1962. The Wild Boy of Aveyron. Appleton-Century-Crofts, New York.

Jackson, D. 1970. The discovery of childhood: A background to pediatrics. Med. J. Aust. 2:763–771.

Jackson, J. F., North, E. R., III, and Thomas, J. G. 1976. Clinical diagnosis of Down's syndrome. Clin. Genet. 9:483–487.

Jacobs, P. A. 1974. Correlations between euploid structural chromosome rearrangements and mental subnormality in humans. Nature 249:164–165.

Jacobs, P. A., Melville, M., and Ratcliffe, S. 1974. A cytogenetic survey of 11,680 newborn infants. Ann. Hum. Genet. 37:359–376.

Jaffe, B. F. 1976. Pinna anomalies associated with congenital conductive hearing loss. Pediatrics 57:332–341.

Jan, J. E., Robinson, G. C., Scott, E., and Kinnis, C. 1975. Hypotonia in the blind child. Dev. Med. Child. Neurol. 17:35–40.

Jeavons, P. M., Bower, B. D., and Dimitrikoudi, M. C. 1973. Long-term prognosis of 150 cases of West syndrome. Epilepsia 14:153–164.

Jeavons, P. M., Harper, J. R., and Bower, B. D. 1970. Long-term prognosis in infantile spasms: A follow-up report on 112 cases. Dev. Med. Child. Neurol. 12:413–421.

Jencks, C., et al. 1972. Inequality: A Reassessment of the Effect of Family and Schooling in America. Basic Books, New York.

Jensen, A. R. 1969. How much can we boost I.Q. and scholastic achievement? Harvard Educ. Rev. 39:1–123.

Jensen, A. R. 1970. A theory of primary and secondary familial mental retardation. In N. R. Ellis (ed.), International Review of Research in Mental Retardation, Vol. 4, pp. 33–105. Academic Press, New York.

Johnson, C. A., and Katz, R. C. 1973. Using parents as change agents for their children: A review. J. Child. Psychol. Psychiatry 14:181–200.

Johnson, G. O. 1968. Special education for the mentally retarded. Ped. Clin. North Am. 15:1005–1016.

Johnson, R. C. 1970. Prediction of independent functioning and of problem behavior from measures of I.Q. and S.Q. Am. J. Ment. Defic. 74:591–593.

Johnson, R. T. 1972. Effects of viral infections on the developing nervous system. N. Engl. J. Med. 287:599–604.

Jones, K. L., and Smith, D. W. 1973. Recognition of the fetal alcohol syndrome in early infancy. Lancet. ii:999–1001.

Jones, K. L., and Smith, D. W. 1975. The fetal alcohol syndrome. Teratology 12:1–10.

Jones, K. L., Smith, D. W., Streissguth, A. P., and Myrianthopoulos, N. C. 1974. Outcome in offspring of chronic alcoholic women. Lancet i:1076–1078.

Jones, K. L., Smith, D. W., Ulleland, C. N., and Streissguth, A. P. 1973. Pattern of malformation in offspring of alcoholic mothers. Lancet i:1267–1271.

Jonsen, A. R., and Garland, M. J. (eds.). 1976. Ethics of Newborn Intensive Care. Institute of Governmental Studies, Berkeley.

Joseph, M., and Dawbarn, C. 1970. Measurement of the Facies: A

Study in Down's Syndrome. S.I.M.P. Research Monograph No. 3. Spastics International Medical Publications, in association with William Heinemann Medical Books, Ltd., London.

Kagan, J. 1971. Change and Continuity in Infancy. John Wiley & Sons, New York.

Kahn, J. V. 1975. Relationship of Piaget's sensorimotor period to language acquisition of profoundly retarded children. Am. J. Ment. Defic. 79:640–643.

Kahn, J. V. 1976. Moral and cognitive development of moderately retarded, mildly retarded, and nonretarded individuals. Am. J. Ment. Defic. 81:209–214.

Kang, E. S., Sollee, N. D., and Gerald, P. S. 1970. Results of treatment and termination of the diet in phenylketonuria (PKU). Pediatrics 46:881–890.

Kanner, L. 1943. Autistic disturbances of affective contact. Nerv. Child. 2:217–250.

Kanner, L. 1949. A Miniature Textbook of Feeblemindedness. Child Care Publications, New York.

Kanner, L. 1964. A History of the Care and Study of the Mentally Retarded. Charles C Thomas Publisher, Springfield.

Kanner, L. 1967. History of attitudes toward the mentally retarded. In J. A. Askin, R. E. Cooke, and J. A. Haller (eds.), A Symposium on the Child, pp. 345–354. The Johns Hopkins University Press, Baltimore.

Karelitz, S., and Fisichelli, V. R. 1962. The cry thresholds of normal infants and those with brain damage: An aid in the early diagnosis of severe brain damage. J. Pediatr. 61:679–685.

Karelitz, S., Fisichelli, V. R., Costa, J., Karelitz, R., and Rosenfeld, L. 1964. Relation of crying activity in early infancy to speech and intellectual development at age three years. Child. Dev. 35:769–777.

Katz, C. M., and Taylor, P. M. 1967. The incidence of low birthweight in children with severe mental retardation. Am. J. Dis. Child. 114:80–87.

Kauffman, J. M., and Hallahan, D. P. 1974. The medical model and the science of special education. Except. Child. 41:97–102.

Kaufman, A. S. 1976. Verbal-performance I.Q. discrepancies on the WISC-R. J. Consult. Clin. Psychol. 44:739–744.

Kaye, H. 1976. Some suggestions for reclassification of ontogenetically relevant early psychomotor behavior. In E. Schopler, and R. Reichler (eds.), Psychopathology and Child Development, pp. 51–76. Plenum Press, New York.

Kendler, H. H., and Kendler, T. S. 1962. Vertical and horizontal processes in problem solving. Psychol. Rev. 69:1–16.

Kessler, J. W. 1970. Contributions of the mentally retarded toward a theory of cognitive development. In J. Hellmuth (ed.), Cognitive Studies, Vol. 1, pp. 111–209. Brunner/Mazel, New York.

Kim, H. J., Hsu, L. Y. F., Paciuc, S., Christian, S., Quintana, A., and Hirschhorn, K. 1975. Cytogenetics of fetal wastage. N. Engl. J. Med. 293:844–947.

Kindred, M., Cohen, J., Penrod, D., and Shaffer, T. S. (eds.). 1976. The Mentally Retarded Citizen and the Law. The Free Press, New York.

Kirk, S. A., and McCarthy, J. J. 1961. The Illinois Test of Psycho-Linguistic Abilities—an approach to differential diagnosis. Am. J. Ment. Defic. 66:399–412.

Kittrie, N. N. 1971. The Right to Be Different. The Johns Hopkins University Press, Baltimore.

Klaber, M. M., and Butterfield, E. C. 1968. Stereotyped rocking as a measure of institution and ward effectiveness. Am. J. Ment. Defic. 73:13–20.

Klein, N. K., and Safford, P. L. 1977. Application of Piaget's theory to the study of thinking of the mentally retarded: A review of research. J. Spec. Educ. 11:201–216.

Knobloch, H., and Pasamanick, B. 1959. Syndrome of minimal cerebral damage in infancy. JAMA 170:1384–1387.

Knobloch, H., and Pasamanick, B. 1960. Environmental factors affecting human development before and after birth. Pediatrics 26:210–218.

Knobloch, H., and Pasamanick, B. 1963. Predicting intellectual potential in infancy. Am. J. Dis. Child. 106:43–51.

Knobloch, H., and Pasamanick, B. 1974. Gesell and Amatruda's Developmental Diagnosis: The Evaluation and Management of Normal and Abnormal Neuropsychologic Development in Infancy and Early Childhood. Harper & Row Publishers, New York.

Knobloch, H., and Pasamanick, B. 1975. Some etiologic and prognostic factors in early infantile autism and psychosis. Pediatrics 55:182–191.

Knobloch, H., Pasamanick, B., and Sherard, E. S. 1966. A

developmental screening inventory for infants. Pediatrics 38:1095–1108.

Koch, R., Graliker, B. V., Sands, R., and Parmelee, A. H., Sr. 1959. Attitude study of parents with mentally retarded children. I. Evaluation of parental satisfaction with the medical care of a retarded child. Pediatrics 23:582–584.

Koch, R., Share, J., Webb, A., and Graliker, B. V. 1963. The predictability of Gesell developmental scales in Mongolism. J. Pediatr. 62:93–97.

Kohlberg, L. 1968. Early education: A cognitive-developmental view. Child. Dev. 39:1013–1062.

Kohn, B. A. 1976. The differential diagnosis of cataracts in infancy and childhood. Am. J. Dis. Child. 130:184–192.

Kolodny, E. H. 1976. Lysosomal storage diseases. N. Engl. J. Med. 294:1217–1220.

Konigsmark, B. W. 1969. Hereditary deafness in man. N. Engl. J. Med. 281:713–720, 774–778, 827–832.

Konigsmark, B. W., and Gorlin, R. J. 1976. Genetic and Metabolic Deafness. W. B. Saunders Company, Philadelphia.

Kopp, C. B. 1974a. An application of Piagetian theory: Sensorymotor development. Am. J. Occup. Ther. 28:217–219.

Kopp, C. B. 1974b. Fine motor abilities of infants. Dev. Med. Child. Neurol. 16:629–636.

Koppitz, E. M. 1963. The Bender Gestalt Test for Young Children. Grune & Stratton, New York.

Koppitz, E. M. 1968. Psychological Evaluation of Children's Human Figure Drawings. Grune & Stratton, New York.

Korsch, B., Cobb, J., and Ashe, B. 1961. Pediatricians' appraisals of patients' intelligence. Pediatrics 27:990–1003.

Korsch, B. M., Gozzi, E. K., and Francis, V. 1968. Gaps in doctor-patient communication. I: Doctor-patient interaction and patient satisfaction. Pediatrics 42:855–871.

Korsch, B. M., and Negrete, V. F. 1972. Doctor-patient communication. Sci. Am. 227(2):66–74.

Kounin, J. S. 1941a. Experimental studies of rigidity. I: The measurement of rigidity in normal and feeble-minded persons. Character Person. 9:251–272.

Kounin, J. S. 1941b. Experimental studies of rigidity. II: The explanatory power of the concept of rigidity as applied to feeble-mindedness. Character Person. 9:273–282.

Kounin, J. S. 1948. The meaning of rigidity: A reply to Heinz Werner. Psychol. Rev. 55:157–166.

Krasner, W. 1977. Labeling the Children. Mental Health Studies and Reports Branch, U.S. Government Printing Office, Washington, D.C.

Kraus, B. S., Jordan, R. E., Nery, E. B., and Kaplay, S. 1967. Abnormalities of dental morphology in mentally retarded individuals: A preliminary report. Am. J. Ment. Defic. 71:828–839.

Krumboltz, J. D., and Krumboltz, H. B. 1972. Changing Children's Behavior. Prentice-Hall, Englewood Cliffs.

Kubler-Ross, E. 1969. On Death and Dying. Macmillan Publishing Company, New York.

Kügel, R. B., and Mohr, J. 1963. Mental retardation and physical growth. Am. J. Ment. Defic. 68:41–48.

Kuhlmann, F. 1940. One hundred years of special care and training. Am. J. Ment. Defic. 45:8–24.

Kutt, H., and Penry, J. K. 1974. Usefulness of blood levels of antiepileptic drugs. Arch. Neurol. 31:283–288.

Lachs, J. 1976. Humane treatment and the treatment of humans. N. Engl. J. Med. 294:838–840.

Lain Entralgo, P. 1969. Doctor and Patient. McGraw-Hill Book Company, New York.

Landrigan, P. J., Whitworth, R. H., Baloh, R. W., Staehling, N. W., Barthel, W. F., and Rosenblum, B. F. 1975. Neuropsychological dysfunction in children with chronic low-level lead absorption. Lancet i:708–712.

Lane, H. 1977. The Wild Boy of Aveyron. Bantam Books, New York.

Langer, J. 1969. Theories of Development. Holt, Rinehart & Winston, New York.

Langer, W. L. 1974. Infanticide: A historical survey. Hist. Childhood Quart. 1:353–365.

Lashley, K. S. 1963. Brain Mechanisms and Intelligence. Dover Publications, New York.

Lawrence, E. A., and Winschel, J. F. 1973. Self concept and the retarded: Research and issues. Except. Child. 39:310–319.

Lawrence, K. M. 1969. Neurological and intellectual sequelae of hydrocephalus. Arch. Neurol. 20:73–81.

Lee, C. W. G., Yu, J. S., Turner, B. B., and Murray, K. E. 1976. Trimethylaminuria: Fishy odors in children. N. Engl. J. Med. 295:937–938.

Leibowitz, J. M., and Holcer, P. 1974. Building and maintaining self-feeding skills in a retarded child. Am. J. Occup. Ther. 28:545–548.

Lemkau, P. V., and Imre, P. D. 1969. Results of a field epidemiologic study. Am. J. Ment. Defic. 73:858–863.

Lemke, H. 1974. Self-abusive behavior in the mentally retarded. Am. J. Occup. Ther. 28:94–98.

Lemke, H., and Mitchell, R. 1972. Controlling the behavior of a profoundly retarded child: A self-feeding program. Am. J. Occup. Ther. 26:261–264.

Lenneberg, E. H. 1964. Language disorders in childhood. Harvard Educ. Rev. 34:152–177.

Lenneberg, E. H. 1967. Biological Foundations of Language. John Wiley & Sons, New York.

Lenneberg, E. H., and Lenneberg, E. (eds.). 1975. Foundations of Language Development: A Multidisciplinary Approach. 2 Vols. Academic Press, New York.

Leonard, C. O., Chase, G. A., and Childs, B. 1972. Genetic counseling: A consumer's view. N. Engl. J. Med. 287:433–439.

Levin, S., Nir, E., and Mogilner, B. M. 1975. T System immunedeficiency in Down's Syndrome. Pediatrics 56:123–126.

Levy, J. 1973. Baby Exercise Book. Random House, New York.

Lewandowski, R. C., Jr., and Yunis, J. J. 1975. New chromosomal syndromes. Am. J. Dis. Child. 129:515–529.

Lewis, D. V., and Freeman, J. M. 1977. The electroencephalogram in pediatric practice: Its use and abuse. Pediatrics 60:324–330.

Lewis, J. F. 1973. The community and the retarded. In G. Tarjan, R. K. Eyman, and C. E. Meyers (eds.), Sociobehavioral Studies in Mental Retardation. Monogr. Am. Assoc. Ment. Defic. 1:164–174.

Lewis, M. 1971. Individual differences in the measurement of early cognitive growth. In J. Hellmuth (ed.), Exceptional Infant, Vol. 2, Studies in Abnormalities, pp. 172–210. Brunner/Mazel, New York.

Lewis, M. (ed.). 1976a. Origins of Intelligence. Plenum Press, New York.

Lewis, M. 1976b. What do we mean when we say "infant intelligence scores?" A sociopolitical question. In M. Lewis (ed.), Origins of Intelligence, pp. 1–17. Plenum Press, New York.

Lewis, M., and McGurk, H. 1972. Evaluation of infant intelligence: Infant intelligence scores—true or false? Science 178: 1174–1177.
Lewko, J. H. 1976. Current practices in evaluating motor behavior of disabled children. Am. J. Occup. Ther. 30:413–419.
Lewontin, R. C. 1974. The analysis of variance and the analysis of causes. Am. J. Hum. Genet. 26:400–411.
Lichtenberg, P., and Norton, D. G. 1970. Cognitive and Mental Development in the First Five Years of Life. U.S. Government Printing Office, Washington, D.C.
Lillywhite, H. 1958. Doctor's manual of speech disorders. JAMA 167:850–858.
Lillywhite, H. S., and Bradley, D. P. 1969. Communication Problems in Mental Retardation. Harper & Row Publishers, New York.
Lillywhite, H. S., Young, N. B., and Olmsted, R. W. 1970. Pediatrician's Handbook of Communication Disorders. Lea & Febiger, Philadelphia.
Lindsley, D. B. 1976. Mental retardation: Historical and psychophysiological perspective. In R. Karrer (ed.), Developmental Psychophysiology of Mental Retardation, pp. 3–38. Charles C Thomas Publisher, Springfield.
Lipton, H. L., and Svarstad, B. 1977. Sources of variation in clinicians' communication to parents about mental retardation. Am. J. Ment. Defic. 82:155–161.
Lobl, M., Welcher, D. W., and Mellits, E. D. 1971. Maternal age and intellectual functioning of offspring. Johns Hopkins Med. J. 128:347–361.
Locke, J. 1959. An Essay Concerning Human Understanding, 2 vols. Dover Publications, New York.
Loesch, D. 1973. The contributions of L. S. Penrose to dermatoglyphics. J. Ment. Defic. Res. 17:1–17.
Lorenz, K. 1967. Evolution and Modification of Behavior. University of Chicago Press, Chicago.
Lowrey, G. H., Bacon, G. E., Fisher, S., and Knoller, H. 1968. Fasting growth hormone levels in mentally retarded children of short stature. Am. J. Ment. Defic. 73:474–476.
Luria, A. R. 1961. The Role of Speech in the Regulation of Normal and Abnormal Behavior. Liveright Publishing Co., New York.
Luria, A. R. 1973. The Working Brain: An Introduction to Neuropsychology. Basic Books, New York.

Lyle, J. G. 1959. The effect of an institution environment upon the verbal development of imbecile children. I. Verbal intelligence. J. Ment. Defic. Res. 3:122–128.

Lynch, J., and Bricker, W. A. 1972. Linguistic theory and operant procedures: Toward an integrated approach to language training for the mentally retarded. Ment. Retard. 10(2):12–16.

Maag, U. R., and Gold, R. J. M. 1975. A simple combinatorial method for calculating genetic risks. Clin. Gent. 7:361–367.

MacAndrew, C., and Edgerton, R. 1964. I.Q. and the social competence of the profoundly retarded. Am. J. Ment. Defic. 69:385–390.

McCall, R. B. 1974. Exploratory manipulation and play in the human infant. Monogr. Soc. Res. Child. Dev. 39(2).

McCall, R. B. 1976. Toward an epigenetic conception of mental development in the first three years of life. In M. Lewis (ed.), Origins of Intelligence, pp. 97–122. Plenum Press, New York.

McCall, R. B. 1977. Challenges to a science of developmental psychology. Child. Dev. 48:333–344.

McCall, R., Hogarty, P. S., and Hurlburt, N. 1972. Transitions in infant sensorimotor development and the prediction of childhood I.Q. Am. Psychol. 27:728–748.

McClelland, D. C. 1973. Testing for competence rather than for "intelligence." Am. Psychol. 28:1–14.

Maccoby, E. E., and Bee, H. L. 1965. Some speculations concerning the lag between perceiving and performing. Child. Dev. 36:367–377.

Mace, J. W., Goodman, S. I., Centerwall, W. R., and Chinnock, R. F. 1976. The child with an unusual odor. Clin. Pediatr. 15:57–62.

MacFarlane, D. W., Boyd, R. D., Dodrill, C. B., and Tufts, E. 1975. Intrauterine rubella, head size, and intellect. Pediatrics 55:707–801.

McFie, J., and Robertson, J. 1973. Psychological test results of children with thalidomide deformities. Dev. Med. Child. Neurol. 15:719–727.

McGraw, M. B. 1942. Appraising test responses of infants and young children. J. Psychol. 14:89–100.

McGraw, M. B., and Molloy, L. B. 1941. The pediatric anamnesis: Inaccuracies in eliciting developmental data. Child. Dev. 12:255–265.

McIntire, R., and Dingman, H. F. 1963. Mental age vs. learning ability: An investigation of transfer of training between hierarchical levels. Am. J. Ment. Defic. 68:396–403.

McKusick, V. A. 1975. Mendelian Inheritance in Man. The Johns Hopkins University Press, Baltimore.

McLaughlin, J. A., and Stephens, B. 1974. Interrelationships among reasoning, moral judgment, and moral conduct. Am. J. Ment. Defic. 79:156–161.

MacMillan, D. L., Jones, R. L., and Aloia, G. F. 1974. The mentally retarded label: A theoretical analysis and review of research. Am. J. Ment. Defic. 79:241–261.

Madsen, C. H., Jr., and Madsen, C. K. 1974. Teaching/Discipline: A Positive Approach for Educational Development. Allyn and Bacon, Boston.

Magary, J. F., Poulsen, M. K., Levinson, P. J., and Taylor, P. A. 1977. Piagetian Theory and Its Implications for the Helping Professions. Emphasis: The Handicapped Child. University of Southern California Press, Los Angeles.

Magoun, H. W. 1960. Evolutionary concepts of brain function following Darwin and Spencer. In S. Tax (ed.), Evolution After Darwin, Vol. 2, The Evolution of Man: Mind, Culture and Society, pp. 187–209. University of Chicago Press, Chicago.

Mahaney, E. R., Jr., and Stephens, B. 1974. Two-year gains in moral judgment by retarded and nonretarded persons. Am. J. Ment. Defic. 79:134–141.

Mahoney, K., Van Wagenen, R. K., and Meyerson, L. 1971. Toilet training of normal and retarded children. J. Appl. Behav. Anal. 4:173–181.

Malson, L. 1972. Wolf Children and the Problem of Human Nature. Monthly Review Press, New York.

Mann, L. 1971. Perceptual training revisited: The training of nothing at all. Rehabil. Lit. 32:322–327, 335.

Mann, L., and Goodman, L. 1976. Perceptual training: A critical retrospect. In E. Schopler and R. J. Reichler (eds.), Psychopathology and Child Development, pp. 271–289. Plenum Press, New York.

Marker, G., and Friedman, P. R. 1973. Rethinking children's rights. Child. Today 2(6):8–11.

Marquis, P. 1976. Cognitive stimulation. Am. J. Dis. Child. 130:410–415.

Marriage, K. J., and Davies, P. A. 1977. Neurological sequelae in children surviving mechanical ventilation in the neonatal period. Arch. Dis. Child. 52:176–182.

Martin, H. P. 1970. Microcephaly and mental retardation. Am. J. Dis. Child. 119:128–131.

Martin, J. P., and Bell, J. 1943. A pedigree of mental defect showing sex-linkage. J. Neurol. Psychiatry 6:154–157.

Massengill, R. M., Jr. 1969. Comparison of the swallowing patterns of mental retardates and normals. Am. J. Ment. Defic. 73:950–955.

Matheny, A. P. 1966. Improving diagnosis forecasts made on a developmental scale. Am. J. Ment. Defic. 71:371–375.

Matheny, A. P., Jr., Dolan, A. B., and Wilson, R. S. 1974. Bayley's infant behavior record: Relations between behaviors and mental test scores. Dev. Psychol. 10:696–702.

Matheny, A. P., Jr., and Vernick, J. 1969. Parents of the mentally retarded child: Emotionally overwhelmed or informationally deprived? J. Pediatr. 74:953–959.

Matthews, C. G., and Manning, G. C. 1964. Psychological test performances in three electroencephalographic classifications of mentally retarded subjects. Am. J. Ment. Defic. 68:485–492.

Mecham, M. J. 1971. Verbal Language Development Scale. American Guidance Service, Circle Pines, Minnesota.

Mednick, B. R. 1977. Intellectual and behavioral functioning of ten to twelve-year old children who showed certain transient symptoms in the neonatal period. Child. Dev. 48:844–853.

Meier, J. 1973. Screening and Assessment of Young Children at Developmental Risk. President's Committee on Mental Retardation, Washington, D.C.

Menkes, J. H., Andrews, J. M., and Cancilla, P. A. 1971. The cerebroretinal degenerations. J. Pediatr. 79:183–196.

Menolascino, F. J. 1969. Emotional disturbances in mentally retarded children. Am. J. Psychiatry 126:168–176.

Menolascino, F. J. (ed.). 1970. Psychiatric Approaches to Mental Retardation. Basic Books, New York.

Menolascino, F. J. (ed.). 1971. Psychiatric Aspects of the Diagnosis and Treatment of Mental Retardation. Special Child Publications, Seattle.

Menolascino, F. 1973. Primitive, atypical, and abnormal-psychotic behavior in institutionalized mentally retarded children. J. Autism Child. Schizo. 3:49–64.

Mental Health Law Project. 1973. Basic Rights of the Mentally Handicapped. Mental Health Law Project, Washington, D.C.

Milgram, N. A. 1969. The rationale and irrational in Zigler's motivational approach to mental retardation Am. J. Ment. Defic. 73:527–532.

Miller, G. A. 1956. The magical number seven, plus or minus two: Some limits on our capacity for processing information. Psychol. Rev. 63:81–97.

Miller, L. G. 1968. Toward a greater understanding of the parents of the mentally retarded child. J. Pediatr. 73:699–705.

Miller, O. J., and Breg, W. R. 1976. Autosomal chromosomal disorders and variations. N. Engl. J. Med. 294:596–598.

Milunsky, A. (ed.). 1975. The Prevention of Genetic Disease and Mental Retardation. W. B. Saunders Company, Philadelphia.

Milunsky, A. 1976. Prenatal diagnosis of genetic disorders. N. Engl. J. Med. 295:377–380.

Minkowski, A. (ed). 1967. Regional Development of the Brain in Early Life. Blackwell Scientific Publications, Oxford.

Mitchell, R., and Etches, P. 1977. Rhythmic habit patterns (stereotypies). Dev. Med. Child. Neurol. 19:545–550.

Mittler, P. 1964. The use of form boards in developmental assessment. Dev. Med. Child. Neurol. 6:510–516.

Montessori, M. 1971. The Montessori Method. Schocken Books, New York.

Moore, C. B., and Morton, K. G. 1976. A Reader's Guide for Parents of Children with Mental, Physical, or Emotional Disabilities. DHEW Publication Number (HSA) 77-5290.

Moore, G., and Stephens, B. 1974. Two-year gains in moral conduct by retarded and nonretarded persons. Am. J. Ment. Defic. 79:147–153.

Moric-Petrovic, S., and Garzicic, B. 1970. Mother with Down's syndrome and her child. J. Ment. Defic. Res. 14:68–76.

Mosier, H. D., Grossman, H. J., and Dingman, H. F. 1965. Physical growth in mental defectives. Pediatrics 36:465–519.

Mosier, H. D., Grossman, H. J., and Dingman, H. F. 1966. Laboratory values in severely stunted mental defectives. Am. J. Ment. Defic. 71:230–236.

Mulvihill, J. J., and Smith, D. W. 1969. The genesis of dermatoglyphics. J. Pediatr. 75:579–589.

Munsinger, H., and Douglass, A., II. 1976. The syntactic abilities of identical twins, fraternal twins, and their siblings. Child. Dev. 47:40–50.

Murdock, C. W. 1973. Civil rights of the mentally retarded—some critical issues. Family Law Quart. 7:1–74.

Mussen, P. H. (ed.). 1970. Carmichael's Manual of Child Psychology. John Wiley & Sons, New York.

Naylor, A. F., and Warburton, D. 1974. Genetics of obstetrical variables: A study from the collaborative perinatal project. Clin. Genet. 6:351–369.

Neaman, J. S. 1975. Suggestion of the Devil: The Origins of Madness. Anchor Books, New York.

Neisworth, J. T., and Greer, J. G. 1975. Functional similarities of learning disability and mild retardation. Except. Child. 42:17–21.

Neligan, G. A., Kolvin, I., Scott, D. Mcl., and Garside, R. F. 1976. Born Too Soon or Born Too Small. Clinics in Developmental Medicine No. 61. Spastics International Medical Publications. William Heinemann Medical Books, Ltd., London.

Nellhaus, G. 1968. Head circumference from birth to eighteen years: Practical composite international and interracial graphs. Pediatrics 41:106–114.

Nelson, K. B., and Ellenberg, J. H. 1976. Predictors of epilepsy in children who have experienced febrile seizures. N. Engl. J. Med. 295:1029–1033.

Newman, R. 1975. A Reply to Zigler and Seitz. Am. J. Ment. Defic. 79:493–505.

Newman, R., Roos, P., McCann, B. M., Menolascino, F. J., and Heal, L. W. 1975. Experimental evaluation of sensorimotor patterning used with mentally retarded children. Am. J. Ment. Defic. 79:372–384.

Newton, M. S., Jacobs, P. A., Price, W. H., Woodcock, G., and Fraser, I. A. 1972a. A chromosome survey of a hospital for the mentally subnormal. Part 1: Sex chromosome abnormalities. Clin. Genet. 3:215–225.

Newton, M. S., Cunningham, C., Jacobs, P. A., Price, W. H., and Fraser, I. A. 1972b. Chromosome survey of a hospital for the mentally subnormal. Part 2: Autosome abnormalities. Clin. Genet. 3:226–248.

Nicholls, E. M., and Stark, A. E. 1971. Bayes' Theorem. Med. J. Aust. 2:1335–1339.

Nichols, P. L., and Broman, S. H. 1974. Familial resemblance in infant mental development. Dev. Psychol. 10:442–446.

Nichtern, S. 1974. Helping the Retarded Child. Grosset & Dunlap, New York.

Niedermeyer, E. 1972. The Generalized Epilepsies: A Clinical Electroencephalographic Study. Charles C Thomas Publishers, Springfield.

Niedermeyer, E. 1973. The value of the EEG in diagnosis, treatment, and prognosis of childhood epilepsy. Pediatr. Ann. 2(8):42–74.

Niedermeyer, E. 1974. Compendium of the Epilepsies. Charles C Thomas Publishers, Springfield.

Nitowsky, H. M., and Legum, C. P. 1974. Genetic counseling. Adv. Pediatr. 18:13–74.

Northern, J., and Downs, M. 1974. Hearing in Children. Williams & Wilkins, Baltimore.

Nowrey, J. E. 1945. A brief synopsis of mental deficiency. Am. J. Ment. Defic. 49:319–357.

Nyhan, W. L. 1977. An approach to the diagnosis of overwhelming metabolic disease in early infancy. Curr. Probl. Pediatr. 7(6):1–20.

Oakland, T. (ed). 1977. Psychological and Educational Assessment of Minority Children. Brunner/Mazel, New York.

Oates, R. K., and Harvey, D. 1976. Congenital rubella associated with hypsarrhythmia. Arch. Dis. Child. 51:77–79.

O'Brien, D. 1970. Rare Inborn Errors of Metabolism in Children with Mental Retardation. PHS Publication No. 2049.

O'Brien, F., Bugle, C., and Azrin, N. H. 1972. Training and maintaining a retarded child's proper eating. J. Appl. Behav. Anal. 5:67–72.

O'Connell, E. J., Feldt, R. H., and Stickler, G. B. 1965. Head circumference, mental retardation, and growth failure. Pediatrics 36:62–66.

Olshansky, S., and Kettell, M. 1963. Attitudes of some interns and first-year residents toward the institutionalization of mentally retarded children. Train. School Bull. 59:116–120.

Olshansky, S., and Sternfeld, L. 1962. Attitudes of some pediatricians toward the institutionalization of mentally retarded children. Train. School Bull. 59:67–73.

Osterrieth, P. A. 1944. Le test de copie d'une figure complexe. Arch. Psychol. 30:205–356.

Ostwald, P. F., Phibbs, R., and Fox, S. 1968. Diagnostic use of infant cry. Biol. Neonat. 13:68–82.

Page, E. B. 1975. Miracle in Milwaukee: Raising the I.Q. In B. Z. Friedlander, G. M. Sterritt, and G. E. Kirk (eds.), Exceptional Infant, Vol. 3, Assessment and Intervention, pp. 434–446. Brunner/Mazel, New York.

Paine, R. S., and Oppe, T. E. 1966. Neurological Examination of Children. Clinics in Developmental Medicine 20/21. Medical Education and Information Unit. The Spastics Society, in Association with William Heinemann Medical Books, Ltd., London.

Palo, J., Lydecken, K., and Kivalo, E. 1966. Etiological aspects of mental deficiency in autopsied patients. Am. J. Ment. Defic. 71:401–405.

Papousek, H., and Papousek, M. 1974. Mirror image and self-recognition in young human infants. 1. A new method of experimental analysis. Dev. Psychobiol. 7:149–157.

Pasamanick, B., and Knobloch, H. 1966. Retrospective Studies on the Epidemiology of Reproductive Casualty: Old and New. Merrill-Palmer Quart. 12:7–26.

Patterson, G. R. 1975. Families. Research Press, Champaign.

Patterson, G. R., and Gullion, M. E. 1971. Living with Children: New Methods for Parents and Teachers. Research Press, Champaign.

Pearson, J. F., and Weaver, J. B. 1976. Fetal activity and fetal wellbeing: An evaluation. Br. Med. J. 1:1305–1307.

Pearson, P. H. 1968. The physician's role in diagnosis and management of the mentally retarded. Ped. Clin. North Am. 15:835–859.

Peiper, A. 1963. Cerebral Function in Infancy and Childhood. Consultants Bureau, New York.

Penney, R. K., Seim, R., and De V. Peters, R. 1968. The mediational deficiency of mentally retarded children. I. The establishment of retardates' mediational deficiency. Am. J. Ment. Defic. 72:626–630.

Penrose, L. S. 1963. The Biology of Mental Defect. Sidgwick and Jackson, London.

Penrose, L. S. 1968. Memorandum on dermatoglyphic nomenclature. Birth Defects 4(3):1–13.

Penrose, L. S., and Smith, G. F. 1966. Down's Anomaly. Little, Brown & Company, Boston.

Perozzi, J. A. 1972. Language acquisition as adaptive behavior. Ment. Retard. 10(2):32–34.

Perrin, J. C., Sands, C. R., Tinker, D. E., Dominguez, B. C., Dingle, J. T., and Thomas, M. J. 1976. A considered approach to sterilization of mentally retarded youth. Am. J. Dis. Child. 130:288–290.

Philips, I., and Williams, N. 1975. Psychopathology and mental retardation: A study of 100 mentally retarded children. I. Psychopathology. Am. J. Psychiatry 132:1265–1271.

Phillips, J. L. 1969. The Origins of Intellect: Piaget's Theory. W. H. Freeman and Company, San Francisco.

Piaget, J. 1954. The Construction of Reality in the Child. Basic Books, New York.

Piaget, J. 1955. The Language and Thought of the Child. Meridian, New York.

Piaget, J. 1962. Play, Dreams and Imitation in Childhood. W. W. Norton & Company, New York.

Piaget, J. 1963. The Origins of Intelligence in Children. W. W. Norton & Company, New York.

Piaget, J. 1967. Six Psychological Studies. Vintage, New York.

Piaget, J. 1968. On the Development of Memory and Identity. Clark University Press, Barre.

Piaget, J. 1969a. The Child's Conception of Physical Causality. Littlefield, Adams & Company, Totowa.

Piaget, J. 1969b. The Child's Conception of the World. Littlefield, Adams & Company, Totowa.

Piaget, J. 1969c. Judgment and Reasoning in the Child. Littlefield, Adams & Company, Totowa.

Piaget, J. 1970a. Piaget's theory. In P. H. Mussen (ed.), Carmichael's Manual of Child Psychology, Vol. 1, pp. 703–732. John Wiley & Sons, New York.

Piaget, J. 1970b. Structuralism. Basic Books, New York.

Piaget, J. 1971a. Biology and Knowledge. University of Chicago Press, Chicago.

Piaget, J. 1971b. Genetic Epistemology. W. W. Norton & Company, New York.

Piaget, J. 1971c. Psychology and Epistemology. Grossman Publishers, New York.

Piaget, J. 1973a. The Child and Reality. Grossman Publishers, New York.

Piaget, J. 1973b. To Understand is to Invent. Grossman Publishers, New York.

Picton, T. W., and Hink, R. F. 1974. Evoked potentials: How? What? and Why? Am. J. EEG Technol. 14:9–44.

Pincus, J. H. 1972. Subacute necrotizing encephalomyelopathy (Leigh's Disease): A consideration of clinical features and etiology. Dev. Med. Child. Neurol. 14:87–101.

Pinder, R. M., Brogden, R. N., Speight, T. M., and Avery, G. S. 1977. Sodium valproate: A review of its pharmacological properties and therapeutic efficacy in epilepsy. Drugs 13:81–123.

Pinto, R. S., and Becker, M. H. 1977. Computer tomography in pediatric diagnosis. Am. J. Dis. Child. 131:583–592.

Popich, G. A., and Smith, D. W. 1972. Fontanels: Range of normal size. J. Pediatr. 80:749–752.

Prechtl, H. F. R. 1961. Neurological sequelae of prenatal and paranatal complications. In B. M. Foss (ed.), Determinants of Infant Behaviour, Vol. 1, pp. 45–48. John Wiley & Sons, New York.

Prechtl, H. F. R. 1963. The mother-child interaction in babies with minimal brain damage (a follow-up study). In B. M. Foss (ed.), Determinants of Infant Behaviour, Vol. 2, pp. 53–66. John Wiley & Sons, New York.

Prechtl, H. F. R. 1965. Prognostic value of neurological signs in the newborn infant. Proc. R. Soc. Med. 58:3–4.

Prechtl, H., and Beintema, D. 1964. The Neurological Examination of the Full Term Newborn Infant. Little Club Clinics in Developmental Medicine No. 12. Spastics Society, in association with William Heinemann Medical Books, Ltd., London.

Prechtl, H. F. R., Theorell, K., Gramsbergen, A., and Lind, J. 1969. A statistical analysis of cry patterns in normal and abnormal newborn infants. Dev. Med. Child. Neurol. 11:142–152.

President's Committee on Mental Retardation. 1972. Background Papers of the Boston Conference, October 12–19, 1972, Screening and Assessment of Young Children at Developmental Risk. USDHEW, Washington, D.C.

Preus, M., and Fraser, F. C. 1976. A methodology for establishing a diagnostic index for syndromes of unknown etiology. Clin. Genet. 10:249–259.

Price, M. E., and Burt, R. A. 1976. Nonconsensual medical

procedures and the right to privacy. In M. Kindred, J. Cohen, D. Penrod, and T. S. Shaffer (eds.), The Mentally Retarded Citizen and the Law, pp. 94–112. The Free Press, New York.

Pritkin, R. A. Posture, Movement and Manipulation Evaluation. Submitted for publication.

Provence, S., and Lipton, R. C. 1969. Infants in Institutions. International Universities Press, New York.

Pryor, H. B., and Thelander, H. 1968. Abnormally small head size and intellect in children. J. Pediatr. 73:593–598.

Purpura, D. P. 1974. Dendritic spine "dysgenesis" and mental retardation. Science 186:1126–1128.

Purvis-Smith, S. G. 1972. The Sydney Line: A significant sign in Down's syndrome. Aust. Paediat. J. 8:198–200.

Qazi, Q. H., and Reed, T. E. 1973. A problem in diagnosis of primary versus secondary microcephaly. Clin. Genet. 4:46–52.

Qazi, Q. H., and Reed, T. E. 1975. A possible major contribution to mental retardation in the general population by the gene for microcephaly. Clin. Genet. 7:85–90.

Rapin, I. 1976. Progressive genetic-metabolic diseases of the central nervous system in children. Pediatr. Ann. 5:313–349.

Redman, R. S., Shapiro, B. L., and Gorlin, R. J. 1966. Measurement of normal and reportedly malformed palatal vaults. II. Normal juvenile measurements. J. Dent. Res. 45:266–269.

Reese, H. W. 1962. Verbal mediation as a function of age level. Psychol. Bull. 59:502–509.

Reiss, P. 1967. Implications of Piaget's developmental psychology for mental retardation. Am. J. Ment. Retard. 72:361–369.

Reitan, R. M. 1966. A research program on the psychological effects of brain lesions in human beings. In N. R. Ellis (ed.), International Review of Research in Mental Retardation, Vol. 1, pp. 153–218. Academic Press. New York.

Renfrew, C., and Murphy, K. (eds.). 1964. The Child Who Does Not Talk. Clinics in Developmental Medicine No. 13. Spastics International Medical Publications, in association with William Heinemann Medical Books, Ltd., London.

Rentfrow, R., and Rentfrow, D. 1969. Studies related to toilet training of the mentally retarded. Am. J. Occup. Ther. 23:425–430.

Report of the Committee of Infectious Diseases. 1974. 17th Ed. American Academy of Pediatrics, Evanston.

Reynolds, B. DeV., Puck, M. H., and Robinson, A. 1974. Genetic counseling: An appraisal. Clin. Genet. 5:177–187.

Rhodes, W. C., and Tracy, M. L. (eds.). 1972. A Study of Child Variance, Vol. 1, Conceptual Models. University of Michigan, Ann Arbor.

Rice, J. A., and Brown, L. F. 1967. Validity of the Peabody Picture Vocabulary Test in a sample of low I.Q. children. Am. J. Ment. Defic. 71:602–603.

Richardson, F. (ed.). 1973. Brain and Intelligence. National Educational Press, Hyattsville.

Richardson, T. 1975. Sign language for the SMR and PMR. Ment. Retard. 13(3):17.

The Rights of Children. 1974. Harvard Education Review Reprint Series No. 9. Harvard Educ. Rev., Cambridge.

Rights of Foster Children. 1973. Child. Today 2(4):20–21.

Riley, R. L., Landwirth, J., Kaplan, S. A., and Collipp, P. J. 1968. Failure to thrive: An analysis of 83 cases. Cal. Med. 108:32–38.

Rivinus, T. M., Jamison, D. L., and Graham, P. J. 1975. Childhood organic neurological disease presenting as psychiatric disorder. Arch. Dis. Child. 50:115–119.

Roberts, C. J. 1968. The distribution of neurological signs in early infancy: A population study. In R. MacKeith and M. Bax (eds.), Studies in Infancy, Clinics in Developmental Medicine No. 27, pp. 55–64. Spastics Society, in association with William Heinemann Medical Books, Ltd., London.

Roberts, J. A. F. 1952. The genetics of mental deficiency. Eugen. Rev. 44:71–83.

Robinson, R. 1966. Cerebral function in the newborn. Dev. Med. Child. Neurol. 8:561–567.

Rola-Pleszeznski, M., Frenkel, L. D., Fuccillo, D. A., Hensen, S. A., Vincent, M. M., Reynolds, D., Stagno, S., and Bellanti, J. A. 1975. Specific impairment of cell-mediated immunity in mothers of infants with congenital cytomegalovirus (CMV) infection. Pediatr. Res. 9:334.

Roos, P., and McCann, B. M. (eds.). 1977. Major trends in mental retardation. Int. J. Ment. Health. 6(1):1–119.

Rose, A. L., and Lombroso, C. T. 1970. Neonatal seizure states. Pediatrics 45:404–425.

Rosen, G. 1968. Some notes on Greek and Roman attitudes toward the mentally ill. In L. G. Stevenson and R. P. Multhauf (eds.),

Medicine, Science and Culture, pp. 17–23. The Johns Hopkins University Press, Baltimore.

Rosen, M., Clark, G. R., and Kivitz, M. S. (eds.). 1976. The History of Mental Retardation: Collected Papers. 2 Vols. University Park Press, Baltimore.

Rosenthal, I. M., Markowitz, A. S., and Medenis, R. 1965. Immunologic incompetence in ataxia telangiectasia. Am. J. Dis. Child. 110:69–75.

Rosenthal, R., and Jacobson, L. F. 1968. Teacher expectations for the disadvantaged. Sci. Am. 218(4):19–23.

Rosenzweig, M. R. 1976. Effects of environment on brain and behavior in animals. In E. Schopler and R. J. Reichler (eds.), Psychopathology and Child Development, pp. 33–49. Plenum Press, New York.

Rosenzweig, M. R., Bennett, E. L., and Diamond, M. C. 1972. Brain changes in response to experience. Sci. Am. 226(2):22–29.

Rousseau, J. J. 1899. Emile. Translated by W. H. Payne. D. Appleton and Company, New York.

Routh, D. K. (ed.). 1973. The Experimental Psychology of Mental Retardation. Aldine Publishing Company, Chicago.

Rutter, M. 1968. Concepts of autism: A review of research. J. Child. Psychol. Psychiatry 9:1–25.

Rutter, M. 1970. Psychological development—predictions from infancy. J. Child Psychol. Psychiatry 11:49–62.

Rutter, M. 1972. Maternal Deprivation Reassessed. Penguin Books, Baltimore.

Rutter, M. 1974. Emotional disorder and educational underachievement. Arch. Dis. Child. 49:249–256.

Rutter, M., and Martin, J. A. M. (eds.). 1972. The Child with Delayed Speech. Clinics in Developmental Medicine No. 43. Spastics International Medical Publications, in association with William Heinemann Medical Books, Ltd., London.

Sameroff, A. J. 1975. Early influences on development: Fact or fancy. Merrill-Palmer Quart. Behav. Dev. 21:275–301.

Sandgrund, A., Gaines, R. W., and Green, A. H. 1974. Child abuse and mental retardation: A problem of cause and effect. Am. J. Ment. Defic. 79:327–330.

Sattler, J. M. 1974. Assessment of Children's Intelligence. W. B. Saunders Company, Philadelphia.

Scarr-Salapatek, S. 1976. An evolutionary perspective on infant intelligence: Species patterns and individual variations. In M. Lewis (ed.), Origins of Intelligence, pp. 165–197. Plenum Press, New York.

Scarr-Salapatek, S., and Williams, M. L. 1973. The effects of early stimulation on low-birth-weight infants. Child. Dev. 44:94–101.

Schaumann, B., and Alter, M. 1976. Dermatoglyphics in Medical Disorders. Springer-Verlag, New York.

Schaumburg, H. H., Powers, J. M., Raine, C. S., Suzuki, W., and Richardson, E. P. 1975. Adrenoleukodystrophy: A clinical and pathological study of 12 cases. Arch. Neurol. 32:577–591.

Schiefelbusch, R. L., and Lloyd, L. L. (eds.). 1974. Language Perspectives—Acquisition, Retardation, and Intervention. University Park Press, Baltimore.

Schlanger, B. B. 1954. Environmental influences on the verbal output of mentally retarded children. J. Speech Hear. Disorder. 19:339–343.

Schopler, E., and Reichler, R. J. (eds.). 1976. Psychopathology and Child Development. Plenum Press, New York.

Scott, C. I., and Thomas, G. H. 1973. Genetic disorders associated with mental retardation: Clinical aspects. Pediatr. Clin. N. Am. 20:121–140.

Scriver, C. R., and Rosenberg, L. E. 1973. Amino Acid Metabolism and Its Disorders. W. B. Saunders Company, Philadelphia.

Seguin, E. 1971. Idiocy and Its Treatment by the Physiological Method. Originally published in 1866. Augustus M. Kelley, New York.

Sells, C. J., and Bennett, F. C. 1977. Prevention of mental retardation: The role of medicine. Am. J. Ment. Defic. 82:117–129.

Sells, C. J., Carpenter, R. L., and Ray, C. G. 1975. Sequelae of central-nervous-system enterovirus infections. N. Engl. J. Med. 293:1–4.

Shaffer, G. W. 1965. The nature of intelligence. In S. Osler and R. Cooke (eds.), The Biosocial Basis of Mental Retardation, pp. 17–34. The Johns Hopkins University Press, Baltimore.

Shank, K. H. 1964. Recognition of articulatory disorders in children. Clin. Pediatr. 3:333–334.

Shapiro, B. K., Accardo, P. J., and Capute, A. J. 1978. Factors affecting walking in a profoundly retarded population. Paper presented at the Thirty-Second Annual Meeting of the American Academy for Cerebral Palsy and Developmental Medicine, September 25, Toronto.

Shapiro, S., Ozbek, N., Cataldo, M. F., and Russo, D. C., 1977. A behavioral approach to menstrual hygiene training. Paper presented at American Association on Mental Deficiency, Region IX, November 1, Baltimore.

Share, J., Koch, R., Webb, A., and Graliker, B. 1964. The longitudinal development of infants and young children with Down's syndrome (Mongolism). Am. J. Ment. Defic. 68:689–692.

Shaw, A., Randolph, J. G., and Manard, B. 1977. Ethical issues in pediatric surgery: A national survey of pediatricians and pediatric surgeons. Pediatrics 60:588–599.

Sheehan, J., Martyn, M. M., and Kilburn, K. L. 1968. Speech disorders in retardation. Am. J. Ment. Defic. 73:251–256.

Shepard, T. H. 1973. Catalog of Teratogenic Agents. The Johns Hopkins University Press, Baltimore.

Shepps, R., and Zigler, E. 1962. Social deprivation and rigidity in the performance of organic and familial retardates. Am. J. Ment. Defic. 67:262–268.

Sheridan, M. D. 1958. Simple clinical hearing tests for very young or mentally retarded children. Br. Med. J. ii:999–1004.

Sheridan, M. 1960. Vision screening of very young or handicapped children. Br. Med. J. ii:453–456.

Sheridan, M. D. 1964. Development of auditory attention and language symbols in young children. In C. Renfrew and K. Murphy (eds.), The Child Who Does Not Talk, pp. 1–10. Clinics in Developmental Medicine No. 13. The Spastic Society Medical Education and Information Unit, in association with William Heinemann Medical Books, Ltd., London.

Sheridan, M. D. 1968. The Developmental Progress of Infants and Young Children. Her Majesty's Stationery Office, London.

Sheridan, M. D. 1973a. The STYCAR Graded-Balls Vision Test. Dev. Med. Child. Neurol. 15:423–432.

Sheridan, M. D. 1973b. The Solo-Dot Test. Dev. Med. Child. Neurol. 15:433–436.

Sholl, C., and Scherzer, A. L. 1974. Feeding problems of the cerebral palsied infant. Pediatr. Dig. 16:19–25.

Shotwell, A. M., and Shipe, D. 1964. Effect of out-of-home care on the intellectual and social development of Mongoloid children. Am. J. Ment. Defic. 68:693–699.

Shoumaker, R. D., Bennett, D. R., Bray, P. F., and Curless, R. G. 1974. Clinical and EEG manifestations of an unusual aphasic syndrome in children. Neurology 24:10–16.
Silver, J., Davies, T. J., Kupersmitt, E., Orme, M., Petrie, A., and Vajda, F. 1974. Prevalence and treatment of vitamin D deficiency in children on anticonvulsant drugs. Arch. Dis. Child. 49:344–350.
Simon, N. 1975. Echolalic speech in childhood autism: Consideration of possible underlying loci of brain damage. Arch. Gen. Psychiatry 32:1439–1446.
Singer, H. S., and Freeman, J. M. 1975. Seizures in adolescents. Med. Clin. North Am. 59:1461–1472.
Sinha, S. K., Kaveggia, E., and Gordon, M. C. 1972. The incidence of cytomegalovirus among mentally retarded and microcephalic children in a state institution. J. Ment. Defic. Res. 16:90–96.
Skeels, H. M. 1966. Adult status of children with contrasting early life experience: A follow-up study. Monogr. Soc. Res. Child. Dev. 31(3):1–65.
Skinner, B. F. 1953. Science and Human Behavior. Macmillan Publishing Company, New York.
Smith, D. H. 1974. On letting some babies die. Hastings Cent. Stud. 2(2):37–46.
Smith, D. W. 1976. Recognizable Patterns of Human Malformation: Genetic, Embryologic and Clinical Aspects. W. B. Saunders Company, Philadephia.
Smith, D. W. 1977. Teratogenicity of anticonvulsant medications. Am. J. Dis. Child. 131:1337–1339.
Smith, D. W., and Gong, B. T. 1974. Scalp-hair patterning: Its origin and significance relative to early brain and upper facial development. Teratology 9:17–34.
Smith, D. W., and Simons, F. E. R. 1975. Rational diagnostic evaluation of the child with mental deficiency. Am. J. Dis. Child. 129:1285–1290.
Smith, G. F., Schindeler, J., Elbualy, S., and Shear, C. 1970. Limb abnormalities and mental retardation. J. Ment. Defic. Res. 14:319–341.
Smith, J. F., Reynolds, E. O. R., and Taghizadeh, A. 1974. Brain maturation and damage in infants dying from chronic pulmonary insufficiency in the postneonatal period. Arch. Dis. Child 49:359–366.

Solnit, A. J., and Stark, M. H. 1961. Mourning and the birth of a defective child. In R. Eissler et al. (eds.), The Psychoanalytic Study of the Child, Vol. 16, pp. 523–537. International Universities Press, New York.

Solomons, G., and Solomons, H. C. 1973. The physician and psychological appraisal. Dev. Med. Child. Neurol. 15:95–103.

Soule, D. 1972. Teacher bias effects with severely retarded children. Am. J. Ment. Defic. 77:208–211.

Spitz, H. H., and LaFontaine, L. 1973. The digit span of idiots-savants. Am. J. Ment. Defic. 77:757–759.

Spitz, R. A. 1957. No and Yes: On the Genesis of Human Communication. International Universities Press, New York.

Spitz, R. A. 1965. The First Year of Life. International Universities Press, New York.

Spreen, O. 1965a. Language functions in mental retardation: A review. I. Language development, types of retardation, and intelligence level. Am. J. Ment. Defic. 69:482–494.

Spreen, O. 1965b. Language functions in mental retardation: A review. II. Language in higher level performance. Am. J. Ment. Defic. 70:351–362.

Stanbury, J. B., Wyngaarden, J. B., and Fredrickson, D. S. (eds.). 1978. The Metabolic Basis of Inherited Disease. McGraw-Hill Book Company, New York.

Stein, Z., and Susser, M. 1963. The social distribution of mental retardation. Am. J. Ment. Defic. 67:811–821.

Steiner, K. G., and Smith, H. A. 1973. Application of cost-benefit analysis to a PKU screening program. Inquiry 10:34–40.

Steisel, I. M. 1969. Some pitfalls in interpretation of the I.Q. J. Pediatr. 75:969–976.

Stephens, B., and McLaughlin, J. A. 1974. Two-year gains in reasoning by retarded and nonretarded persons. Am. J. Ment. Defic. 79:116–126.

Stephens, W. B. 1966. Piaget and Inhelder—application of theory and diagnostic techniques to the area of mental retardation. In M. L. Denburg (ed.), Readings for the Psychology of the Exceptional child, pp. 207–218. MSS Information Corporation, New York.

Stott, L. H., and Ball, R. S. 1965. Infant and preschool mental tests: Review and evaluation. Monogr. Soc. Res. Child. Dev. 30(3).

Strauss, A. A., and Lehtinen, L. 1947. Psychopathology and Education of the Brain Injured Child. Grune & Stratton, New York.

Summitt, R. L. 1969. Cytogenetics in mentally defective children with anomalies: A controlled study. J. Pediatr. 74:58–66.

Sweedler, D., and Kraushaar, A. 1975. The Brothers and Sisters Game. United Community Planning Corporation, Boston.

Sylvester, P. E. 1966. Parietal lobe deficit in the mentally retarded. J. Neurol. Neurosurg. Psychiatry 29:176–180.

Szasz, T. S. 1970. The Manufacture of Madness. Harper & Row Publishers, New York.

Szasz, T. 1974. Ideology and Insanity. Penguin Books, Baltimore.

Taft, L. T. (ed.). 1973. The mentally retarded child. Pediatr. Ann. 2(7).

Talbot, M. E. 1964. Edouard Seguin: A Study of an Educational Approach to the Treatment of Mentally Defective Children. Teachers College Press, New York.

Tanner, J. M., and Inhelder, B. 1971. Discussions on Child Development. 4 Vols. International Universities Press, New York.

Tarjan, G., Wright, S. W., Eyman, R. K., and Keeran, C. V. 1973. Natural history of mental retardation: Some aspects of epidemiology. Am. J. Ment. Defic. 77:369–379.

Taylor, E. M. 1961. Psychological Appraisal of Children with Cerebral Defects. Harvard University Press, Cambridge.

Taylor, J. J., and Achenbach, T. M. 1975. Moral and cognitive development in retarded and nonretarded children. Am. J. Ment. Defic. 80:43–50.

Templin, M. C. 1966. The study of articulation and language development during the early school years. In S. Smith and G. A. Miller (eds.), The Genesis of Language, pp. 173–180. MIT Press, Cambridge.

Tew, B. J., Payne, H., and Lawrence, K. M. 1974. Must a family with a handicapped child be a handicapped family? Dev. Med. Child. Neurol. (Suppl.) 32:95–98.

Thomas, A., and Chess, S. 1977. Temperament and Development. Brunner/Mazel, New York.

Thomas, G. H., and Howell, R. R. 1973. Selected Screening Tests for Genetic Metabolic Diseases. Year Book Medical Publishers, Chicago.

Thomas, G. H., and Scott, C. I. 1973. Laboratory diagnosis of genetic disorders Pediatr. Clin. North Am. 20:105–119.

Thompson, T., and Grabowski, J. (eds.). 1972. Behavior Modification of the Mentally Retarded. Oxford University Press, New York.

Thomson, A. J., Searle, M., and Russell, G. 1977. Quality of survival after severe birth asphyxia. Arch. Dis. Child 52:620–626.

Thorburn, M. J., and Martin, P. A. 1971. Chromosome studies in 101 mentally handicapped Jamaican children. J. Med. Genet. 8:59–64.

Thorpe, H. W., and Werner, E. E. 1974. Developmental screening of preschool children: A critical review. Pediatrics 53:362–370.

Thurston, J., Thurston, D. L. and O'Leary, J. 1972. Prognosis in childhood epilepsy: Follow-up study of 148 cases in which therapy had been suspended after prolonged anticonvulsant control. N. Engl. J. Med. 286:169–174.

Timor-Tritsch, I., Zador, I., Hertz, R. H., and Rosen, M. G. 1976. Classification of human fetal movement. Am. J. Obstet. Gynecol. 126:70–77.

Todres, I. D., Krane, D., Howell, M. C., and Shannon, D. C. 1977. Pediatricians' attitudes affecting decision-making in defective newborns. Pediatrics 60:197–201.

Tolman, E. C. 1948. Cognitive maps in rats and men. Psychol. Rev. 55:189–208.

Topper, S. T. 1975. Gesture language for a non-verbal severely retarded male. Ment. Retard. 13(1):30–31.

Torrey, E. F. 1974. The Death of Psychiatry. Radnor, Chilton.

Touwen, B. C. L. 1972. Laterality and dominance. Dev. Med. Child. Neurol. 14: 747–755.

Touwen, B. C. L., and Prechtl, H. F. R. 1970. The Neurological Examination of the Child with Minor Nervous Dysfunction. Clinics in Developmental Medicine No. 38. Spastics Society, in association with William Heinemann Medical Books, Ltd., London.

Towbin, A. 1971. Organic causes of minimal brain dysfunction. JAMA 217:1207–1214.

Townsend, G. L., Morimoto, A. M., and Kralemann, H. 1973. Management of sialorrhea in mentally retarded patients by transtympanic neurectomy. Mayo Clin. Proc. 48:776–779.

Turner, G., Collins, E., and Turner, B. 1971. Recurrence risk of mental retardation in sibs. Med. J. Aust. i:1165–1166.

Twardosz, S. (ed.). 1976. Guidelines for the use of behavioral procedures in state programs for retarded persons. NARC Research Advisory Committee Monograph Vol. 1, No. 1.

Twitchell, T. E. 1965. The automatic grasping responses of infants. Neuropsychologia 3:247–259.

Uzgiris, I. C. 1967. Ordinality in the development of schemas for relating to objects. In J. Hellmuth (ed.), Exceptional Infant, Vol. 1, Normal Infant, pp. 315–334. Brunner/Mazel, New York.

Uzgiris, I. C. 1976. Organization of sensorimotor intelligence. In M. Lewis (ed.), Origins of Intelligence, pp. 123–263. Plenum Press, New York.

Uzgiris, I. C., and Hunt, J. McV. 1975. Assessment in Infancy: Ordinal Scales of Psychological Development. University of Illinois Press, Urbana.

Valente, M. 1972. Counseling parents of retarded children. Cal. Med. 116:21–26.

Vanderheiden, D. H., Brown, W. P., Reinen, S., MacKenzie, P., and Scheibel, C. 1975. Symbol communication for the mentally handicapped. Ment. Retard. 13(1):34–37.

VanderVeer, B., and Schweid, E. 1974. Infant assessment: Stability of mental functioning in young retarded children. Am. J. Ment. Defic. 79:1–4.

Vanier, J. 1971. Eruption to Hope. Griffin House, Toronto.

Veatch, R. M. 1973a. Generalization of expertise. Hastings Cent. Stud. 1(2):29–40.

Veatch, R. M. 1973b. The medical model: Its nature and problems. Hastings Cent. Stud. 1(3):59–76.

Vogel, W., Kun, K. J., Meshorer, E., Broverman, D. M., and Klaiber, E. L. 1969. The behavioral significance of EEG abnormality in mental defectives. Am. J. Ment. Defic. 74:62–68.

Volpe, J. J. 1976. Perinatal hypoxic-ischemic brain injury. Ped. Clin. North Am. 23:383–397.

Vygotsky, L. S. 1962. Thought and Language. MIT Press, Cambridge.

Wachs, T. D. 1975. Relation of infants' performance on Piaget scales between twelve and twenty-four months and their Stanford-Binet performance at thirty-one months. Child. Dev. 46:929–935.

Waldrop, M. F., and Halverson, C. F., Jr. 1971. Minor physical anomalies and hyperactive behavior in young children. In J.

Hellmuth (ed.), Exceptional Infant, Vol. 2., Studies in Abnormalities, pp. 343–380. Brunner/Mazel, New York.

Walker, A. E., Caveness, W. F., and Critchley, M. (eds.). 1969. Late Effects of Head Injury. Charles C Thomas Publisher, Springfield.

Warkany, J. 1971. Congenital Malformations. Year Book Medical Publishers, Chicago.

Watson, A. O., Massler, M., and Perlstein, M. A. 1964. Tooth ring analysis in cerebral palsy. Am. J. Dis. Child. 107:370–382.

Watson, J. B. 1962. Behaviorism. University of Chicago Press, Chicago.

Wehbring, K., and Ogren, C. 1976. Community Residences for Mentally Retarded Persons. NARC Research Advisory Committee Monograph 3.

Weinberg, E. G. 1971. A Child's Cry: A Clue to Diagnosis. (33⅓ R.P.M. recording). Pfizer Laboratories, New York.

Weisz, J. R. 1976. Studying cognitive development in retarded and nonretarded groups: The role of theory. Am. J. Ment. Defic. 81:235–239.

Wenar, C., and Coulter, J. B. 1962. A reliability study of developmental histories. Child. Dev. 33:453–462.

Werner, E. E. 1972. Denver Developmental Screening Test. In O. K. Buros (ed.), The Seventh Mental Measurements Yearbook, pp. 734–736. Gryphon Press, Highland Park.

Werner, E. E., Bierman, J. M., and French, F. E. 1971. The Children of Kauai. University of Hawaii Press, Honolulu.

Werner, E. E., and Smith, R. S. 1977. Kauai's Children Come of Age. University of Hawaii Press, Honolulu.

Werner, H. 1946. The concept of rigidity: A critical evaluation. Psychol. Rev. 53:43–52.

Werner, H. 1948. Comparative Psychology of Mental Development. International Universities Press, New York.

White, B. 1970. The initial coordination of sensorimotor schemas in human infants: Piaget's ideas and the role of experience. In J. Hellmuth (ed.), Cognitive Studies, Vol. 1, pp. 24–43. Brunner/Mazel, New York.

White, B. L., Held, R., and Castle, P. 1967a. Experience in early human development. Part 1. Observations on the development of visually-directed reaching. In J. Hellmuth (ed.), Exceptional Infant, Vol. 1, Normal Infant, pp. 267–289. Brunner/Mazel, New York.

White, B. L., and Held, R. 1967b. Experience in early human development. Part 2. Plasticity of sensorimotor development in the human infant. In J. Hellmuth (ed.), Exceptional Infant, Vol. 1, Normal Infant, pp. 291–313. Brunner/Mazel, New York.
White, J. H. 1977. Pediatric Psychopharmacology. Williams & Wilkins, Baltimore.
White, R. W. 1959. Motivation reconsidered: The concept of competence. Psychol. Rev. 66:297–333.
Whitehouse, D. 1966. Diagnostic value of the café au lait spot in children. Arch. Dis. Child. 41:316–319.
Whitney, L. R., and Barnard, K. E. 1966. Implications of operant learning theory for nursing care of the retarded child. Ment. Retard. 4(6):26–29.
Wilson, J. 1972. Investigation of degenerative disease of the central nervous system. Arch. Dis. Child. 47:163–170.
Wilson, M. G. 1975. Genetic counseling. Curr. Probl. Pediatr. 5(7):1–51.
Windle, W. F. 1968. Brain damage at birth. JAMA 206:1967–1972.
Winnacker, J. L., Yeager, H., Saunders, J. A., Russell, B., and Anast, C. S. 1977. Rickets in children receiving anticonvulsant drugs: Biochemical and hormonal markers. Am. J. Dis. Child. 131:286–290.
Witkin, H. A., Mednick, S. A., Schulsinger, F., Bakkestrom, E., Christiansen, K. O., Goodenough, D. R., Hirschhorn, K., Lundsteen, C., Owen, D. R., Philip, J., Rubin, D. B., and Stocking, M. 1976. Criminality in XYY and XXY men. Science 193:547–555.
Wolfensberger, W. 1972. The Principle of Normalization in Human Services. National Institute on Mental Retardation, Toronto.
Wolfensberger, W. (ed.). 1973. A Selective Overview of the Work of Jean Vanier and the Movement of L'Arche. NIMR Monograph 1. National Institute on Mental Retardation, Toronto.
Wolfensberger, W., and Kurtz, R. A. (eds.). 1969. Management of the Family of the Mentally Retarded. Follett Publishing Company, Chicago.
Wolfensberger, W., and Menolascino, F. 1968. Basic considerations in evaluating ability of drugs to stimulate cognitive development in retardates. Am. J. Ment. Defic. 73:414–423.

Wolff, P. H. 1960. The developmental psychologies of Jean Piaget and psychoanalysis. Psychol. Issues Monograph 5. 1–181.

Wolinsky, G. F. 1962. Piaget and the psychology of thought: Some implications for teaching the retarded. Am. J. Ment. Defic. 67:250–256.

Woodward, M. 1959. The behavior of idiots interpreted by Piaget's theory of sensorimotor development. Br. J. Educ. Psychol. 29:60–71.

Wright, B. J., and Isenstein, V. R. 1977. Psychological Tests and Minorities. Mental Health Studies and Reports Branch, U.S. Government Printing Office, Washington, D.C.

Wursten, H. 1974. On the relevancy of Piaget's theory to occupational therapy. Am. J. Occup. Ther. 28:213–217.

Yakovlev, P. I., and Lecours, A. R. 1967. The myelogenetic cycles of regional maturation of the brain. In A. Minkowski (ed.), Regional Development of the Brain in Early Life, pp. 3–65. Blackwell Scientific Publications, Oxford.

Yang, D. C., Ting, R. Y., and Kennedy, C. 1968. The predictive value of the neurologic examination in infancy for mental status at four years of age. In R. MacKeith and M. Bax (eds.), Studies in Infancy, Clinics in Developmental Medicine No. 27, pp. 94–99. Spastics Society, in association with William Heinemann Medical Books, Ltd., London.

Zangwill, O. L. 1963. The cerebral localization of psychological function. Advance. Sci. 20:335–344.

Zaporozhets, A. V., and Elkonin, D. B. (eds.). 1971. The Psychology of Preschool Children. MIT Press, Cambridge.

Zarin-Ackerman, J., Lewis, M., and Driscoll, J. M. 1977. Language development in 2-year-old normal and risk infants. Pediatrics 59:982–986.

Zeaman, D., and House, B. J. 1963. The role of attention in retardate discrimination learning. In N. R. Ellis (ed.), Handbook of Mental Deficiency, pp. 159–223. McGraw-Hill Book Company, New York.

Zigler, E. 1967. Familial mental retardation: A continuing dilemma. Science 155:292–298.

Zigler, E. 1969. Developmental versus difference theories of mental retardation and the problems of motivation. Am. J. Ment. Defic. 73:536–556.

Zigler, E., and Butterfield, E. C. 1966. Rigidity in the retarded: A further test of the Lewin-Kounin formulation. J. Abnorm. Psychol. 71:224–231.

Zigler, E., and Butterfield, E. C. 1968. Motivational aspects of changes in I.Q. test performance of culturally deprived nursery school children. Child. Dev. 39:1–14.

Zigler, E., and Seitz, V. 1975. On "An Experimental Evaluation of Sensorimotor Patterning": A critique. Am. J. Ment. Defic. 79:483–492.

Zuk, G. H., Miller, R. L., Bartram, J. B., and Kling, F. 1961. Maternal acceptance of retarded children: A questionnaire study of attitudes and religious background. Child. Dev. 32:525–540.

INDEX

Abortion, 51, 52, 155
Academic achievement, 20–23
Acceptance, 172–175
Accommodation, 38
Adaptive behavior, 15
Adenoma sebaceum, 92
Alcohol, *see* Fetal alcohol syndrome
Alerting, 135
Amniocentesis, 54, 155
Anal atresia, 67
Angiography, cerebral, 48, 73
Anoxia, 18, 45, 46
Anticipatory guidance, 35–36, 155, 173
Anticonvulsants, 99, 100, 148
Aortic stenosis, 67
Apgar score, 50, 62
Aphasia, 45, 148
Articulation, 144, 145
Asphyxia, 18, 45, 62
Assimilation, 38
Associated handicaps, 17–19
Asymmetry, 69
Ataxia, 65, 100
Ataxia telangiectasia, 49, 80, 95
Attitudes toward the retarded, 3, 30, 170, 175, 176
Audiology, 74, 79
Auditory orienting, 33, 34, 84, 122, 138–141
Autism, 146, 148–150
Axillary freckling, 87, 91

Banding, chromosomal, 52, 53, 61, 103
Bayes' theorem, 55
Behavior problems, 21, 159–164
Behavioral psychology, 23, 39, 150, 158–160, 184
Benign cerebral hypotonia, 64
Binet, A., 8
Birth weight
small, 48, 49
large, 69
Blindness, 18, 65
Block figures, 122
Brain damage, 27, 30, 32–36, 45, 46, 96, 124, 147, 150, 161
Brain malformation, 31, 46–48, 96
Breech, 48, 51
Brushfield spots, 68

Café au lait, 87, 90
Calcification, intracranial, 46, 75, 76, 94
Camptodactyly, 89
Carey questionnaire, 41
Cataract, 79, 94
Central auditory imperception, 148
Cerebellum, 45
Cerebral palsy, 18–20, 28, 33, 36, 54, 64, 65, 81, 94, 119, 121, 123, 124
Choreoathetosis, 18
Chromatogram, amino acid, 60, 61
Chromosomal disorder, 31, 49, 51, 52, 60, 69
Chun gun, 64, 73
Cleft lip/cleft palate, 84
Cleidocranial dysostosis, 73
Clinodactyly, 68, 89
"Clumsy child," 28
Cognitive theory, 38, 39
Coloboma, 67, 80, 83
Communication disorder, 28, 121, 124, 146, 148
Computerized tomography (CT), 73, 75, 78
Consanguinity, 61
Constipation, 161
Contraception, 182, 183
Convulsions, *see* Epilepsy
Cooing, 137
Coprolalia, 163
Craniosynostosis (craniostenosis), 73
Cretinism, *see* Hypothyroidism
Criminality, 55
Crowe's rule, 87
Cryptorchidism, 68
Cutis verticis gyrata, 94
Cytomegalovirus, 49, 75

Daily fetal movement count (DFMC), 62
Deafness, 5, 18, 79, 103, 146, 148, 150
Defect theory, 30
Degenerative disease, 38, 61, 65, 66, 73, 102
Deinstitutionalization, 23, 175
Depakene, 102
Deprivation, 8, 31, 32, 41
Dermatoglyphics, 85, 86
Developmental pediatrician, 9, 59
Developmental quotient (DQ), 19, 63
Deviancy, 124, 141
Difference theory, 30
Difficult child temperament, 35, 36
Dissociation, 109, 123, 124, 143, 144, 149, 150, 158
Drawing tests 125–131
Drugs
  chloral hydrate, 163
  chlorpromazine, 162
  clonazepam, 97, 100
  Depakene, 102
  Dilantin, 99, 100
  diphenhydramine, 161, 163
  lithium carbonate, 163, 164
  Mysoline, 120
  phenobarbital, 100
  stilbestrol, 62
  Tegretol, 100
  tetracycline, 88
  thioridazine, 161, 162
  trifluoperazine, 163
Duodenal atresia, 68
Dyslexia, 28
Dysmorphology, 13, 60, 67

Ear, 73, 81
Echolalia, 147, 148
Educable retardation, *see* Retardation, mild
Electroencephalogram (EEG), 54, 79, 87, 96–99
Elfin facies, 67
Emotional problems, 36, 38
Employment, 21
Environment, 31, 32, 39
  average expectable, 30
Epicanthal fold, 81
Epilepsy, 8, 17, 18, 51, 54, 61, 65, 87, 94, 95–100, 102
Equilibrium, 38
Erikson, E., 36–37
Eugenics, 3, 9
Euthanasia, 3, 186
Evoked potentials, 79, 87
Eye, 69, 73, 74, 79, 81, 82, 94

Failure to thrive (FTT), 69
Familial retardation, *see* Retardation, mild
Febrile convulsion, 95, 96
Feebleminded, 19
Fetal alcohol syndrome, 6, 69
Fetal hydantoin syndrome, 85
Fetal movement, 62
Fetal wastage, 50, 51, 52
Fontanel, 73
Freud, S., 9, 33, 37

Galactosemia, 155
Genetic counseling, 55, 155
Genetic scare, 3, 9
Genetics, 30–32, 60, 124
Genotype, 31
Gesell, A., 9, 13, 34, 39, 108
Gesell figures, 125
Gesture, 139
Gingival hyperplasia, 99–101
Grade levels, 20, 21
Growth failure, 67–69
Guilt, 173

Habituation, 64
Head banging, 160, 161
Head circumference (OFC), 70–73
Hearing loss, 17, 73, 121, 123, 148
Hemiplegia, 18
Herpes, 49
Hiccups, fetal, 62

History, developmental, 108–111, 119
Holmes, O. W., Jr., 182
Home Observation for the Measurement of the Environment (HOME), 41
Hydranencephaly, 70, 186
Hydrocephalus, 8, 70, 147, 186
Hydrocephalus ex vacuo, 71
Hyperactivity, 67, 160, 161
Hyperammonemia, 155
Hyperbilirubinemia, 18, 51
Hypertelorism, 73
Hypoactive fetus, 62
Hypocalcemia, 50
Hypoglycemia, 50, 54, 96
Hypomagnesemia, 50
Hypopigmented macules, 89, 91
Hypospadias, 67
Hypotelorism, 73
Hypothyroidism, 8, 67, 73, 138, 155
Hypotonia, 64, 65, 68, 69
Hypoxia, 45, 46, 96
Hypsarrhythmia 97, 98

Ichthyosis, 94
Idiot, 19
Imbecile, 19
Imitation, 19, 39
Immunization, 55, 96
Immunodeficiency, 49, 55
Impedance audiometry, 79
Incontinentia pigmenti, 93
Infant cry, 138
Infant-maternal interaction, 34, 35
Infant stimulation, 41, 59, 155, 156
Infant tests, 19
Infant temperament, 35, 40
Infantile spasms, 8, 95–98
Infection, intrauterine, 46, 49
Insanity, 3, 5
Institution, 6, 8, 30, 161, 175
Instruments, *see* Tests
Intelligence quotient (IQ), 13, 19, 27, 29, 30, 39, 59
Ireland, W., 6, 10
Irritibility, 35, 62
Itard, J. M. G., 3, 10

Jargon, 142

Kauai study, 35
Ketogenic diet, 97
Kohlberg, L., 37, 39

Labeling, 23, 156
Language, 19, 31, 39, 45, 121, 135–151
Laterality, 65
Lashley, K. S., 33
Law, 4, 5, 9
Lead, 35
Learning disability, 14, 28, 161
Learning theory, *see* Behavioral psychology
Lennox-Gastaut, 97, 99
Lewin-Kounin model, 29, 30
Literacy, 21, 22, 148
Luria, A. R., 33

Macrocephaly, 61, 70
Mainstreaming, 21, 156
Malnutrition, 31, 45, 69
Maple syrup urine disease, 155
Marriage, 170, 173, 182, 183
Mass action, 33
Maternal deprivation, 41
Maturational model, 32–35, 39, 109
Meconium, 50, 51, 54
Medical model, 27
Megancephaly, 8
Meningitis, 8
Menstrual hygiene, 184
Metabolic disorders, 150, 155
Microcephaly, 6, 49, 54, 61, 69–71, 73, 74, 84, 138
Minimal brain dysfunction (MBD), 28, 36, 160
Montessori, M., 6
Moral judgment, 39, 40
Moron, 19
Mortality, 17
Motor abilities, 108–121
Mouthing, 35, 36
Mutation, 27, 52
Myelination, 33, 34

Neonatal convulsions, 95
Neurocutaneous syndromes, 86–94
Neurofibromatosis, 86
Neuropsychology, 33
Neuroradiology, 48, 73, 75, 76, 78
Nevus sebaceus of Jadassohn, 94
New York Longitudinal Study, 35
Newborn examination, 46, 70, 77
Nonverbal communication, 147, 148, 151
Normalization, 23, 184

Occupational therapy, 23, 109, 157, 158
Odontoglyphics, 81, 84, 88
Operant conditioning, *see* Behavioral psychology
Ophthalmologic evaluation, 73–74
Optokinetic nystagmus, 64, 74
Orienting
  auditory, 33, 34, 84, 122, 138–141
  tactile, 138
  visual, 33, 34, 138

Palate, 6, 84, 103
Parents, 21, 22, 54, 59, 60, 62, 123, 137, 156, 157, 158, 160, 167–176, 184, 185
"Parrot talk," 149
Pavlov, I., 33
Perception, 121–123
Perceptual disorder, 28
Petit mal variant, 97, 99
Phakomatoses, 86–95
Phenotype, 31
Phenylketonuria, 94, 96
Physical therapy, 23, 109, 157, 158
Physiologic method, 5
Piaget, J. 37–39, 121
Pica, 35
Placenta, 54
Pneumoencephalography (PEG), 48, 73, 76
Polydactyly, 69
Porencephaly, 78, 96
Postmaturity, 54
Predictability, 15, 19, 31, 32, 46, 64, 107, 131, 135
Prematurity, 62, 63
Prenatal etiology, 47, 48
Primitive reflexes, 65
Pseudoretardation, 74
Psychiatry, 5, 160
Psychiatric disorders 17, 18
Psychoanalytic theory, 36, 37
Psychohistory, 3
Psychometric model, 32, 33
Psychotropic drugs, 161–164

Recurrence risks, 52, 54, 55
Religion, 175, 186
Retardation
  associated handicaps, 17–19
  definition, 13–16
  levels, 19–23
  mild, 17–22, 27, 29, 30, 40, 59, 60, 156
  moderate, 22, 146, 147, 157
  profound, 19, 23, 24, 71, 109, 160, 161, 181
  severe, 16, 19, 23, 24, 27–29, 40, 46–48, 123, 125, 157, 158
Retina, 69, 82
Rickets, 99–100, 102
Rocking, 160, 161
Rooting reflex, 144
Rosenthal effect, 23
Rousseau, J. J., 5, 155, 158
Rubella, 49, 79, 82, 96
"Rule of five," 20, 21

Saint Dymphna, 5
Scales, *see* Tests
Scatter, 14, 15, 124, 158
  see also Splinter skills
Screening, developmental, 107
Seguin, E., 6, 7, 10, 186
Seizures, *see* Epilepsy
Self-mutilation, 161
Sex education, 182
Shagreen patch, 94
Short stature, 68, 69
Simian crease, 65, 68, 69

Simon, T., 8
Sinistrality, 65
Slow learner, 19
Slow virus, 55
Social competence, 15
Social smile, 63, 137
Sociocultural retardation, *see* Retardation, mild
Socioeconomic status (SES), 46
Soft neurologic signs, 65
Speech therapy, 23, 145
Special education, 15, 21, 23, 155, 156, 157
Splinter skills, 15, 124, 143, 150, 158
Sterilization, 3, 9, 182–186
Stillbirth, 52
Strauss syndrome, 36, 160
Structuralism, 39
STYCAR tests, 79, 84, 85, 86, 104
Subtrainable level of retardation, 19
Suck, 62
Sydney line, 89
Syndromes
  ataxia telangiectasia, 49, 80, 95
  cat eye, 67
  "cocktail talk," 147
  Cornelia de Lange, 67, 138
  cri du chat (5p-), 67, 138
  Down (trisomy 21), 6, 19, 24, 49, 65, 67, 68, 73, 81, 86, 89, 103, 175, 186
  Edwards (trisomy 18), 86, 138
  fetal alcohol, 6
  fetal hydantoin, 85
  Gilles de la Tourette, 163
  Hartnup's disease, 46, 94
  hyperammonemia, 66
  Lawrence-Moon-Bardet-Biedl, 69
  Lennox-Gastaut, 97, 99
  Martin-Bell, 54
  Menkes, 67
  Prader-Willi, 69
  Rubinstein-Taybi, 89
  Russell-Silver, 69
  Sjögren-Larsson, 94
  Smith-Lemli-Opitz, 67
  Sotos, 69
  Strauss, 36, 160
  Sturge-Weber, 78, 96
  Vulnerable child, 177
  West, 8, 95, 98
  Wiedemann-Beckwith, 69
  Williams, 67
  Wilson's disease, 66
Synophrys, 67

Tay-Sachs disease, 82
Teeth, *see* Odontoglyphics
Temple Longitudinal Study, 39, 40
Temporal lobe, 96, 148
Teratogen, 62
Territoriality, 159
Tests
  Alpern-Boll, 15
  Bayley, 13, 107
  Bender Gestalt, 126, 127
  Binet-Simon, 8
  Cattell, 13
  Clancy, 149, 150
  Denver
    DASE, 145
    DDST, 107
  Developmental Screening Inventory (DSI), 131
  Gesell, 13, 108, 125, 126
  Goodenough DAP, 126, 128, 129
  Hiskey Nebraska, 148
  Leiter (Arthur), 148
  Peabody (PPVT), 151
  Rey-Osterreith, 126, 129–131
  Stanford-Binet, 13, 19
  STYCAR, 79, 84, 86, 102
  Vineland, 15
  Wechsler
    WISC, 13, 14
    WPPSI, 13
Toilet training, 159, 184
Tongue tie, 145
TORCH, 49
Toxin, 45, 69
Toxoplasmosis, 49
Trainable retardation, *see* Retardation, moderate
Transillumination, 64, 73